W9-AWF-265

| Passenger | Age | Class | Lost/Saved |
|---|---|---|---|
| Mr. Anthony Abbing | 42 | 3rd | Lost |
| Master Eugene Joseph Abbott | 13 | 3rd | Lost |
| Mr. Rossmore Edward Abbott | 16 | 3rd | Lost |
| Mrs. Stanton (Rosa) Abbott | 35 | 3rd | Saved |
| Miss Anna Karen Abelseth | 16 | 3rd | Saved |
| Mrs. Johanna Persdotter Ahlin | 40 | 3rd | Lost |
| Mr. Ali Ahmed | 24 | 3rd | Lost |
| Mr. Isak Aijo-Nirva | 41 | 3rd | Lost |
| Mrs. Sam (Leah Rosen) Aks | 18 | 3rd | Saved |
| Master Philip (Frank) Aks | 10m | 3rd | Saved |
| Mr. Charles Augustus Aldworth | 30 | 2nd | Lost |
| Mr. William Alexander | 23 | 3rd | Lost |
| Mr. Ilmari Rudolf Alhomaki | 20 | 3rd | Lost |
| Mr. William Ali | 25 | 3rd | Lost |
| Miss Elisabeth Walton Allen | 29 | 1st | Saved |
| Mr. William Henry Allen | 35 | 3rd | Lost |
| Master Hudson Trevor Allison | 11m | 1st | Saved |
| Miss Helen Lorraine Allison | 2 | 1st | Lost |
| Mr. Hudson Joshua C. Allison | 30 | 1st | Lost |
| Mrs. Hudson J.C. (Bessie Waldo Daniels) Allison | 25 | 1st | Lost |
| Mr. Owen George Allum | 18 | 3rd | Lost |
| Mr. Thor Olsvigen Andersen | 20 | 3rd | Lost |
| Mr. Albert Karvin Andersen | 32 | 3rd | Lost |
| Mr. Harry Anderson | 47 | 1st | Saved |
| Miss Ellis Anna Maria Andersson | 2 | 3rd | Lost |
| Mr. Johan Samuel Andersson | 26 | 3rd | Lost |
| Miss Sigrid Elizabeth Andersson | 11 | 3rd | Lost |
| Master Sigvard Harald Elias Andersson | 4 | 3rd | Lost |

# TITANIC
## *fortune & fate*

*Catalogue from*
*The Mariners' Museum Exhibition*

BEVERLY McMILLAN

STANLEY LEHRER

And the Staff of The Mariners' Museum

The Mariners' Museum, Newport News, Virginia
Simon & Schuster

SIMON & SCHUSTER
Rockefeller Center
1230 Avenue of the Americas
New York, NY 10020



Director, The Mariners' Museum,
Claudia L. Pennington

Photographic Services by
Jason Copes, Christian Higgins, Claudia Jew,
John Pemberton, Gregg Vicik,
The Mariners' Museum

Collections management by
Jeanne Willoz-Egnor, Lori Mastemaker,
The Mariners' Museum

Design and composition by
Matt Hahn, ThinkDesign, Buellton, California

Printed in the United States of America

Library of Congress Cataloging-in-Publication Data is available.

ISBN 0-684-85710-3

On April 10, 1912, the RMS *Titanic*—the largest, most luxurious, most technologically advanced ocean liner the world had ever seen—set out on her maiden voyage from Southampton, England, to New York.

More than 2,200 passengers and crew were aboard the RMS *Titanic* as she embarked on her fateful voyage. They represented many countries and many segments of society—from American tycoons to Syrian emigrants, from French babies to English maids.

At 11:40 P.M. on Sunday, April 14, the *Titanic* struck an iceberg in the calm, frigid waters off the Newfoundland Banks. Within two and a half hours, the liner once billed as "unsinkable" went down. Only 705 of her passengers and crew were saved.

# RMS TITANIC

Today the *Titanic* sails on across the expanse of the human imagination. The fascination lies in the stories of her people, in her remarkable design and her famous opulence, in the tragedy of her last night, and in her enduring legacy of safer ships. In these pages, which commemorate an acclaimed exhibition of *Titanic* artifacts and memorabilia organized by The Mariners' Museum in 1998, we invite you to explore the *Titanic* and her fate from the point of view of the people who sailed aboard her. In the final analysis, their stories—some tragic, others heroic, and still others shrouded in controversy or in the shifting mists of speculation—are the stories of us all.

—JOHN B. HIGHTOWER, PRESIDENT AND CEO
The Mariners' Museum
Newport News, Virginia

ROYAL
SOUTHAMPTON
LIVERPOOL TO
STEAMERS
THE WORLD
(BUILDING)
WHITE STAR
LINE
THOS. COOK & SON 92, St. James Street, BURNLEY.

# TITANIC

*fortune & fate*

As the RMS *Titanic* departed on her maiden voyage on April 10, 1912, her graceful hull stretched more than four city blocks and towered eleven stories high. Released gently from her Southampton moorings into a rising sea, she set out upon the ocean as the embodiment of the belief that human minds and hands had produced one of the signature technological achievements of a still-young century. The *Titanic* boasted unprecedented size, awesome power, and more. She surrounded

# PRIDE

her passengers with no less than the best that maritime engineers, designers, and crafters had to offer: lush accommodations and amenities, including supremely elegant restaurants for the first class, staterooms that ranged from lavish to uncommonly comfortable, and public rooms featuring rich carpeting, elaborate carvings, and the finest paneling. In short, as her owners, passengers, and the whole world knew, she was grand.

Opposite Page:
WHITE STAR–AMERICAN LINE. SOUTHAMPTON–NEW YORK.
THE ROYAL MAIL TRIPLE-SCREW STEAMER *TITANIC*.
Poster, 1912
Courtesy Stanley Lehrer Collection

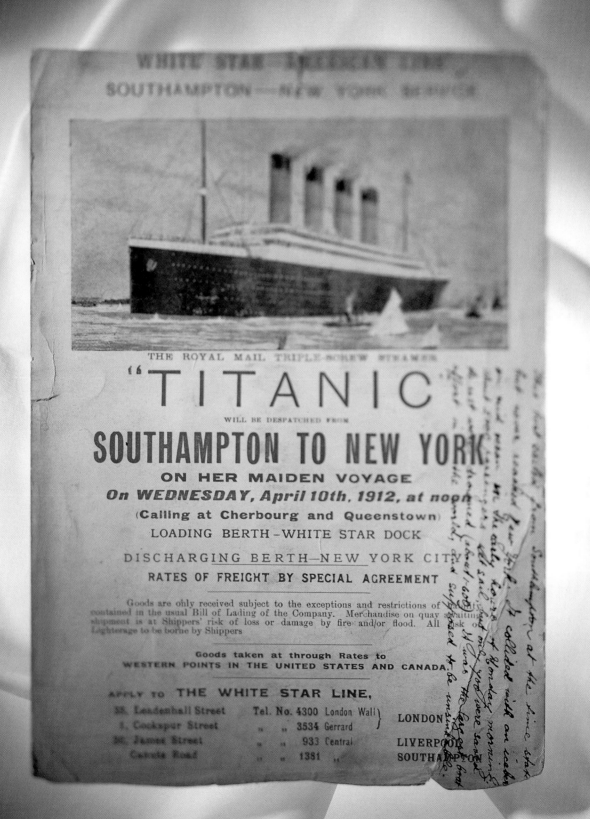

WHITE STAR AMERICAN LINE

SOUTHAMPTON—NEW YORK SERVICE

THE ROYAL MAIL TRIPLE-SCREW STEAMER

# "TITANIC"

WILL BE DESPATCHED FROM

## SOUTHAMPTON TO NEW YORK

### ON HER MAIDEN VOYAGE

***On WEDNESDAY, April 10th, 1912, at noon***

**(Calling at Cherbourg and Queenstown)**

LOADING BERTH—WHITE STAR DOCK

DISCHARGING BERTH—NEW YORK CITY

**RATES OF FREIGHT BY SPECIAL AGREEMENT**

---

Goods are only received subject to the exceptions and restrictions of liability contained in the usual Bill of Lading of the Company. Merchandise on quay awaiting shipment is at Shippers' risk of loss or damage by fire and/or flood. All risk of Lighterage to be borne by Shippers

---

**Goods taken at through Rates to**
**WESTERN POINTS IN THE UNITED STATES AND CANADA.**

---

APPLY TO **THE WHITE STAR LINE,**

| | | | |
|---|---|---|---|
| 38, Leadenhall Street | Tel. No. 4300 London Wall | } | LONDON |
| 1, Cockspur Street | " " 3534 Gerrard | | |
| 30, James Street | " " 933 Central | | LIVERPOOL |
| Canute Road | " " 1381 " | | SOUTHAMPTON |

| PASSENGER | AGE | CLASS | LOST/SAVED |
|---|---|---|---|
| Miss Erna Andersson | 17 | 3rd | Saved |
| Miss Ebba Iris Andersson | 6 | 3rd | Lost |
| Mrs. Anders (Alfrida K. Brogren) Andersson | 39 | 3rd | Lost |
| Miss Ingeborg Constancia Andersson | 9 | 3rd | Lost |
| Mr. Anders Johan Andersson | 39 | 3rd | Lost |
| Miss Ida Augusta M. Andersson | 38 | 3rd | Lost |

{*The Shipbuilder*, a trade magazine, declared the *Titanic* "practically unsinkable."}

## PRIDE

Built by Belfast's Harland and Wolff shipyard, the *Titanic* incorporated the latest in technological advances and—even with lifeboats for fewer than half of the passengers and crew—exceeded the safety standards of the day.

Below:
WHITE STAR INSIGNIA PIN
Courtesy The Family of Frank P. Aks

"EVERYTHING HAS BEEN DONE IN REGARD TO THE FURNITURE AND FITTINGS TO MAKE THE FIRST CLASS ACCOMMODATIONS MORE THAN EQUAL TO THAT PROVIDED IN THE FINEST HOTELS ON SHORE." —*The Shipbuilder*

Right:
THE LARGEST STEAMERS IN THE WORLD
Poster, ca. 1910
*As the twentieth century unfolded, the lucrative transatlantic passenger trade was hotly competitive. The White Star Line touted the* Titanic's *immense proportions and safety features such as the double-bottom hull—features that supposedly made the vessel unsinkable.*
Courtesy James E. O'Neill, Jr.

Below:
MODEL OF THE RMS *TITANIC*
Courtesy Maritime Replicas International

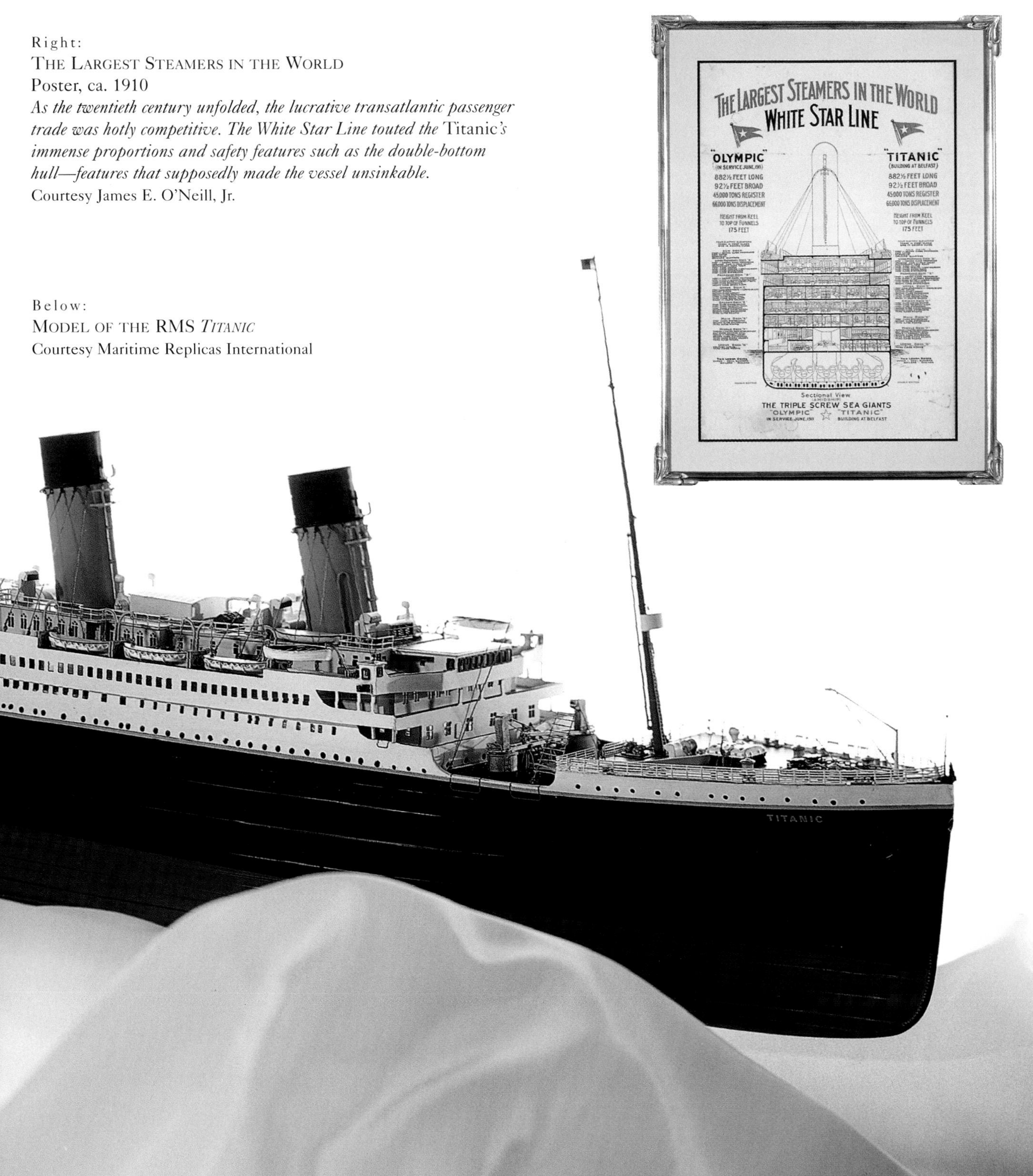

**DEEP IN THE BOWELS OF THE SHIP, STOKERS WORKED AROUND THE CLOCK IN HEAT AND DIRT, SHOVELING COAL INTO THE TWENTY-NINE BOILERS THAT DROVE THE TITANIC'S GIANT STEAM ENGINES.**

{In 1912, the *Titanic* was the largest movable object ever made.}

## PRIDE

The RMS *Titanic*
*Length:* 882′6″
*Beam:* 92′6″
*Gross weight:* 46,328 tons
*Displacement:* 66,000 tons
*Propulsion:* Two 990-ton triple-expansion steam engines and a 420-ton steam turbine engine generating a combined 46,000 horsepower
*Power:* Twenty-nine coal-fired 15-foot-high boilers, each weighing nearly 100 tons
*Top cruising speed:* 23–24 knots
*Decks:* 9 steel;
16 watertight compartments with electrically operated doors

Opposite Page:
BOILERS FOR THE *TITANIC*
Harland & Wolff photograph
Courtesy Ken Marschall Collection

Above:
ADVERTISING CALENDAR, 1910
Artist, Alf Cooke
Courtesy The Miottel Collection, San Francisco

| PASSENGER | AGE | CLASS | LOST/SAVED |
|---|---|---|---|
| Mr. Paul Edvin Andreasson | 20 | 3rd | Lost |
| Mr. Frank Andrew | | 2nd | Lost |
| Mr. Edgar Samuel Andrew | 18 | 2nd | Lost |
| Miss Kornelia Theodosia Andrews | 63 | 1st | Saved |
| Mr. Thomas, Jr. Andrews | 39 | 1st | Lost |
| Mr. Minko Angheloff | 26 | 3rd | Lost |

**"I CANNOT IMAGINE ANY CONDITION WHICH WOULD CAUSE A SHIP TO FOUNDER. I CANNOT CONCEIVE OF ANY VITAL DISASTER HAPPENING TO THIS VESSEL. MODERN SHIPBUILDING HAS GONE BEYOND THAT."**

*—Captain Edward Smith*

## PRIDE

The *Titanic*'s crew of nearly 900 included engineers, firemen, trimmers, stokers, lookouts, bakers, caterers and cooks, icemen, scullions, waiters and stewards, barbers, florists, and cashiers. Then there were the special crew—postal clerks, wireless operators, and orchestra musicians.

Below:
WHITE STAR UNIFORM BUTTON, CA. 1911
MILLER & SON, SOUTHAMPTON, ENGLAND
Courtesy The Family of Frank P. Aks

Left:
CAPTAIN EDWARD SMITH
Cork *Examiner*,
courtesy Ken Marschall Collection

| PASSENGER | AGE | CLASS | LOST/SAVED |
|---|---|---|---|
| Mr. William A. Angle | 34 | 2nd | Lost |
| Mrs. William A. (Florence) Angle | 32 | 2nd | Saved |
| Mrs. Edward Dale (Charlotte Lamson) Appleton | 58 | 1st | Saved |
| Mr. Josef Arnold | 25 | 3rd | Lost |
| Mrs. Josef (Josephine Frank) Arnold | 18 | 3rd | Lost |
| Mr. Ernst Axel Algot Aronsson | 24 | 3rd | Lost |
| Mr. Ramon Ramon Artagaveytia | | 1st | Lost |

{A formal portrait captured Captain Smith and his officers shortly before the *Titanic* sailed.}

Above:
CAPTAIN SMITH AND OFFICERS OF THE *TITANIC*
*Four of the nine survived the disaster.*
Courtesy Stanley Lehrer Collection

# "A British crew for a British ship."

## Pride

Left:
BAKER CHARLES JOUGHIN
Courtesy *Illustrated London News* Picture Library

Opposite Page:
STEWARDESS VIOLET JESSOP
*Jessop, a stewardess assigned to first-class ladies, was one of twenty-one females among the* Titanic's *crew. She survived the sinking and, later, the sinking of the* Britannic.
Courtesy Sheridan House

Right:
SECOND OFFICER
CHARLES H. LIGHTOLLER
*Second Officer Charles Lightoller had been shipwrecked and prospected for gold in the Yukon. He hoped to command his own ship one day, but never was given the opportunity.*
Courtesy *Illustrated London News* Picture Library

{Violet Jessop was saying her prayers when the *Titanic* collided with the iceberg.}

| PASSENGER | AGE | CLASS | LOST/SAVED |
|---|---|---|---|
| Mr. John Ashby | 57 | 2nd | Lost |
| Mr. Adola Asim | 35 | 3rd | Lost |
| Mrs. Carl Oscar (Selma Augusta Johansson) Asplund | 38 | 3rd | Saved |
| Miss Lillian Gertrud Asplund | 5 | 3rd | Saved |
| Master Filip Oscar Asplund | 13 | 3rd | Lost |
| Master Edwin Rojj Felix Asplund | 3 | 3rd | Saved |
| Master Carl Edgar Asplund | 5 | 3rd | Lost |
| Mr. John Charles Asplund | 23 | 3rd | Saved |
| Mr. Carl Oscar Asplund | 40 | 3rd | Lost |
| Master Clarence Gustaf Hugo Asplund | 9 | 3rd | Lost |
| Lady Cynthia Asquith | | 1st | Saved |

# In an era in which the Social Register listed the vessels on which the socially prominent sailed, a certain prestige was associated with sailing on the maiden voyage of the newest, biggest, most luxurious ship.

{Luxury accoutrements for the first class included a Turkish bath, a tennis and handball court, and a saltwater swimming pool.}

## Pride

The *Titanic* carried 900 tons of baggage and first-class freight—everything from steamer trunks to motor cars to lace bound for New York fashion houses. As a Royal Mail ship, the *Titanic* also had a post office for processing mail from England to the United States. A water-stained label was found in the pocket of Oscar S. Woody, the postal clerk, after his body was recovered from the frigid Atlantic.

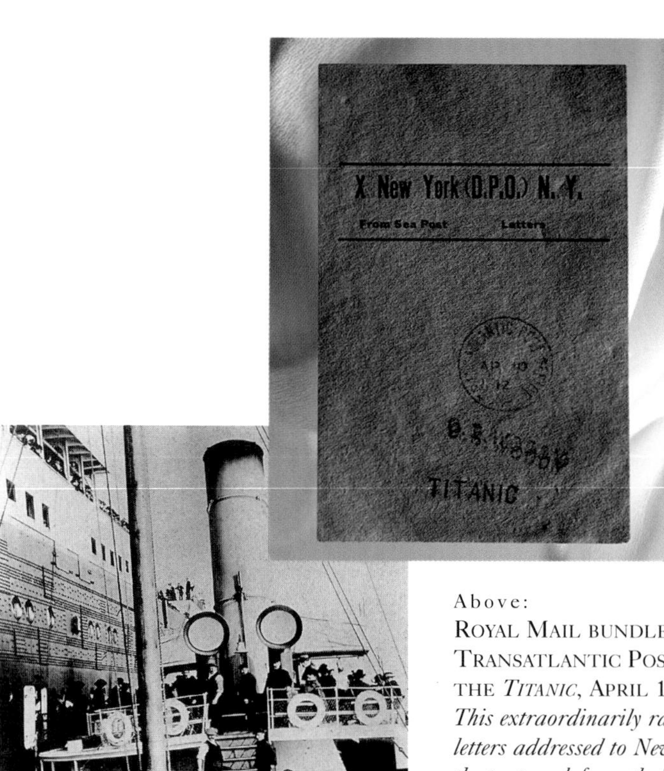


Above:
ROYAL MAIL BUNDLE TAG,
TRANSATLANTIC POST OFFICE,
THE *TITANIC*, APRIL 10, 1912
*This extraordinarily rare tag, intended for letters addressed to New York City, bears the postmark from the Transatlantic Post Office aboard the* Titanic. *It is stamped the first day of the maiden departure.*
Courtesy Stanley Lehrer Collection

Right:
LUGGAGE WAITING TO BE LOADED ABOARD THE *OLYMPIC*
Courtesy Brown Brothers, Sterling, Pennsylvania

Opposite Page:
STEAMER TRUNKS, CA. 1909;
LOUIS VUITTON & CO., PARIS
Courtesy Joanne's This, That and the Other, Poquoson, Virginia

| PASSENGER | AGE | CLASS | LOST/SAVED |
|---|---|---|---|
| Mrs. Mariana Assaf | 45 | 3rd | Saved |
| Mr. Gerios Assaf | | 3rd | Lost |
| Mr. Ali Assam | 23 | 3rd | Lost |
| Mrs. John Jacob (Madeleine Talmadge Force) Astor | 19 | 1st | Saved |
| Col. John Jacob Astor | 47 | 1st | Lost |
| Mr. Solomon Attala (Kalil) | 27 | 3rd | Lost |

Public fascination with the *Titanic* began long before the disaster. Posters and newspaper articles shouted her enticements—superior accommodations, fine food, and remarkable speed. For the wealthy, there was the allure of an opulent maiden voyage on this fairest of transatlantic liners. For others,

# ANTICIPATION

the appeal lay beyond status, in a sure, swift reunion with a lover, a child, a friend—or an encounter with a future they could only begin to imagine. And so, along with brown mountains of luggage and mail, the *Titanic*'s cargoes were ease and pleasure for some, and for others trepidation, hope, and desire.

Opposite Page:
TUGBOATS ASSIST THE *TITANIC* AS SHE EMBARKS FROM BELFAST.
Courtesy Stanley Lehrer Collection

| PASSENGER | AGE | CLASS | LOST/SAVED |
|---|---|---|---|
| Miss Malaka Attalah | 17 | 3rd | Lost |
| Mrs. Leontine Pauline Aubert | | 1st | Saved |
| Mr. Albert Augustsson | 23 | 3rd | Lost |
| Mr. Rafout Baccos | 20 | 3rd | Lost |
| Mrs. Karl Alfred (Maria Mathilda Gustafsson) Backstrom | 33 | 3rd | Saved |
| Mr. Karl Alfred Backstrom | 32 | 3rd | Lost |

{On May 31, 1911, some 100,000 people turned out for the *Titanic*'s launch in Belfast.}

## ANTICIPATION

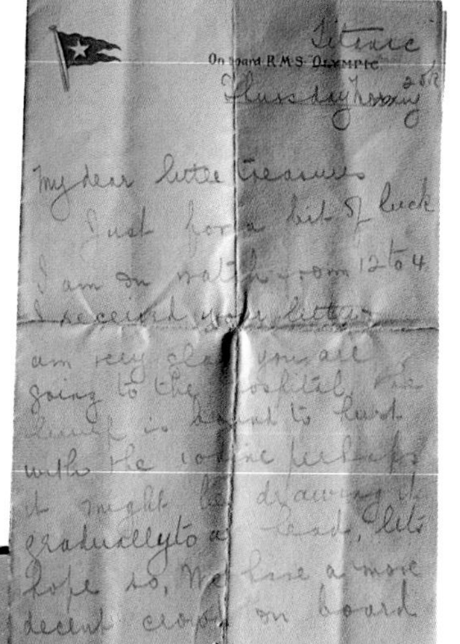

Titanic
On board R.M.S. Olympic
Thursday morning

My dear little treasures
Just for a bit of luck
I am on watch from 12 to 4
I received your letter
am very glad ...
going to the hospital ...
... it might be drawing it
gradually to a head, let's
hope so. We have a more
decent crowd on board

LETTER FROM ROOM STEWARD GEORGE A. BEEDEM
*"My dear little treasures," begins the letter written by room steward George Beedem to his wife and son. Beedem, who worked from midnight to 4:00* A.M., *had recently been transferred to the* Titanic *from the* Olympic *and apparently was writing to his family in the wee hours of the morning of April 11, 1912.*
Courtesy Stanley Lehrer Collection

Opposite Page:
"HANDS ACROSS THE SEA"
Postcards, jacquard silk, 1911–1912
*Silk-work pictures were popular during the late nineteenth and early twentieth centuries. Though such articles were often handcrafted, these were probably woven by machine.*
Courtesy Stanley Lehrer Collection and The Mariners' Museum

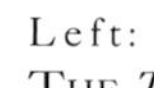

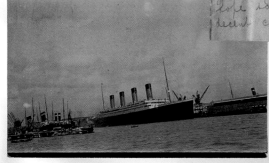

Left:
THE *TITANIC* IN SOUTHAMPTON HARBOR
*Presumably photographed on April 10, 1912, a few hours before the* Titanic *sailed*
Courtesy Stanley Lehrer Collection

**"A LOT [OF PEOPLE ARE] TO COME ON AT QUEENSTOWN . . . THE MORE THE MERRIER."**

—Titanic *steward George A. Beedem*

WOVEN IN SILK
R.M.S. TITANIC.
HANDS ACROSS THE SEA.
WOVEN IN SILK
R.M.S. TITANIC.

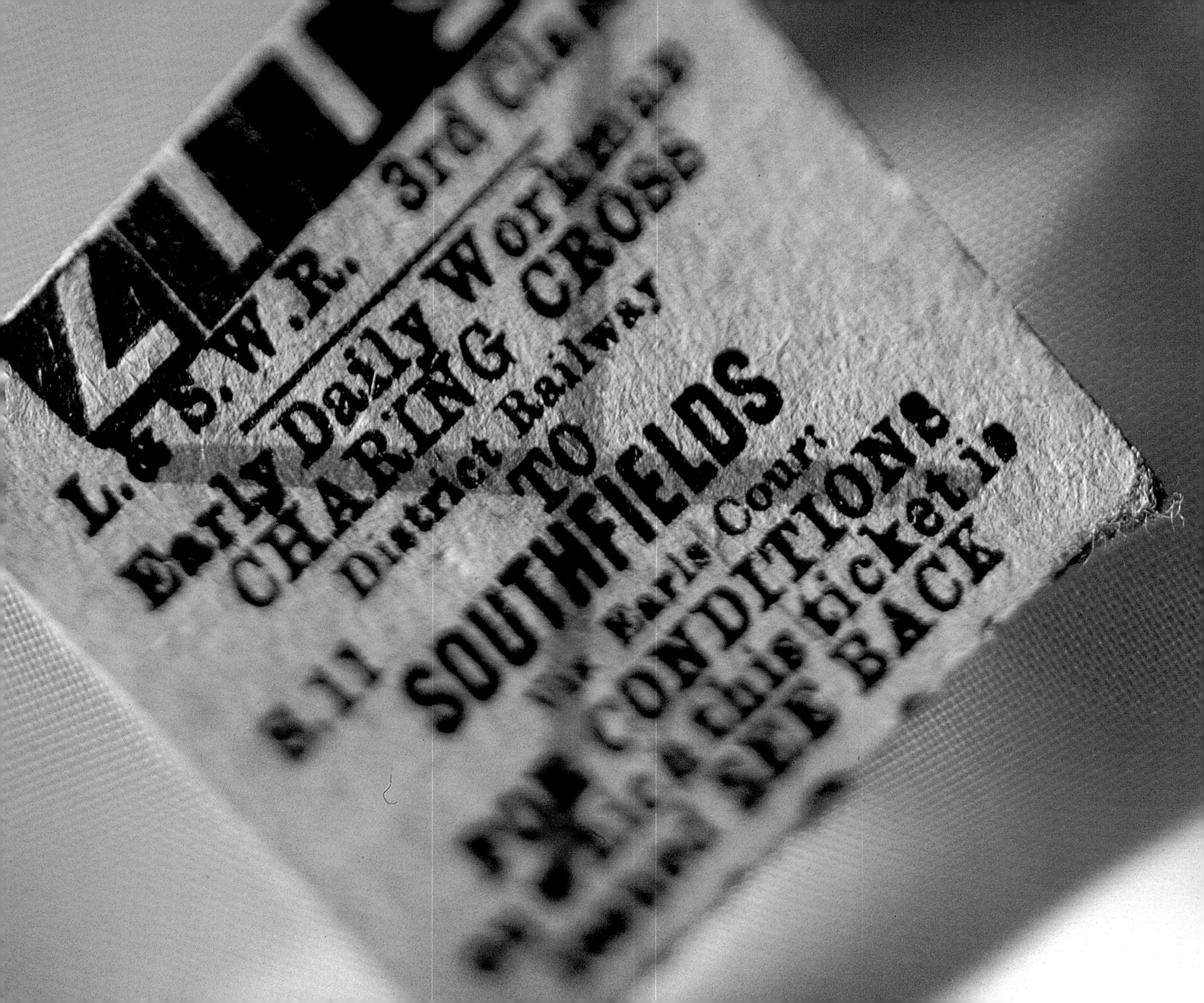
L. & S. W. R. 3rd
Early Daily Work
CHARING CROSS
District Railway
TO
SOUTHFIELDS
via Earls Court
CONDITIONS
SEE BACK

# AMONG THE 1,026 THIRD-CLASS PASSENGERS WERE MANY IMMIGRATING TO AMERICA TO PURSUE THEIR DREAMS.

{Leah Aks's parents refused to allow her to leave for America on any ship other than the new, "unsinkable" giant, the *Titanic*.}

## ANTICIPATION

The *Titanic*'s third-class quarters rang with many languages—English, French, Polish, Italian, Dutch, even Arabic.

Left:
THE AKS FAMILY
*Eighteen-year-old Leah Aks and her son, Frank (Filly), were third-class passengers, traveling from England to Norfolk, Virginia, to join Mrs. Aks's husband, Frank.*
Courtesy The Family of Frank P. Aks

Opposite Page:
THIRD-CLASS L. & S.W.R. RAILROAD TICKET STUB, CHARING CROSS DISTRICT TO SOUTHFIELDS, 1912
Titanic *passenger Selena R. Cook kept the railroad ticket stub from the train trip to the docks where she boarded the* Titanic. *She befriended Leah Aks, and later reportedly helped the young mother care for her son aboard the* Carpathia.
Courtesy The Family of Frank P. Aks

| PASSENGER | AGE | CLASS | LOST/SAVED |
|---|---|---|---|
| Miss Helene Baclini | | 3rd | Saved |
| Miss Eugenie Baclini | 3 | 3rd | Saved |
| Miss Maria Baclini | | 3rd | Saved |
| Mrs. Solomon (Latifa) Baclini | 24 | 3rd | Saved |
| Miss Emily Louisa Badman | 18 | 3rd | Saved |
| Mr. Mohammed Badt | 40 | 3rd | Lost |
| Mr. Mohammed Badt | 40 | 3rd | Lost |
| Mr. Percy Andrew Bailey | 18 | 2nd | Lost |
| Mr. Charles R. Baimbrigge | 23 | 2nd | Lost |

{Dr. J. Edward Simpson's request to serve aboard the *Titanic* was granted. He did not survive.}

**"THE SHIP IS SO BIG THAT I HAVE NOT YET FOUND MY WAY ABOUT: I HOPE I SHAN'T GET LOST ON BOARD BEFORE I ARRIVE IN NEW YORK!! THE SEA IS CALM AND WE ARE HAVING A JOLLY TIME."**

—*From a postcard [Stanley Lehrer Collection] mailed by a* Titanic *passenger*

## ANTICIPATION

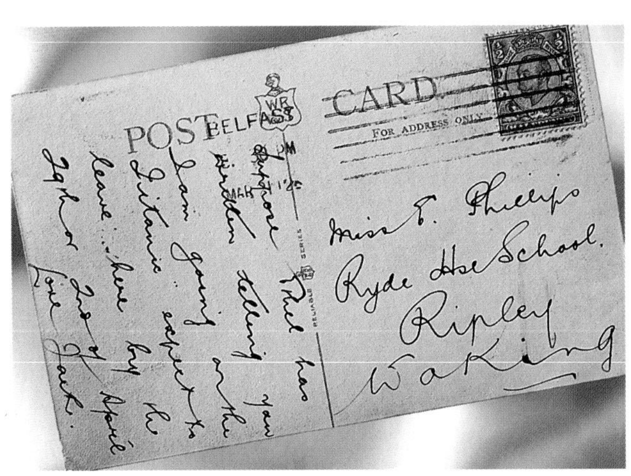
POST CARD
FOR ADDRESS ONLY
BELFAST
Suppose Phil has written telling you I am going on the Titanic. expect to leave here by the 2nd of April. Love Jack.
Miss E. Phillips
Ryde Hse School.
Ripley
Woking

Above:
POSTCARD MAILED BY *TITANIC* SENIOR WIRELESS OPERATOR JACK PHILLIPS TO HIS SISTER, ELSIE PHILLIPS, MARCH 21, 1912
*Writing to his sister from Belfast, Phillips's message read in part, "Suppose Phil has written telling you I am going on the* Titanic."
Courtesy Stanley Lehrer Collection

Opposite Page:
LETTER FROM J. EDWARD SIMPSON, APRIL 9, 1912
*Writing on* Titanic *stationery (note watermark) the day before the vessel's departure from Southampton, assistant surgeon Simpson asked to be transferred from the Royal Army Medical Corps so he could serve aboard the* Titanic.
Courtesy Stanley Lehrer Collection

| PASSENGER | AGE | CLASS | LOST/SAVED |
|---|---|---|---|
| Mr. Cerin Balkic | 26 | 3rd | Lost |
| Mrs. Ada E. Hall Balls | 36 | 2nd | Lost |
| Mr. Frederick J. Banfield | 28 | 2nd | Lost |
| Miss Ayout Banoura | 15 | 3rd | Lost |
| Mrs. Catherine Barbara | 45 | 3rd | Lost |
| Miss Saude Barbara | 18 | 3rd | Lost |

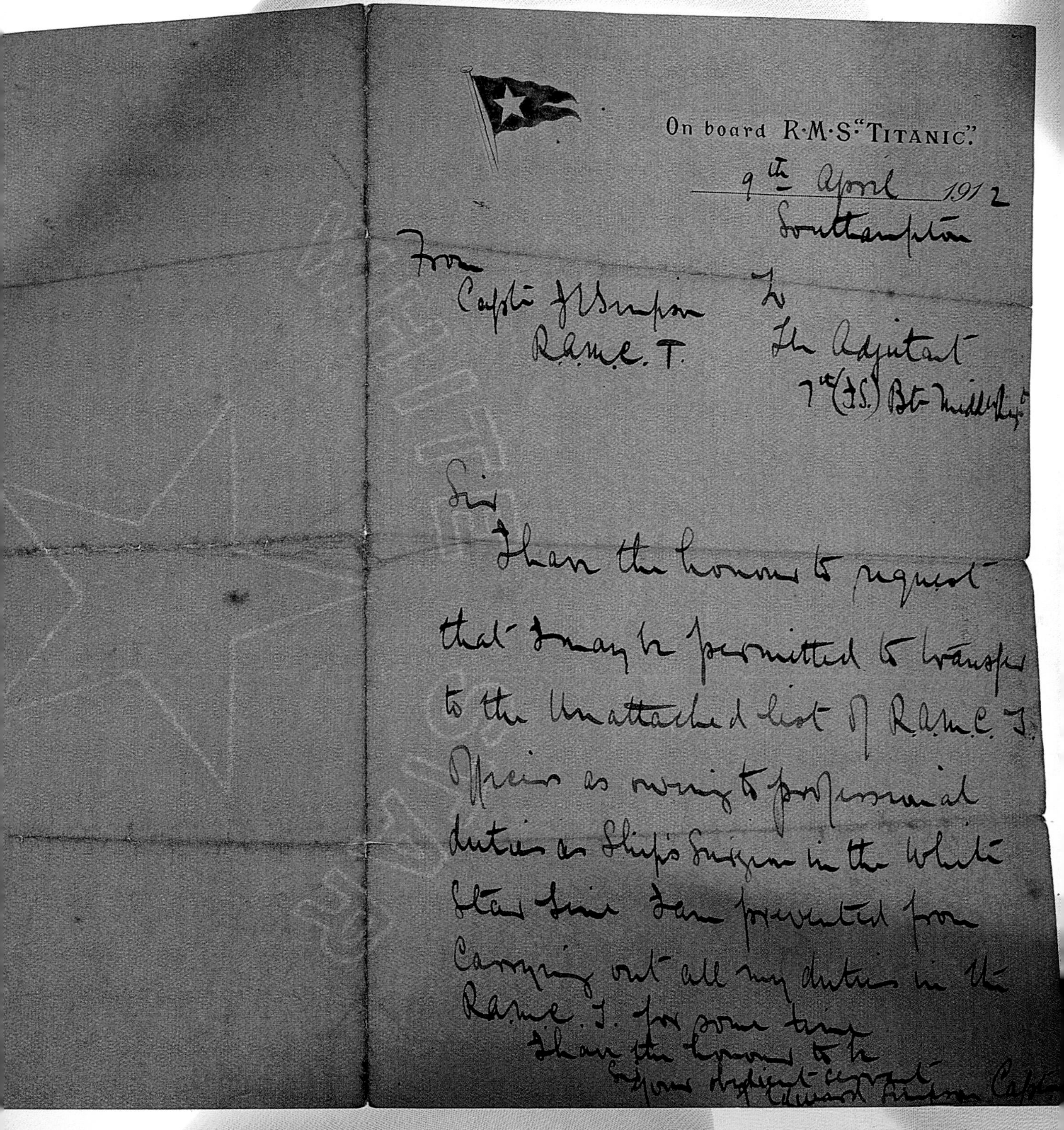

On board R·M·S "TITANIC".

9th April 1912
Southampton

From
Captn J E Simpson
R.A.M.C.T.

To
The Adjutant
7th (T.S.) Bn Middx Regt

Sir

I have the honour to request that I may be permitted to transfer to the Unattached list of R.A.M.C.T. Officers as owing to professional duties as Ship's Surgeon in the White Star Line I am prevented from carrying out all my duties in the R.A.M.C.T. for some time

I have the honour to be
Sir your obedient servant
Edward Simpson Captn

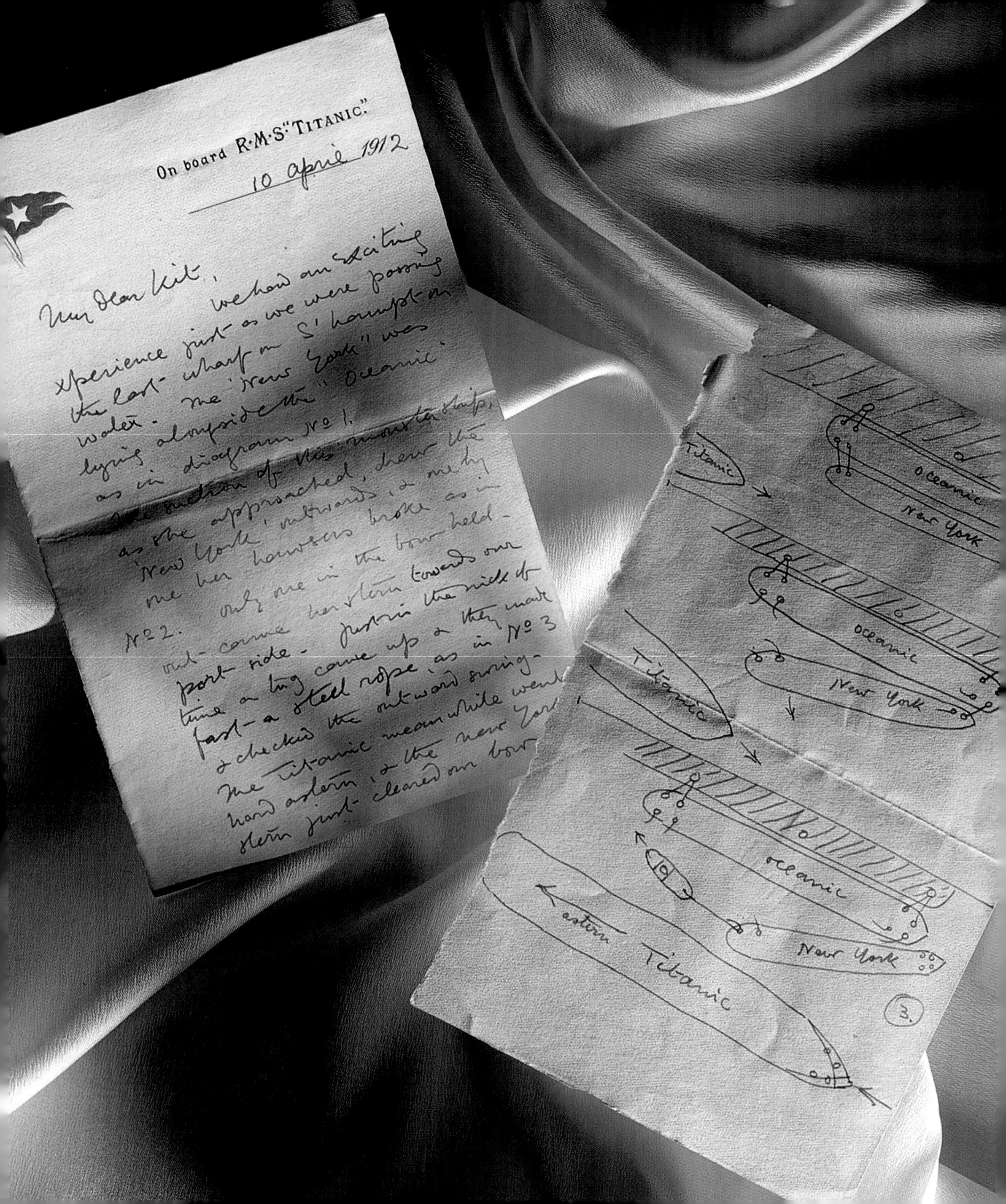

On board R·M·S· "TITANIC."

10 April 1912

My Dear Kit,

We had an exciting experience just as we were passing the last wharf in S'hampton water. The 'New York' was lying alongside the "Oceanic" as in diagram No 1. The suction of this monster ship, as she approached, drew the 'New York' outwards, & [illegible] her hawsers broke as in No 2. only one in the bow held - out-come her stern towards our port side. Just in the nick of time a tug came up & they made fast - a steel rope, as in No 3 & checked the outward swing. The Titanic meanwhile went hard astern, & the New York stern just cleared our bow

Titanic

Oceanic

New York

Titanic

Oceanic

New York

Oceanic

New York

astern

Titanic

3.

# "Great excitement! Jack got five photos of it, which he is cabling to sell to papers at home."

*—Marconigram sent by Mrs. Marian Longstreth Morris Thayer to her sister, April 10, 1912*

## Anticipation

As the *Titanic* left the dock, the nearby liner *New York* suddenly snapped her moorings and nearly rammed the mammoth White Star Line vessel. Adept maneuvering averted the collision, although some *Titanic* passengers feared the near miss was a bad omen.

Opposite Page:
Letter from Hugh Woolner on board the RMS *Titanic*, April 10, 1912
*Using* Titanic *stationery, first-class passenger Hugh Woolner made diagrams of the near collision with the* New York. *Prophetically, he wrote, "I hope not to have any more accidents."*
Courtesy Stanley Lehrer Collection

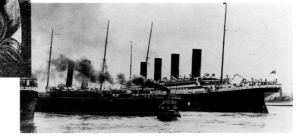

Left:
John B. and Marian Thayer
*John Thayer, who started his career as a freight clerk, was taking an extended leave of absence from his demanding job as second vice president of the Pennsylvania Railroad. Little is known about Thayer's wife, Marian, who survived the sinking—as did their teenage son, Jack.*
Courtesy *Illustrated London News* Picture Library

Above:
The *New York* nearly collided with the *Titanic* minutes after she left Southampton dock.
Courtesy Stanley Lehrer Collection

| Passenger | Age | Class | Lost/Saved |
|---|---|---|---|
| Mr. Algernon H. Barkworth | | 1st | Saved |
| Miss Julia Barry | 27 | 3rd | Lost |
| Mr. David Barton | 22 | 3rd | Lost |
| Rev Robert James Bateman | 51 | 2nd | Lost |
| Mr. John D. Baumann | | 1st | Lost |
| Mrs. James (Helene DeLaudeniere Chaput) Baxter | 50 | 1st | Saved |

{"*Titanic* will be despatched from Southampton to New York on her maiden voyage."}

{For the rest of her life, Kate Buss was not able to discuss the *Titanic* disaster without weeping.}

| Passenger | Age | Class | Lost/Saved |
|---|---|---|---|
| Mr. Quigg Edmond Baxter | 24 | 1st | Lost |
| Mr. Edward Beane | 32 | 2nd | Lost |
| Mrs. Edward (Ethel Clarke) Beane | 19 | 2nd | Lost |
| Mr. Thomson Beattie | 36 | 1st | Lost |
| Mr. Henry James Beauchamp | 28 | 2nd | Lost |
| Mr. William Thomas Beaven | 19 | 3rd | Lost |

## Anticipation

Above:
THE *TITANIC* FORGES HER WAY AT HIGH SPEED THROUGH THE ICE FIELD.
Illustration by Ken Marschall, from *Titanic: An Illustrated History* (Hyperion/Madison Press, 1992)

Opposite Page:
KATE BUSS
Courtesy Don Lynch Collection

**ENGLISHWOMAN KATE BUSS, AGE THIRTY-SIX, WAS ON HER WAY TO CALIFORNIA TO MARRY SAMUEL WILLIS—WHICH SHE DID, TWENTY-NINE DAYS AFTER THE SINKING.**

I am yours truly
W. T. Stead
Lafayette LTD
674 J
MR. W. T. STEAD
J. BEAGLES & Co.
E.C.

# "Thanks for message success to you NW wind fine and clear. Commander."

*—Marconigram from Captain Smith to the captain of the* Olympic, *April 3, 1912*

{As the *Titanic* left Queenstown on her way to New York, Captain Smith was photographed peering from the bridge.}

Opposite:
William T. Stead
*A leading British spiritualist, reformer, educator, and journalist, Stead was one of the most powerful opinion-makers of the Edwardian era. At the behest of President Taft, he was sailing to America to address a peace conference slated for April 21, 1912, at New York's Carnegie Hall. He never made it to the engagement.*
Courtesy Stanley Lehrer Collection

## Anticipation

Right:
The *Titanic*'s bridge and one of the lifeboats
Courtesy Corbis-Bettmann

Below:
Marconigram from Captain Smith to the captain of the *Olympic*

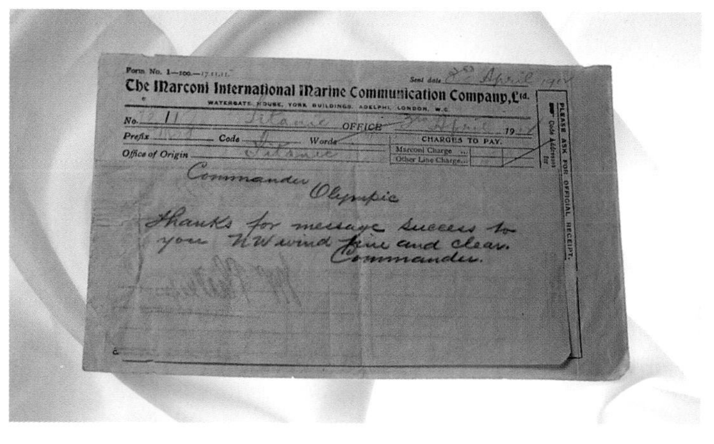

The Marconi International Marine Communication Company, Ltd.
WATERGATE HOUSE, YORK BUILDINGS, ADELPHI, LONDON, W.C.
No. Prefix Code Words OFFICE
Office of Origin Titanic
CHARGES TO PAY. Marconi Charge Other Line Charge
PLEASE ASK FOR OFFICIAL RECEIPT.

Commander
Olympic

Thanks for message success to you NW wind fine and clear.
Commander.

| Passenger | Age | Class | Lost/Saved |
| --- | --- | --- | --- |
| Mrs. Allen Oliver (Nellie E. Baumgardner) Becker | 36 | 2nd | Saved |
| Miss Marion Louise Becker | 4 | 2nd | Saved |
| Master Richard F. Becker | 1 | 2nd | Saved |
| Miss Ruth Elizabeth Becker | 12 | 2nd | Saved |
| Mrs. Richard (Sally Monypeny) Beckwith | 47 | 1st | Saved |
| Mr. Richard Leonard Beckwith | 37 | 1st | Saved |

In 1912, conspicuous class distinctions informed many of life's events—including an ocean crossing aboard the *Titanic*. Yet there was a difference with the White Star Line's ambitious beauty. On the *Titanic*, opulence unparalleled at sea embraced the first-class passengers. By design, the "inferior" classes too were elevated. Second-class passengers slept, strolled, and dined amid surroundings

# CLASS

that would have been reserved for the first class on another steamer. Third-class travelers enjoyed ample food and comfortable lodgings which, for many, must have surpassed all they knew in everyday life. So, though separate and clearly unequal, each of the *Titanic*'s three classes of travelers had booked a passage that lifted them out of the mundane into the extraordinary.

Opposite Page:
DETAIL OF CARVED OAK PANEL FROM FIRST-CLASS STAIRCASE
*This richly carved panel from the first-class grand staircase was installed aboard the* Titanic*'s sister ship, the* Olympic, *and gives a good idea of the elaborate woodwork aboard the doomed ship.*
Courtesy Stanley Lehrer Collection

| PASSENGER | AGE | CLASS | LOST/SAVED |
|---|---|---|---|
| Mr. Laurence Beesley | 34 | 2nd | Saved |
| Mr. Karl Howell Behr | 26 | 1st | Saved |
| Mr. John Viktor Bengtsson | 26 | 3rd | Lost |
| Miss Lillian W. Bentham | 19 | 2nd | Saved |
| Mr. Karl Ivar Sven Berglund | 22 | 3rd | Lost |
| Mr. William S. Berrimman | 23 | 2nd | Lost |

{U.S. government regulations required health inspections only for third-class passengers, the group thought most likely to contain "undesirables."}

## CLASS

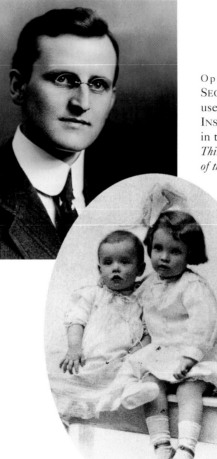

Right:
HUDSON J. ALLISON
*First-class passengers Hudson Allison, his wife, Bess, and their two small children, Trevor and Loraine, were traveling with their cook, chauffeur, nurse, and Bess's personal maid. Only Trevor and the maid survived. Two-year-old Loraine was the only first-class child lost in the sinking.*
Courtesy McCord Museum of Canadian History, Montreal

Right:
TREVOR AND LORAINE ALLISON
Courtesy Don Lynch Collection

Opposite Page:
SECOND-CLASS TICKET. Reproduction used in the 1997 film *Titanic.*
INSPECTION CARD. Reproduction used in the 1997 film *Titanic.*
*Third-class passengers—many, if not most, of them immigrants—were inspected by officials of the shipping line, who looked mainly for evidence of infectious diseases such as tuberculosis and for other conditions that would prevent the passenger from being self-sufficient in America.*
Courtesy Twentieth Century Fox Film Corporation and Twentieth Century Fox Film Archives

**THE DIFFERENT CLASSES ATE THEIR MEALS IN SEPARATE DINING ROOMS, DRANK IN SEPARATE BARS, STROLLED ON SEPARATE PROMENADES, EVEN HAD THEIR HAIR CUT IN SEPARATE BARBERSHOPS.**

№ 94395

SECOND CLASS

WHITE STAR LINE

ROYAL AND UNITED STATES MAIL STEAMERS

ISMAY, IMRIE & CO.

LONDON

JAMES STREET LIVERPOOL

CANUTE ROAD, SOUTHAMPTON

Agent at PARIS
NICHOLAS MARTIN, 9, Rue Scribe

WHITE STAR LINE

GENOA
NAPLES
BOSTON
NEW YORK
QUEBEC
MONTREAL

JAMES SCOTT & CO. Agents
QUEENSTOWN

OCEANIC STEAM NAVIGATION COMPANY, LIMITED, OF GREAT BRITAIN.

PASSENGER'S CONTRACT TICKET.
(NOT TRANSFERABLE).

Tons Register

19

SHIP ______ of ______ for ______

to sail from ______ day of ______

on the ______

| NAMES | AGES | Equal to statute to Adults |
|---|---|---|
| | | |

BILL OF FARE

SHIP ......

Tons Register ...... to sail from

...... on the

for ...... 19

day of ......

day of ......

| NAMES | AGES | Equal to statute to Adults |
|---|---|---|
| | | |

INSPECTION CARD.

Contract Ticket No. ......

Date of Departure ......

Port of Departure, QUEENSTOWN

Name of Ship ......

Name of Immigrant ......

Last Residence ......

## Class

The *Titanic*'s first-class passenger list glittered with names like Astor, Guggenheim, Widener, and Straus.

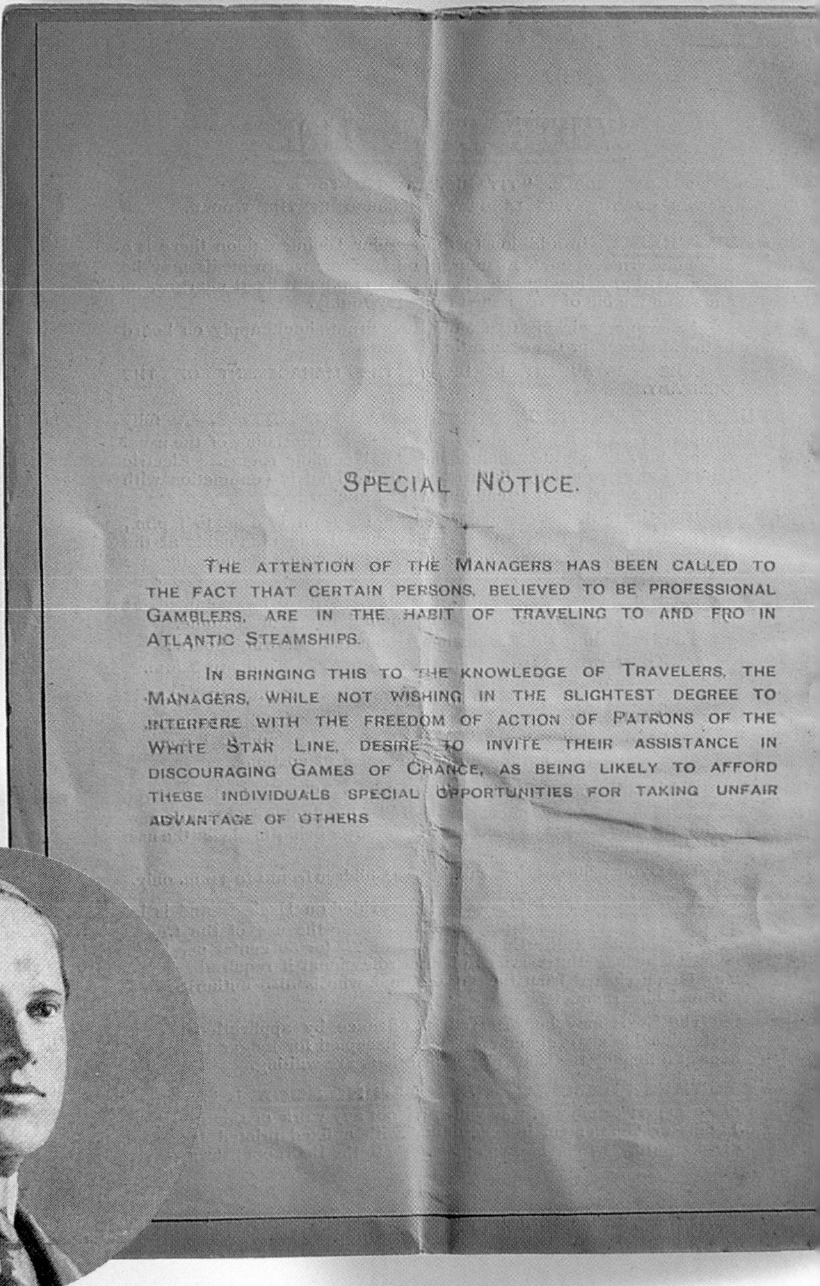

SPECIAL NOTICE.

THE ATTENTION OF THE MANAGERS HAS BEEN CALLED TO THE FACT THAT CERTAIN PERSONS, BELIEVED TO BE PROFESSIONAL GAMBLERS, ARE IN THE HABIT OF TRAVELING TO AND FRO IN ATLANTIC STEAMSHIPS.

IN BRINGING THIS TO THE KNOWLEDGE OF TRAVELERS, THE MANAGERS, WHILE NOT WISHING IN THE SLIGHTEST DEGREE TO INTERFERE WITH THE FREEDOM OF ACTION OF PATRONS OF THE WHITE STAR LINE, DESIRE TO INVITE THEIR ASSISTANCE IN DISCOURAGING GAMES OF CHANCE, AS BEING LIKELY TO AFFORD THESE INDIVIDUALS SPECIAL OPPORTUNITIES FOR TAKING UNFAIR ADVANTAGE OF OTHERS

Right:
BENJAMIN GUGGENHEIM
*Benjamin Guggenheim, age forty-six, was the scion of a Swiss immigrant family that had experienced a rags-to-riches rise to great wealth in the United States. In 1911, however, he had broken away to go into business on his own and was apparently suffering embarrassing financial losses. Though married, he was traveling aboard the* Titanic *with his Parisian mistress, Madame Aubert, who boarded Lifeboat 9. Guggenheim stayed behind.*
The Mariners' Museum

**"WE'VE DRESSED IN OUR BEST AND ARE PREPARED TO GO DOWN LIKE GENTLEMEN."**

*—Ascribed to Benjamin Guggenheim*

FIRST CLASS PASSENGER LIST
PER
ROYAL AND U.S. MAIL
S.S. "Titanic,"
FROM SOUTHAMPTON AND CHERBOURG
TO NEW YORK
(Via QUEENSTOWN).

*Wednesday, 10th April, 1912.*

Captain, E. J. Smith, R.D. (Commr. R.N.R.).
geon, W. F. N. O'Loughlin.
. Surgeon, J. E. Simpson.
Pursers { H. W. McElroy / R. L. Barker.
Chief Steward, A. Latimer.

Allen, Miss Elizabeth Walton
Allison, Mr. H. J.
Allison, Mrs. H. J. and Maid
Allison, Miss
Allison, Master and Nurse
Anderson, Mr. Harry
Andrews, Miss Cornelia I.
Andrews, Mr. Thomas
Appleton, Mrs. E. D.
Artagaveytia, Mr. Ramon
Astor, Colonel J. J. and Manservant
Astor, Mrs. J. J. and Maid
Aubert, Mrs. N. and Maid

Above:
GEORGE AND ELEANOR WIDENER
The Mariners' Museum

Left:
FIRST-CLASS PASSENGER LIST
Courtesy Independence Seaport Museum Library, Thayer Collection

"A MAN WHO HAS A MILLION DOLLARS
IS ALMOST AS WELL OFF AS IF HE WERE WEALTHY."

—*Col. John Jacob Astor*

Opposite Page:
14-KARAT GOLD, 19-JEWEL WALTHAM CASE POCKET WATCH, 1901–1902, TIFFANY & CO.
*Col. John Jacob Astor carried this monogrammed watch aboard the* Titanic. *It was recovered from his body on or about April 27, 1912, along with $2,500 in cash in his pockets. Astor's son, Vincent, had the watch put in working order and carried it for several years.*
Courtesy The Miottel Collection, San Francisco

Below:
MADELINE ASTOR
Courtesy Corbis-Bettmann

Left:
COL. JOHN JACOB ASTOR
Courtesy Collection of the New York Public Library, Astor, Lennox, and Tilden Foundations

Below:
18-KARAT GOLD MONOGRAMMED CUFF LINKS, EARLY TWENTIETH CENTURY, TIFFANY & CO.
*Also bearing the monogram "J.J.A.," these cuff links were given to William Dobbyn IV, Col. Astor's executive secretary, by the Astor family.*
Courtesy The Miottel Collection, San Francisco

## CLASS

First-class passage was expensive, but well within the means of passengers like John Jacob Astor, who paid just over £224 for himself, his wife, her maid, and his manservant. A single man could travel first class for £28.

{With a fortune totaling $87 million ($1.3 billion today), John Jacob Astor was by far the wealthiest person on board the *Titanic*.}

| PASSENGER | AGE | CLASS | LOST/SAVED |
|---|---|---|---|
| Mr. Ernst Herbert Bjorklund | 18 | 3rd | Lost |
| Mr. Mauritz Hakan Bjornstrom | 28 | 1st | Saved |
| Mr. Stephen Weart Blackwell | 45 | 1st | Lost |
| Mr. Henry Blank | 39 | 1st | Saved |
| Miss Caroline Bonnell | 29 | 1st | Saved |

{F. Dent Ray transferred from the *Olympic* to the *Titanic* before her maiden voyage. He was among the surviving crew.}

# THE SHIP EVEN OFFERED A DINING ROOM FOR SERVANTS AND SPECIAL ACCOMMODATIONS FOR FIRST-CLASS DOGS.

Right:
SECTION OF CARPET, STATEROOM, C DECK, RMS *TITANIC*, CA. 1911
*Steward F. Dent Ray obtained a remnant of green carpeting from a stateroom. He took it home to show his wife and later used it to cushion a music stool. In the early 1960s, the carpeting was donated to the Titanic Historical Society, which cut it into one-inch squares and traded it for other acquisitions.*
Courtesy Stanley Lehrer Collection

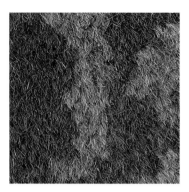

Opposite Page:
WOODEN FRAGMENT FROM FIRST-CLASS STAIRCASE
*The chunk of wood shown here was wrenched from the first-class staircase as the ship sank; it was found drifting in the Atlantic during efforts to locate survivors.*
Courtesy Stanley Lehrer Collection

## CLASS

The *Titanic*'s public rooms featured rich carpeting, cut-glass fittings, elaborate carvings, and the finest paneling. First-class passengers also had their own gymnasium, swimming pool, a Turkish bath, a squash court, and even a fully equipped darkroom, and three elevators.

Left:
GRAND STAIRCASE
*The showpiece of the* Titanic*'s opulent first-class interior was the grand staircase. Natural light streamed through the wrought-iron-and-glass dome above the staircase and reflected off the polished oak paneling and carved gilt balustrades.*
Courtesy Library of Congress

| PASSENGER | AGE | CLASS | LOST/SAVED |
|---|---|---|---|
| Miss Elizabeth Bonnell | 58 | 1st | Saved |
| Miss Margaret (Muddy) Boone | | 1st | Saved |
| Mr. John James Borebank | | 1st | Lost |
| Mr. Guentcho Bostandyeff | 26 | 3rd | Lost |
| Mr. William Hull Botsford | 26 | 2nd | Lost |

| PASSENGER | AGE | CLASS | LOST/SAVED |
|---|---|---|---|
| Master Akar Boulos | 6 | 3rd | Lost |
| Miss Laura Boulos | 9 | 3rd | Lost |
| Mr. Hanna Boulos | | 3rd | Lost |
| Mrs. Joseph (Sultana) Boulos | | 3rd | Lost |
| Miss Mary Bourke | | 3rd | Lost |
| Mrs. John (Catherine) Bourke | 32 | 3rd | Lost |
| Mr. John Bourke | 40 | 3rd | Lost |

{Charlotte Cardeza's fourteen-page insurance claim for lost personal items totaled $177,352.75.}

## CLASS

First-class passengers might travel with more than a dozen trunks. Wealthy Philadelphian Charlotte Drake Cardeza and her son, Thomas, were accompanied by fourteen trunks, four suitcases, three crates, and a medicine chest. The contents of the luggage included seventy dresses and ten fur coats. Mrs. Cardeza submitted the largest claim against the White Star Line for loss of life and property resulting from the sinking of the *Titanic.*

Opposite Page:
LADY'S PERIOD DRESS
Courtesy Helen Larson Collection

ABOVE:
MRS. CHARLOTTE DRAKE CARDEZA
Courtesy Titanic Historical Society, Inc., Father Browne Collection

Below:
LUGGAGE LABEL, "WANTED FIRST CLASS."
Reproduction used in the 1997 film *Titanic.*
Courtesy Twentieth Century Fox Film Corporation and Twentieth Century Fox Film Archives

"IT MUST BE ADMITTED THAT A VERY LARGE FRACTION OF OUR TIME WAS SPENT IN DRESSING AND UNDRESSING. WE WERE FOREVER CHANGING OUR CLOTHES, A CUSTOM THAT NECESSITATED TRAVELING WITH A MOUNTAIN OF LUGGAGE." —*Lady Cynthia Asquith*

{Some second-class cabins housed representatives of the *Titanic*'s builder, who were charged with handling problems that might arise on the maiden voyage.}

## "NO EFFORT HAD BEEN SPARED TO GIVE EVEN SECOND-CABIN PASSENGERS . . . THE BEST DINNER THAT MONEY COULD BUY."

*—Attributed to a surviving passenger*

### CLASS

Second class on the *Titanic* was superior to first class on many other liners—and cost as much or more. A couple traveling with their daughter paid just over £26, while a single fare could be had for £13. Among the 271 second-class passengers were businessmen and their families, an American film producer, a pastor, a teacher, and a chauffeur.

On April 14, the *Titanic*'s last night, the second-class dining saloon offered a choice of four main courses: baked haddock, curried chicken, spring lamb, or roast turkey.

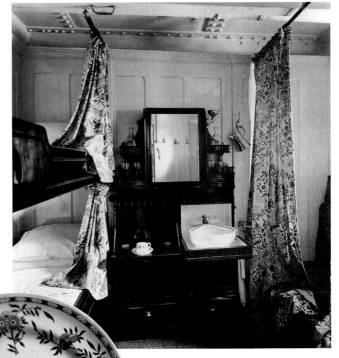

Above:
SECOND-CLASS STATEROOM
Courtesy the National Maritime Museum, Greenwich, England

Right:
WHITE STAR LINE
SECOND-CLASS PLATE, CA. 1910;
STONIER & CO., LIVERPOOL
*Second-class tableware aboard the* Titanic *was more elegant than that of most other ships' first-class service.*
The Mariners' Museum

Opposite Page:
SAMUEL WARD STANTON
*Samuel Ward Stanton spent his entire life around ships. The son of a prominent New York shipbuilder, he edited the* Nautical Gazette *and, prompted by his friendship with renowned steamboat painter James Bard, published a book in 1895 entitled* American Steam Vessels. *Stanton was returning from a research trip to Spain and was among the more than 1,500* Titanic *passengers who perished. He left a wife and three children.*
Courtesy H. Kneeland Whiting

| Passenger | Age | Class | Lost/Saved |
|---|---|---|---|
| Miss Grace Scott Bowen | 45 | 1st | Saved |
| Mr. David Bowen | 45 | 1st | Saved |
| Mr. David Bowen | 26 | 3rd | Lost |
| Mr. Soloman Bowenur | | 2nd | Lost |
| Miss Elsie Edith Bowerman | 22 | 1st | Saved |
| Mrs. James H. Bracken | 27 | 2nd | Lost |

## Class

Third-class travelers were critical to the profitability of the transatlantic route, and the *Titanic* competed by offering cabins and public rooms that were better than the best accommodations of most nineteenth-century liners. The food was hearty and nourishing, and probably better in both quality and quantity than what many third-class passengers were used to at home.

Opposite Page:
THIRD-CLASS SLEEPING ACCOMMODATIONS
*The 222 third-class cabins were surprisingly large and airy, with pine paneling and comfortable floor coverings—a significant improvement over the bare metal walls and floors that had been the norm on most liners.*
Courtesy Ken Marschall Collection

Above:
FREDERICK AND AUGUSTA GOODWIN WITH FIVE OF THEIR SIX CHILDREN; EIGHTEEN-MONTH-OLD SIDNEY GOODWIN (inset)
*Like many third-class passengers, the Goodwins were making their way to America to begin a new life. Third-class accommodations were spread over four different decks, requiring passengers to navigate myriad passageways, stairs, and decks to reach their berths. The berths contained no instructions for lifesaving measures, location of life vests, or directions to other parts of the vessel. The Goodwins never reached Niagara Falls, as they had hoped; all eight perished in the sinking.*
Courtesy Don Lynch Collection

| PASSENGER | AGE | CLASS | LOST/SAVED |
|---|---|---|---|
| Miss Bridget Delia Bradley | 26 | 3rd | Lost |
| Mr. James Bertram Brady | 40 | 1st | Lost |
| Miss Elin Ester Maria Braf | 20 | 3rd | Lost |
| Mr. Youssef Brahim | | 3rd | Lost |
| Mr. Emil Brandeis | 48 | 1st | Lost |
| Mr. Owen Harris Braund | 22 | 3rd | Lost |
| Mr. Lewis Richard Braund | 29 | 3rd | Lost |

{A family with nine children traveled in third class for less than £70, while a mother and son paid just over £9.}

There were 127,000 pieces of tableware on the *Titanic*, including thousands of bone-china dinner plates, 800 cut-glass tumblers and assorted fine crystal, and 100 grape scissors. The *Titanic*'s first-class dining saloon was the largest room afloat. With its nearby reception room, the dining saloon—which extended the full width of the ship and included Jacobean-style alcoves with leaded-glass windows—could seat more than 500 passengers in splendor. Separate

# Luxury

and equally elegant was the à la carte restaurant, where diners could arrange private dinner parties. Such luxuries were not merely an Edwardian fancy. They were ever-so-deliberate attempts to shape a reputation that would set the *Titanic* and her sister, the *Olympic*, apart from their competitors. A White Star Line passage would not be cheap, but the passenger's money would buy the best.

Opposite Page:
White Star Line mustard pot
The Mariners' Museum

{After Captain Smith, head chef Charles Proctor was the *Titanic*'s highest-paid crew member.}

Above:
FIRST-CLASS DINING SALOON
Courtesy Ken Marschall Collection

Below:
LIST OF PURCHASES MADE ON BOARD THE RMS *TITANIC* BY MRS. THAYER
Courtesy Independence Seaport Museum Library, Thayer Collection

## LUXURY

Looking at this rendering of the first-class dining saloon of the *Olympic*, the *Titanic*'s sister ship, one can almost hear the lilting background music and the soft voices and laughter of some of the world's wealthiest people.

Opposite Page:
WHITE STAR LINE TIN CIGARETTE CASE, WITH CIGARETTES, CA. 1910
Courtesy James E. O'Neill, Jr.

Below:
WHITE STAR LINE BUD VASE
The Mariners' Museum

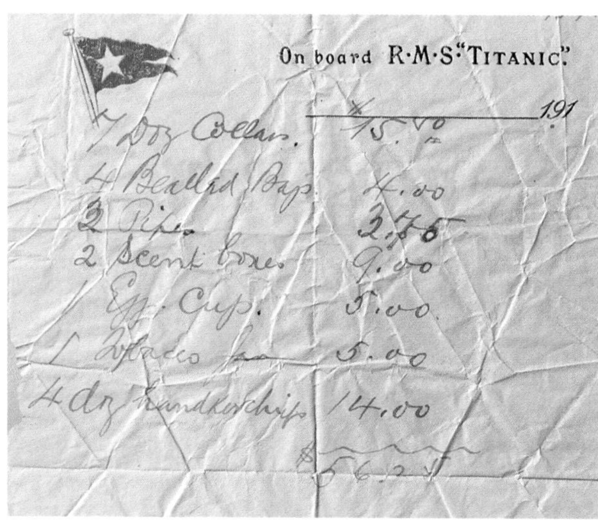

On board R·M·S "TITANIC".

________ 191

1 Doz Collars. 15.50
4 Beaded Bags 4.00
2 Pipes 3.75
2 Scent boxes 9.00
Egg Cups 5.00
1 Tobacco jar 5.00
4 doz handkerchiefs 14.00
$56.25

In an era known for opulence, the White Star Line's Titanic and her twin, the Olympic, were the last word in elegance and comfort.

| Passenger | Age | Class | Lost/Saved |
|---|---|---|---|
| Mr. George Arthur Brayton | | 1st | Saved |
| Dr. Arthur Jackson Brewe | | 1st | Lost |
| Mr. Karl Rudolf Brobeck | 22 | 3rd | Lost |
| Mr. William Alfred Brocklebank | 35 | 3rd | Lost |
| Mr. Thomas William Brown | 45 | 2nd | Lost |
| Miss Edith E. Brown | 15 | 2nd | Saved |

| PASSENGER | AGE | CLASS | LOST/SAVED |
|---|---|---|---|
| Mrs. James Joseph (Margaret Tobin) Brown | 44 | 1st | Saved |
| Mr. John Murray (Caroline Lane Lamson) Brown | 59 | 1st | Saved |
| Miss Mildred Brown | 24 | 2nd | Saved |
| Mrs. Thomas William (Elizabeth C.) Brown | 40 | 2nd | Saved |
| Miss Dagmar Bryhl | 20 | 2nd | Saved |
| Mr. Kurt Arnold G. Bryhl | 25 | 2nd | Lost |
| Miss Katherine Buckley | 20 | 3rd | Lost |
| Mr. Daniel Buckley | 21 | 3rd | Lost |
| Mrs. William Robert (Emma Eliza Ward) Bucknell | 60 | 1st | Saved |

{Frederic Spedden and several other men were allowed into the lifeboat only because, at that moment, there seemed to be no more women or children on deck.}

Right:
SIX-YEAR-OLD DOUGLAS SPEDDEN PLAYING WITH A TOP ON THE *TITANIC*'S FIRST-CLASS PROMENADE DECK
*Douglas was attached to Polar, his Steiff polar bear, and took the bear everywhere with him, including on the* Titanic. *Daisy Spedden's book* Polar, the Titanic Bear *is a delightful children's story written as a Christmas present for Douglas in the months after their rescue. All three Speddens—along with Douglas's nanny, Margaret Burns, and Mrs. Spedden's maid—survived, leaving the sinking* Titanic *in Lifeboat 3.*
Photograph by Father Francis Browne. Courtesy Titanic Historical Society, Inc.

## LUXURY

Opposite Page:
*TITANIC* GYMNASIUM
The Mariners' Museum

Left:
FIRST-CLASS LOUIS XVI LOUNGE
Harland & Wolff photograph, courtesy Ulster Transport and Folk Museum

**THE TITANIC'S PASSENGERS SPENT MUCH OF THEIR TIME READING, PLAYING CARDS, WALKING ON DECK, OR—IN FIRST CLASS—PERHAPS EXERCISING IN THE GYMNASIUM OR SWIMMING POOL.**

| Passenger | Age | Class | Lost/Saved |
|---|---|---|---|
| Mr. Jeremiah Apri Burke | 19 | 3rd | Lost |
| Miss Mary Delia Burns | 18 | 3rd | Lost |
| Miss Kate Buss | 36 | 2nd | Saved |
| Mr. Reginald Fenton Butler | 25 | 2nd | Lost |
| Major Archibald Willingham Butt | 45 | 1st | Lost |

**IN THE ROOMS KNOWN AS THE VERANDAH AND PALM COURT, IVY GREW ON THE TRELLIS-COVERED WALLS. . . . THESE ROOMS WERE POPULAR AREAS FOR PARENTS TO MINGLE AS THEIR CHILDREN PLAYED.**

{Eva Hart lost her father on the fateful voyage and later wrote a book about the tragedy, *Shadow of the* Titanic.}

Right:
FREDERIC, DAISY, AND DOUGLAS SPEDDEN WITH POLAR
1998 Leighton H. Coleman III, Spedden Collection. All rights reserved.

Opposite Page:
STEIFF POLAR BEAR, 1909
Courtesy Steiff USA

LUXURY

Right:
EVA HART AND HER PARENTS, CA. 1912
*Eva Hart was only seven when she experienced the most horrendous sea tragedy in history. Her mother, Esther, had been so plagued by a premonition that the ship would sink that she sat up at night and slept during the day because she felt sure that any tragedy would strike at night.*
Courtesy Stanley Lehrer Collection

Above:
DOLL
Jumeau Company
*This expensive French doll with an elaborate handmade costume is similar to the kind upper-class young girls aboard the* Titanic *might have owned.*
Courtesy Carolyn K. Barry, Suffolk, Virginia

R.M.S. "TITANIC."

APRIL 3, 1912.

LUNCHEON.

CROÛTE-AU-POT SCOTCH BROTH

TURBOT À LA CRÈME

EGG À L'OLGA

HARICOT OX TAIL

VEAL & HAM PIE

FROM THE GRILL.

GRILLED CHICKEN & BACON

MASHED, FRIED & BAKED JACKET POTATOES

SAGO PUDDING

DEVONSHIRE DUMPLINGS PASTRY

BUFFET.

FRESH LOBSTERS POTTED SHRIMPS

SARDINES

ROAST BEEF

ROAST CHICKEN OX TONGUE

BRAISED BEEF À LA GELÉE

CUMBERLAND HAM BOLOGNA SAUSAGE

LETTUCE TOMATOES

CHEESE.

CHESHIRE STILTON

COFFEE

R.M.S. "TITANIC."

APRIL 3, 1912.

FRUIT

QUAKER OATS

FILLETS OF WHITING

KIPPERED HERRINGS

CALVES' LIVER & BACON

GRILLED HAM GRILLED SAUSAGE

MINCED CHICKEN

POACHED & FRIED EGGS

PLAIN & TOMATO OMELETTES

MASHED & SAUTÉ POTATOES

COLD MEAT

ROLLS SCONES

MARMALADE

STRAWBERRY CONSERVE

WATERCRESS

**"WE DINED THE LAST NIGHT IN THE [À LA CARTE] RITZ RESTAURANT. IT WAS THE LAST WORD IN LUXURY. THE TABLES WERE GAY WITH PINK ROSES AND WHITE DAISIES, THE WOMEN IN THEIR BEAUTIFUL SHIMMERING GOWNS, THE MEN IMMACULATE. . . . THE FOOD WAS SUPERB: CAVIAR, LOBSTER, QUAIL FROM EGYPT, PLOVER'S EGGS, AND HOTHOUSE GRAPES AND FRESH PEACHES."**

*—Mrs. Walter Douglas*

## LUXURY

Opposite page:
BREAKFAST AND LUNCH MENUS, THE RMS *TITANIC*, APRIL 3, 1912
*A full breakfast and an elegant lunch were served the day following the* Titanic's *sea trials off the coast of Belfast.*
Courtesy Stanley Lehrer Collection

Left:
TABLE SETTING, FIRST-CLASS WHITE STAR LINE DINING SALOON
*This table is set with reproductions of White Star Line's finest china, crystal, and silver, and represents a typical table setting for dinner aboard the* Titanic. *Some of the items seen here were used in the 1997 film* Titanic.
The Mariners' Museum and courtesy Twentieth Century Fox Film Corporation and Twentieth Century Fox Film Archives

{"... the orchestra [in the first-class dining saloon was] playing music from Puccini and Tchaikovsky."}

| PASSENGER | AGE | CLASS | LOST/SAVED |
|---|---|---|---|
| Rev. Thomas Archibald Willingham Byles | 45 | 1st | Lost |
| Rev. Thomas Roussel D. Byles | | 2nd | Lost |
| Mrs. Carolina Bystrom | | 2nd | Lost |
| Mr. Grego Cacic | 18 | 3rd | Lost |
| Mr. Luka Cacic | 38 | 3rd | Lost |
| Mr. Manda Cacic | | 3rd | Lost |

WHITE
STAR
LINE

63

| PASSENGER | AGE | CLASS | LOST/SAVED |
|---|---|---|---|
| Mr. Maria Cacic | 30 | 3rd | Lost |
| Mr. Edward P. Calderhead | | 1st | Saved |
| Mr. Albert Francis Caldwell | 26 | 2nd | Saved |
| Mrs. Albert Francis (Sylvia Mae Harbaugh) Caldwell | 26 | 2nd | Saved |
| Master Alden Gates Caldwell | 10m | 2nd | Saved |
| Mr. Peter Cacic | 17 | 3rd | Lost |
| Miss Clear Cameron | 31 | 2nd | Saved |
| Mr. Patrick Canavan | 21 | 3rd | Lost |
| Miss Mary Canavan | 21 | 3rd | Lost |

## LUXURY

In the first-class restaurants the service and food rivaled those of the most elegant restaurants on land. Tables were beautifully set with silver and gilded Spode china; the wine list was impressive; the orchestra played nearby, and haute cuisine was the order of the day.

Opposite Page:
WHITE STAR LINE
FIRST-CLASS DINNER PLATE, CA. 1910;
WHITE STAR LINE
DINNER FORK, DINNER KNIFE,
AND TABLESPOON, CA. 1911

Left:
WALLACE HARTLEY SURROUNDED BY MEMBERS OF HIS ORCHESTRA
Courtesy *Illustrated London News* Picture Library

**WHEN THE BUGLER SOUNDED "THE ROAST BEEF OF OLD ENGLAND" —THE TRADITIONAL CALL TO MEALS ABOARD WHITE STAR LINERS— PASSENGERS KNEW THAT ONE OF THE HIGHLIGHTS OF LIFE AT SEA AWAITED THEM.**

{The menu for Sunday night, April 14, included oysters, salmon with mousseline sauce, filet mignon, sauté of chicken lyonnaise, roast duckling, roast squab, and pâté.}

{Bruce Ismay, managing director of White Star, occupied one of two promenade suites, each of which boasted a 50-foot private deck.}

# LUXURY

Below:
CLOSE-UP OF THE FINAL FIRST-CLASS DECK PLAN FOR THE *TITANIC*, RELEASED BY THE WHITE STAR LINE ON MARCH 29, 1912
*One of only three known to exist, unlike previous* Titanic *deck plans, this one revealed the location (by numbers) of deck chairs on A deck.*
Courtesy Stanley Lehrer Collection

Left:
FIRST-CLASS STATEROOM
*One-, two-, and three-berth staterooms were available in first class. Some featured an adjoining cabin for the passenger's personal servant. A drawer from a dressing table like the one seen in this photograph was recovered from the floating debris.*
Courtesy Ken Marschall Collection

Opposite Page:
DRESSING TABLE DRAWER
The Mariners' Museum,
gift of Mrs. Montfort Haslom

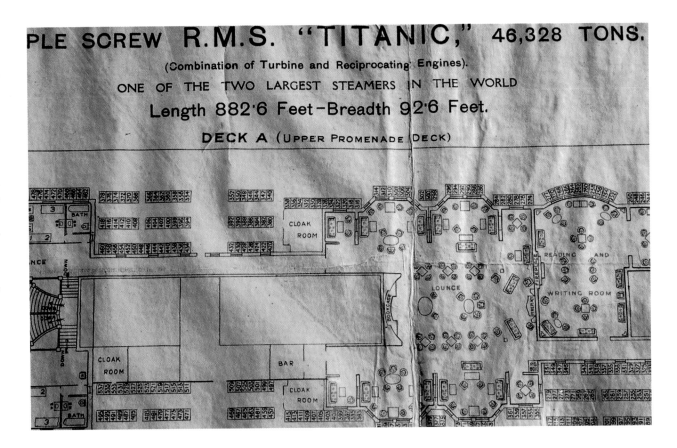

PLE SCREW R.M.S. "TITANIC," 46,328 TONS.
(Combination of Turbine and Reciprocating Engines).
ONE OF THE TWO LARGEST STEAMERS IN THE WORLD
Length 882'6 Feet–Breadth 92'6 Feet.
DECK A (UPPER PROMENADE DECK)

CLOAK ROOM
BATH
LOUNGE
READING AND WRITING ROOM
FIREPLACE
BOOKCASE
BAR
CLOAK ROOM
CLOAK ROOM
BATH

"THE SHIP IS LIKE A PALACE.
THERE IS AN UNINTERRUPTED DECK RUN OF
165 YARDS FOR OUR USE, AND A RIPPING SWIMMING BATH. . . .
MY CABIN IS RIPPING——HOT AND COLD WATER
AND A VERY COMFY-LOOKING BED——AND LOTS OF ROOM."

*—First-class passenger Hugh Woolner*

| PASSENGER | AGE | CLASS | LOST/SAVED |
|---|---|---|---|
| Mrs. Edward (Helen Churchill Hungerford) Candee | 53 | 1st | Saved |
| Mr. Ernest Cann | 21 | 3rd | Lost |
| Mr. Joseph Caram (Kareem) | | 3rd | Lost |
| Mrs. Joseph (Maria Elias) Caram (Kareem) | | 3rd | Lost |
| Mr. William Carbines | 19 | 2nd | Lost |
| Mr. Thomas Drake M. Cardeza | 36 | 1st | Saved |
| Mrs. James Warburton M. Cardeza (Charlotte Wardle Drake) | 58 | 1st | Saved |

On fine days, deck chairs beckoned on the promenade decks, and stewards hovered nearby, ready to satisfy a passenger's every whim.

Below:
LUCILE POLK CARTER
*Socialite Lucile Polk Carter, her son and daughter, and her husband, Billy, traveled in first class—of course. A friend of aristocrat George Widener since boyhood, Billy Carter made the aristocratic sport of polo his game. His beloved polo ponies may have been aboard the* Titanic, *along with his twenty-four polo sticks and his Renault.* Courtesy Don Lynch Collection

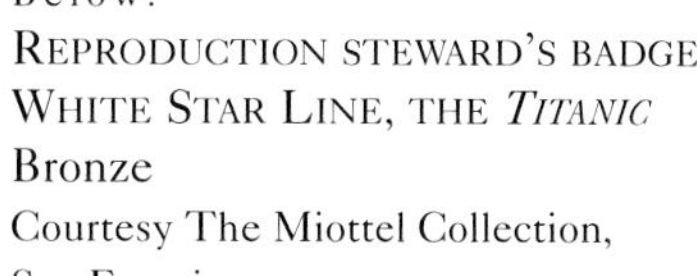

Below:
REPRODUCTION STEWARD'S BADGE, WHITE STAR LINE, THE *TITANIC*
Bronze
Courtesy The Miottel Collection, San Francisco

## LUXURY

Below:
WOODEN DECK CHAIR
Reproduction used in the 1997 film *Titanic*
Courtesy Twentieth Century Fox Film Corporation and Twentieth Century Fox Film Archives

Opposite Page:
DOROTHY GIBSON
*Few people realized that Dorothy Gibson, the proper twenty-two-year-old traveling with her mother in first class, was a professional model and minor movie star. While on board, Gibson received a wireless message from her secret lover, a married man and successful movie backer, which reportedly made her "awfully happy."*
Courtesy Corbis-Bettmann

{After returning safely to New York, Dorothy Gibson went on to star in the first movie about the *Titanic*.}

| PASSENGER | AGE | CLASS | LOST/SAVED |
|---|---|---|---|
| Mr. August Sigfrid Carlsson | 28 | 3rd | Lost |
| Mr. Julius Carlsson | 33 | 3rd | Lost |
| Mr. Carl Robert Carlsson | 24 | 3rd | Lost |
| Mr. Frans Olof Carlsson | 33 | 1st | Lost |
| Miss Helen Carr | 16 | 3rd | Saved |
| Miss Jeannie Carr | 37 | 3rd | Lost |

In the crow's nest, lookout Frederick Fleet strained to see through the moonless night. Spying "a small, dark mass" a mile ahead, Fleet rang the three-bell alarm and telephoned the bridge. Efforts to steer around the iceberg proved fatal: slowly, slowly, the *Titanic* swung to port, grazing the iceberg

# DISASTER

## APRIL 14, 1912: 41°46′N., 50°14′W.

on her starboard side. There was no hint that the ship had been seriously damaged. But below, under tremendous pressure, the sea was pouring in. Six compartments were filling with water, and the *Titanic* could not float with more than four flooded. So, inexorably, disaster began to unfold.

Opposite Page:
LIFE VEST—LINEN, WITH TWELVE CORK BLOCKS
Attributed to the RMS *Titanic*, ca. 1911
The Mariners' Museum, gift of Bonnie M. Brewer

Previous Pages:
THE *TITANIC* IN MIST PULLING AWAY FROM SOUTHAMPTON
Courtesy Stanley Lehrer Collection

**"IT DID NOT SEEM TO ME THERE WAS ANY GREAT IMPACT AT ALL. IT WAS AS THOUGH WE WENT OVER ABOUT A THOUSAND MARBLES."**

*—Mrs. Stuart J. White, passenger*

{"We all walked slowly with the life belts tied on over our clothing, but even then we presumed that this was merely a wise precaution the captain was taking and that we should return in a short time to go to bed."—Lawrence Beesley}

## DISASTER

Most passengers felt only a jar or heard a scrape, then quiet, as the *Titanic* glided to a stop. Several people ran to scoop up bits of ice from the chunks that had fallen on deck, some to place in their alcoholic drinks.

Above:
THE *TITANIC* BEGINS HER FINAL PLUNGE INTO THE ICY WATERS, STERN RISING.
Illustration by Ken Marschall.
From *Titanic: An Illustrated History*
(Hyperion/Madison Press, 1992)

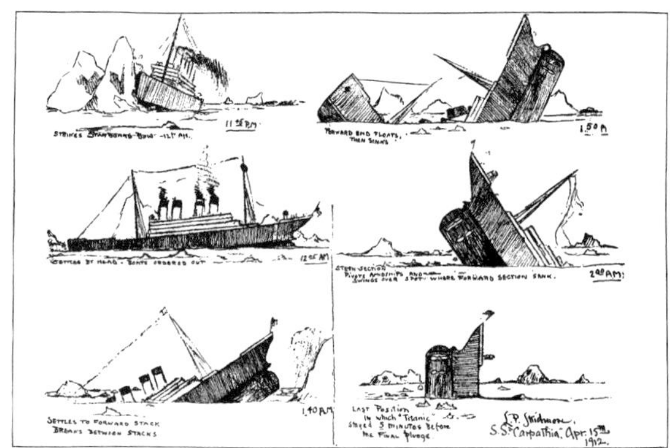

Above:
APRIL 1912 DRAWING OF THE SINKING OF THE *TITANIC*
*Survivor Jack Thayer described the sinking to* Carpathia *passenger L. D. Skidmore, who made this rough drawing.*
The Mariners' Museum

Opposite Page:
LAWRENCE BEESLEY
*Lawrence Beesley, a second-class passenger and science professor from London, was reading in his bunk when the collision occurred. Beesley was taking a voyage to America to try to recover from his wife's death, having left his young son with family in England. He managed to board Lifeboat 13 and took care of a baby until safely aboard the* Carpathia.
Courtesy *Illustrated London News* Picture Library

| PASSENGER | AGE | CLASS | LOST/SAVED |
|---|---|---|---|
| Mr. Francisco Carrau | | 1st | Lost |
| Mr. Jose Pedro Carrau | | 1st | Lost |
| Mr. William Ernest Carter | 36 | 1st | Saved |
| Mrs. William Ernest (Lucile Polk) Carter | 36 | 1st | Saved |
| Miss Lucile Polk Carter | 14 | 1st | Saved |
| Master William Thorton II Carter | 11 | 1st | Saved |

11

A Hymn of Glory Let Us Sing
L. M., with Alleluias
Lasst uns erfreuen
"Geistliche Kirchengesäng"
Cologne, 1623
1: 11
num canamus gloriae
Venerable Bede, 1735
Benjamin Webb, 1854, alt.
1 A hymn of glo - ry let us sing; New songs thro'-out the
2 The ho - ly ap - os - tol - ic band Up - on the Mount of
3 To whom the an - gels, draw - ing nigh, "Why stand and gaze up-
4 "A - gain shall ye be - hold Him so As ye to - day have
world shall ring: Al - le - lu - ia! Al - le - lu - ia! Christ,
Ol - ives stand; Al - le - lu - ia! Al - le - lu - ia! And
on the sky? Al - le - lu - ia! Al - le - lu - ia! This
seen Him go, Al - le - lu - ia! Al - le - lu - ia! In
by a road be - fore un - trod, As - cend - eth to the
with His fol - low - ers they see Je - sus' re - splen - dent
is the Sav - ior," thus they say; "This is His no - ble
glo - rious pomp as - cend - ing high, Up to the por - tals
throne of God. Al - le - lu - ia! Al - le - lu - ia!
maj - es - ty. Al - le - lu - ia! Al - le - lu - ia!
tri - umph - day. Al - le - lu - ia! Al - le - lu - ia!
of the sky." Al - le - lu - ia! Al - le - lu - ia!
Lo, Judah's Lion Wins the
8. 8. 4. 7.
Rev. 5: 5
Aj, ten silný lev udatný
From the Bohemian, c. 1650
Tr., John Bajus, 1940
1 Lo, Ju - dah's Li - on
2 'Tis He whom Da - vi
3 Like Sam - son, Christ
reigns o'er death to
he did strong Go
con - quered hell, its
Oh,
Oh,
Oh,
4 Th
W

| PASSENGER | AGE | CLASS | LOST/SAVED |
|---|---|---|---|
| Mrs. Ernest Courtenay (Lilian Hughes) Carter | 44 | 2nd | Lost |
| Rev. Ernest Courtenay Carter | 54 | 2nd | Lost |
| Mr. Alfred John Carver | 28 | 3rd | Lost |
| Mr. Howard Brown Case | 49 | 1st | Lost |
| Mrs. Henry Arthur, Jr. (Genevieve Fosdick) Cassebeer | | 1st | Saved |
| Mr. Nassef Belmenty Cassem | | 3rd | Saved |

{"Hard a-starboard. Full speed astern." —First Officer Murdoch's order upon hearing that an iceberg had been sighted.}

## DISASTER

Opposite Page:
WHITE STAR LINE HYMNAL
Reproduction used in the 1997 film *Titanic*
Courtesy Twentieth Century Fox Film Corporation and Twentieth Century Fox Film Archives

Below:
TICKET FROM A WEIGHING MACHINE ABOARD THE *TITANIC*, APRIL 8, 1912
*This water-stained ticket most likely records the weight of a member of the* Titanic's *crew. Stamped two days before the vessel sailed from Southampton, the ticket was found floating in a box after the ship sank.*
Courtesy Stanley Lehrer Collection

| STONES | LBS. | S. S. TITANIC |
|---|---|---|
| | 5 | DATE 8 . 4 . 12 |

Above:
ANXIOUS CROWDS BESIEGE THE *NEW YORK AMERICAN* OFFICE IN NEW YORK CITY.
Courtesy Brown Brothers, Sterling, Pennsylvania

**"CRASH! THEN A LOW RENDING, CRUNCHING RIPPING SOUND, AS TITANIC SHIVERED A TRIFLE AND THE SOUND OF HER ENGINES GENTLY CEASED."**

—*Stewardess Violet Jessop*

Captain Smith and Thomas Andrews, managing director of the shipbuilding company, soon knew the truth. At 12:15 A.M. on April 15, Senior Wireless Operator Jack Phillips began sending CQD as the prevailing distress call and then, at 12:45 A.M., switched to SOS, the newly introduced international distress signal. For the first

# DESPAIR

time in history, SOS was used from a ship at sea. The call ended with MGY, the *Titanic*'s radio call sign.

The SS *Californian* was closest to the disaster scene, but the ship's only wireless operator had signed off for the night. Another ship to receive the signal, the *Carpathia*, was more than fifty-eight miles away.

**CQD, CQD, CQD, CQD, CQD,**
**CQD, CQD, SOS, SOS, SOS, MGY**

Opposite Page:
LOGBOOK ENTRY FROM THE *CARONIA*
*Although the* Titanic *had received ice warnings from several ships in the area during the day of April 14, only the one from the* Caronia *was posted so that all officers knew of the possible danger. Calculations derived from the* Caronia *message indicated that the* Titanic *would reach the ice at approximately 11:00 P.M.*
Courtesy Craig A. Sopin Collection

abt [illegible]
got it direct [illegible]
him I missed 33 [illegible]
[illegible]ed 2 SGs for MGY
spoke with MCE re SG
MGY sends following (Titanic)
I require assistance immediately
Struck by iceberg in 41.46N
Long 50.14W. [MGY] 38 Miles East)
(our distance fm MGY
Sent CQD MGY to MBC + CQD
MGY struck iceberg requires
immediate assistance - RD fm ML [CMF]
Titanic MGY called DFT Frankfort
MGY " are you coming to
our assistance, MGY

3.45 MKC CQD - MGY
3.52 SOS - MGY
3.54 MKC - MGY We are CQD here
3.55 MGY to MRA We are CQD here
Posn 41-46N 50.14W. SOS - MGY CQD
3.58 MRA to MBC
in 41-46N 50.14W wants immediate assistance
Advised MBC of above - MBC
about 490 astern of us
4.10 MGY to MKC we are in Collision
with berg sinking head down 41.46N
50.14W. Come soon as possible

39.47 Frankfurt
52.10 posn [illegible]

SOS

(3)

SOS

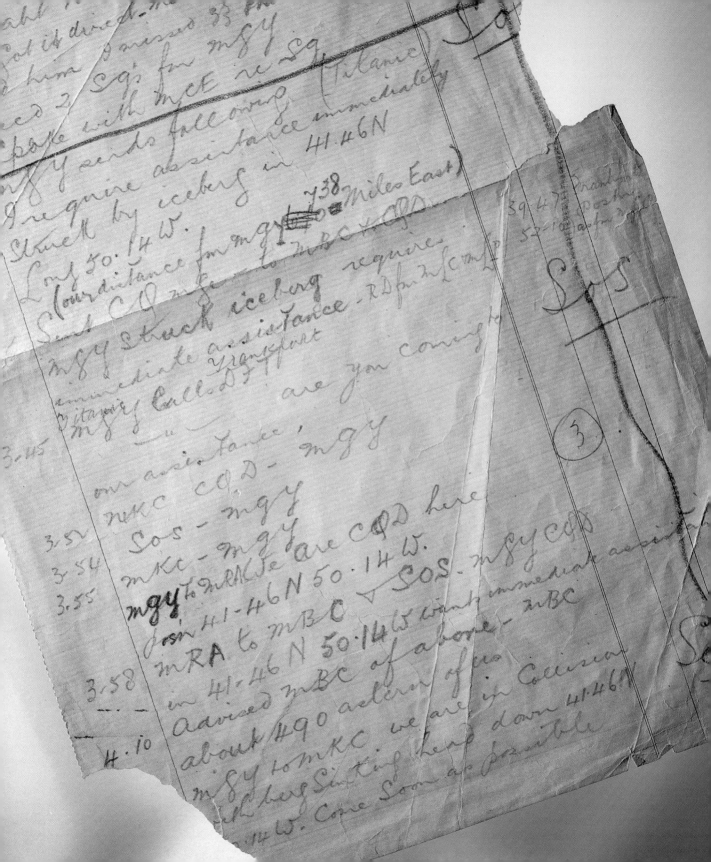

{At 1:15 A.M., the *Titanic's* bow began to settle below water.}

# "IT'S THE NEW CALL, AND IT MIGHT BE YOUR LAST CHANCE TO SEND IT."

*—Junior Wireless Operator Harold Bride to Senior Operator Jack Phillips*

## DESPAIR

Left:
HAROLD BRIDE, SECOND OPERATOR, MARCONI MARINE, RMS *TITANIC*
*Harold Bride worked as a telegrapher in the British Postal Service before joining Marconi Marine in 1911. He was twenty-two years old when he earned a second operator rating. When the great ship sank, Bride joined a group of men attempting to deploy a collapsible lifeboat. Suffering from injuries to his feet and severe frostbite, he managed to cling to the capsized boat—and to life—until rescuers arrived.*
Courtesy GEC–Marconi Archives, Chelmsford, Essex, Great Britain

Left:
MARCONI WIRELESS ROOM ABOARD THE *TITANIC*
*This is the only known photograph of the wireless room aboard the* Titanic. *Harold Bride can be seen working.*
Courtesy Titanic Historical Society, Inc.

Opposite Page:
REPLICA OF MARINE MARCONI ROOM
Courtesy James and Felicia Kreuzer Collection, New Wireless Pioneers

| PASSENGER | AGE | CLASS | LOST/SAVED |
|---|---|---|---|
| Mr. Tyrell William Cavendish | 36 | 1st | Lost |
| Mrs. Tyrell William (Julia Florence Siegel) Cavendish | | 1st | Saved |
| Mr. Francesco Celotti | 24 | 3rd | Lost |
| Mr. Herbert Fuller Chaffee | 46 | 1st | Lost |
| Mrs. Herbert Fuller (Carrie Toogood) Chaffee | 47 | 1st | Saved |
| Mr. Norman Campbell Chambers | 27 | 1st | Saved |

MARCONI
WIRELESS TELEGRAPH
CO. of AMERICA
COMMERCIAL MESSAGES RECEIVED HERE
MARCONIGRAM

| Passenger | Age | Class | Lost/Saved |
|---|---|---|---|
| Mr. Norman Campbell (Bertha Griggs) Chambers | 31 | 1st | Saved |
| Mrs. John Henry (Elizabeth Lawry) Chapman | 28 | 2nd | Lost |
| Mr. Charles H. Chapman | 52 | 2nd | Lost |
| Mr. John Henry Chapman | 30 | 2nd | Lost |
| Mr. David Chartens | 21 | 3rd | Lost |
| Mr. Emir Farres Chehab | | 3rd | Lost |

Opposite Page:
John "Jack" Phillips, chief operator, Marconi Marine, RMS *Titanic*
*On April 11, 1912, Jack Phillips celebrated his twenty-fifth and final birthday. Harold Bride always remembered Phillips as "the man who saved us all."*
Courtesy GEC–Marconi Archives, Chelmsford, Essex, Great Britain

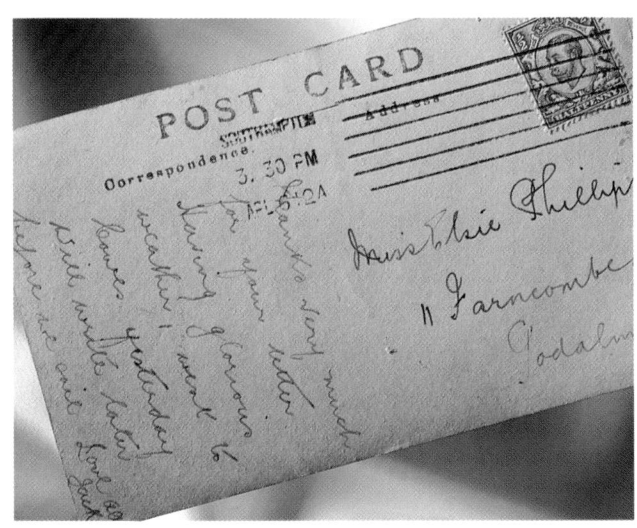


Above:
Postcard from Jack Phillips to his sister, Elsie Phillips, April 6, 1912
Courtesy Kenneth Schultz Collection

## Despair

Русское Восточно Азіатское Пароходство

The Russian East Asiatic S. S. Co. Radio-Telegram.

S. S. Birma

Titanic 11.50 april 14/15 Distress Call Sig Good

CQD - SOS from MGY
We have struck iceberg sinking fast come to our assistance
Position Lat 41.46 n. Lon 50.14 w
MGY

[illegible]

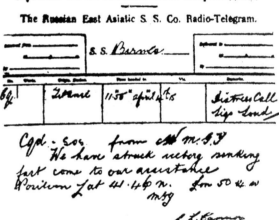

Above:
SOS Marconigram sent from the *Titanic* to the Russian ship SS *Birma*
Courtesy George Behe Collection

**"CQD-SOS from MGY we are sinking fast passengers being put into boats."**

—*SOS Marconigram sent from the* Titanic *to the SS* Birma

{"Look out for yourselves—you can do no more!" —Captain Smith to the Marconi operators}

**NO GENERAL ALARM WAS SOUNDED, BUT STEWARDS BEGAN TO URGE PASSENGERS TO DRESS AND PUT ON LIFE VESTS.**

## DESPAIR

Opposite Page:
RUTH BECKER AND HER BROTHER, RICHARD, CA. 1912
*Ruth Becker, age twelve, got her younger brother and sister on deck and into Lifeboat 11. As the boat was being lowered, her mother screamed, "Oh, let me go with my children," and jumped in—leaving Ruth on deck. Sixth Officer James Moody picked Ruth up and dropped her into the already loaded Lifeboat 13, where the resourceful child comforted crying women, tore her own blankets in half to keep others warm, and even bandaged one passenger's finger.*
Courtesy Don Lynch Collection

Above:
"WOMEN AND CHILDREN FIRST. GOOD-BYE; GOOD-BYE; MEET ME IN NEW YORK," CA. 1912
Offset lithograph after Fortunino Matania
The Mariners' Museum

Above:
BRASS NAMEPLATE FROM *TITANIC* LIFEBOAT 5, CA. 1911
Courtesy Stanley Lehrer Collection

| PASSENGER | AGE | CLASS | LOST/SAVED |
|---|---|---|---|
| Miss Gladys Cherry | | 1st | Saved |
| Mr. Paul Chevre | | 1st | Saved |
| Mrs. Edit Chibnall | | | Saved |
| Mr. Paul Chevre | | 1st | Saved |
| Mrs. Edith Martha Chibnall | | 1st | Saved |
| Mr. Chang Chip | 32 | 3rd | Lost |
| Mr. Roderick Robert Chisholm | | 1st | Lost |

{Only thirteen of the *Titanic*'s lifeboats were brought to New York by the *Carpathia*. What happened to them is uncertain, although there was speculation that the *Olympic* brought the boats to Southampton.}

**"WE WERE A MASS OF HOPELESS,**
**DAZED HUMANITY ATTEMPTING,**
**AS THE ALMIGHTY AND NATURE MADE US,**
**TO KEEP OUR FINAL BREATH**
**UNTIL THE LAST POSSIBLE MOMENT."**

—*Jack Thayer*

Left:
EDWINA TROUTT
*When disaster struck, twenty-seven-year-old Edwina Troutt refused to board a lifeboat, insisting that it was criminal for a single woman to be saved in place of a man with a family. Suddenly an infant was thrust into Troutt's arms by a man who claimed he would not seek a lifeboat position in the place of a woman. Troutt took the baby and found her way to one of the last boats to be lowered, collapsible Lifeboat D.*
Courtesy Don Lynch Collection

## DESPAIR

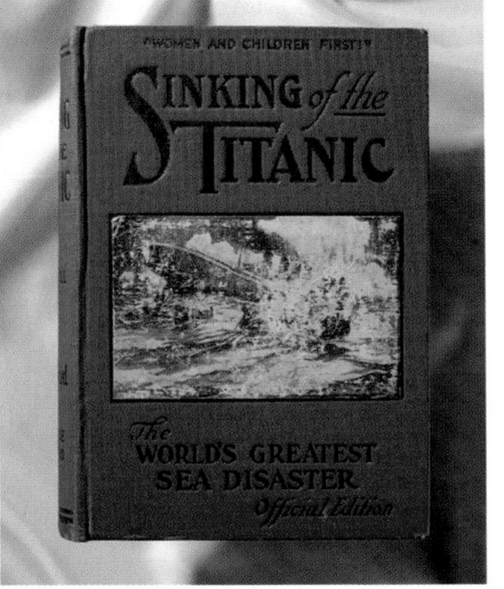


Right:
*SINKING OF THE* TITANIC: *THE WORLD'S GREATEST SEA DISASTER*
National Bible House,
Chicago. T. A. Russell, ed.

Opposite Page:
CALF-DEEP IN ICY WATER
IN COLLAPSIBLE LIFEBOAT D
Courtesy Don Lynch Collection

| PASSENGER | AGE | CLASS | LOST/SAVED |
|---|---|---|---|
| Mr. Emil Christmann | 29 | 3rd | Lost |
| Mrs. Alice Frances Christy | | 2nd | Saved |
| Miss Julie Christy | | 2nd | Saved |
| Mr. Apostolos Chronopoulos | 26 | 3rd | Lost |
| Mr. Demetrios Chronopoulos | 18 | 3rd | Lost |
| Mr. Walter Miller Clark | 27 | 1st | Lost |

{At 2:17 A.M., her stern heaved up in the air, and the *Titanic* poised vertically in the sea. Left on board were over 1,500 men, women, and children.}

The *Titanic* was sinking. By 2:00 A.M., freezing seawater was lapping within 10 feet of the promenade deck. Steaming toward the scene was the Cunard ship *Carpathia*, commanded by Captain Arthur Henry Rostron. On her way from New York to Gibraltar, *Carpathia* received the *Titanic*'s distress

# COURAGE

call just as her wireless operator was preparing to shut down for the night. Rostron turned the *Carpathia* around, becoming, in that unflinching moment, a hero. Aboard the *Titanic* herself, and adrift in her lifeboats like waifs in the North Atlantic, other heroic figures were emerging.

Opposite Page:
COMMEMORATIVE MEDAL, CA. 1912
*The "unsinkable" Molly Brown led a campaign to honor the captain, the officers, and crew of the* Carpathia *for their efforts to rescue victims of the* Titanic *disaster. The medal features a bas-relief image of the Cunard Line vessel approaching a* Titanic *lifeboat and the inscription (reverse side) "in recognition of gallant and heroic services."*
Courtesy Stanley Lehrer Collection

**AFTER HELPING TO LOAD THE LIFEBOATS WITH WOMEN AND CHILDREN, GRACIE SWAM FROM THE BOAT DECK IN THE FRIGID WATERS AS THE GREAT SHIP SANK.**

## COURAGE

Right:
MINNIE COUTTS
*Minnie Coutts, with her two sons, age three and nine, was sailing to New York to join her husband. Finding only two life vests in her cabin, she was able to obtain a third one from a passing crewman, who told her, "There! If the boat goes down, you'll remember me." After briefly becoming lost in the bowels of the great liner, Coutts and her children finally found another crewman, who showed them an alternate route to the outer deck.*
Courtesy Haynes Publishing

Opposite Page:
COL. ARCHIBALD GRACIE IV
*On the roof of the officers' quarters, Gracie was caught in a whirlpool and pulled down. He managed to free himself and swam furiously, eventually reaching the overturned collapsible Lifeboat B.*
Courtesy Titanic Historical Society, Inc.

| PASSENGER | AGE | CLASS | LOST/SAVED |
|---|---|---|---|
| Mr. Walter Miller (Virginia McDowell) Clark | 26 | 1st | Saved |
| Mrs. Charles V. (Ada Maria) Clarke | 28 | 2nd | Saved |
| Mr. Charles V. Clarke | 29 | 2nd | Lost |
| Mr. George Quincy Clifford | | 1st | Lost |
| Mr. Domingos Fernandes Coelho | 20 | 3rd | Lost |
| Mr. Gurshon (Gus) Cohen | 19 | 3rd | Saved |
| Mr. Patrick Colbert | 24 | 3rd | Lost |

| Passenger | Age | Class | Lost/Saved |
|---|---|---|---|
| Mr. Peyo Coleff | 36 | 3rd | Lost |
| Mr. Fotio Coleff | 24 | 3rd | Lost |
| Mr. Reginald Charles Coleridge | 29 | 2nd | Lost |
| Mr. Erik Collander | 27 | 2nd | Lost |
| Mr. Sidney C. Stuart Collett | 24 | 2nd | Saved |
| Mr. Edward Pomeroy Colley | | 1st | Lost |
| Mr. Harvey Collyer | 35 | 2nd | Lost |
| Mrs. Harvey (Charlotte Tate) Collyer | 31 | 2nd | Saved |
| Miss Marjory Collyer | 8 | 2nd | Saved |

{Of the Titanic's almost 900 crew members, more than 200 were saved.}

## Courage

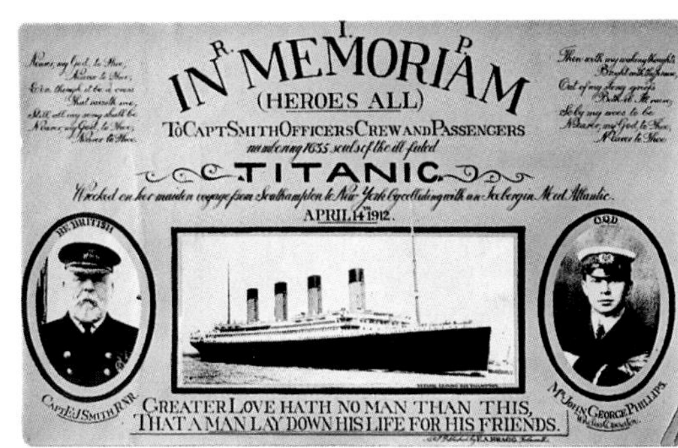


Right:
R.I.P. IN MEMORIAM (HEROES ALL)
Postcard featuring John George "Jack" Phillips and Captain Smith
*For staying at his post relaying distress signals until the last possible moment, Marconiman Jack Phillips was lionized by the media as a man who "gave his life so that others could be saved." Phillips managed to escape the rapidly sinking ship but died of hypothermia before rescuers arrived.*
Courtesy James and Felicia Kreuzer Collection, New Wireless Pioneers

Opposite Page:
*CARPATHIA* WIRELESS OPERATOR
HAROLD THOMAS COTTAM
*After the sinking, Harold Cottam was lauded as "the man who saved over 700 lives."*
The Mariners' Museum

**"The band was still playing,**
**and I guess they all went down.**
**They were playing 'Autumn' then.**
**I swam with all my might."**

*—Marconi Operator Harold Bride*

| PASSENGER | AGE | CLASS | LOST/SAVED |
|---|---|---|---|
| Miss Sara Rebecca Compton | 39 | 1st | Saved |
| Mrs. Alexander Taylor (Mary Eliza Ingersoll) Compton | 64 | 1st | Saved |
| Mr. Alexander Taylor, Jr. Compton | 37 | 1st | Lost |
| Mr. Thomas Henry Conlin | 31 | 3rd | Lost |
| Mr. Michael Connaghton | 31 | 3rd | Lost |

{"If the old ship goes down, you'll find my affairs in shipshape condition." —Major Archibald Butt}

Right:
WHITE STAR LINE RMS *TITANIC* POSTCARD, APRIL 10, 1912
*An unidentified second-class passenger mailed this postcard to a Miss Needham in Staffordshire, England, just before the* Titanic *sailed from Southampton.*
Courtesy Stanley Lehrer Collection

## COURAGE

Right:
MAJ. ARCHIBALD W. BUTT
*Forty-five-year-old Archie Butt, an aide to President Taft, was playing cards in the first-class smoking room when the* Titanic *collided with the iceberg. Survivors recalled his quiet but heroic efforts to ensure that women and children got safely away before he, and the ship, disappeared into the icy Atlantic.*
Courtesy *Illustrated London News* Picture Library

Left:
SILK SCARF
*Madeline Astor, wife of the famous millionaire, reportedly gave this scarf to Leah Aks to cover her child's head as they ascended to the cold air on the* Titanic*'s upper deck.*
Courtesy The Family of Frank P. Aks

**"BE BRAVE. NO MATTER WHAT HAPPENS, BE BRAVE."**

*—First-class passenger Dr. W.E. Minahan to his wife as he stepped back with the other men*

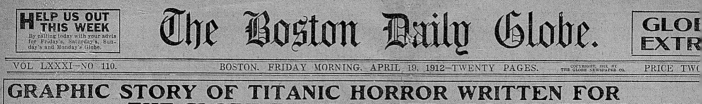

The Boston Daily Globe.

GLOB EXTR

VOL LXXXI—NO 110. BOSTON, FRIDAY MORNING, APRIL 19, 1912—TWENTY PAGES. PRICE TWO



# GRAPHIC STORY OF TITANIC HORROR WRITTEN FOR THE GLOBE BY REPORTER ABOARD THE CARPAT

# TITANIC STRIKES ON STARBOAR BOW AS ENGINES ARE STOPP

## Only Brief Warning of Coming Crash---Vessel's S Badly Torn and Ship Settles Rapidly.

## NO RUSH FOR BOATS

### Vivid Story of a Passenger.

### Awful Cries When Titanic Went Down.

### No Panic Following Crash, Mr Beasley Says.

By L. BEASLEY

(Cambridge University man whose home is in London. He was a second-cabin passenger on the Titanic.)

NEW YORK, April 18—The following thrilling story of the sinking of the Titanic and the rescue of her survivors was told tonight by Mr Beasley:

"The voyage from Queenstown had been quiet and uneventful. Very fine weather was experienced and the sea was quite calm. The wind had been westerly to southwesterly the whole way, but very cold, particularly the last day; in fact, after dinner on Sunday evening, it was almost too cold to be out on deck at all.

"I had been in my berth for about

Contaued on the Fourth Page.

THE CARPATHIA AS SHE STEAMED INTO NEW YORK LAST EVENING SURROUNDED BY SMALL CRAFT CHARTERED BY ANXIOUS RELATIVES OF SURVIVORS AND DEAD AND BY THE NEWSPAPERS.

(Drawn by Worden Wood, the Globe's Marine Artist, From Telegraphic Description.)

## Passengers Su By Order to B

### Boilers Explode Final Plunge C

### Capt Smith Shoots As Ship Goes D

BY CARLOS F. HUR

Staff Correspondent of the New York W the Carpathia.



NEW YORK, April 18—Seventeen h the figures will hardly vary in either dir than a few dozen—were lost in the sinking which struck an iceberg at 11.45 p m Su at the ocean's bottom two hours and 35 m

The checked up lists show that of passengers 126 are missing, most of them of 262 second cabin 116 came in on the Ca these 102 are women. The survivors of passengers numbered 136, of whom 83 a children. Just 207 members of the cr classed as follows: Officers 10, ablebodi firemen 71, stewards 64, stewardesses 18, c seaman named Long was picked up dead. carried 2388 souls.

### CORRECT TABLE OF SURV IN THE TITANIC D

Compiled by C. F. Hurd, on SS Carpa

Women and

## TODAY'S GLOBE CONTENTS.



## THE WEATHER.

WASHINGTON, April 18—Forecast for Northern New England — Rain or snow Friday; Saturday fair; brisk east shifting to west winds.

For Southern New England—Rain followed by clearing Friday; Saturday fair; brisk east shifting to west winds.

For Eastern New York—Cloudy, with probable rain north portion Friday; Saturday fair, moderate to brisk west winds.

## RIPPED OPEN BY ICE.

### Titanic Broke in Two Parts Just Before She Went Down.

NEW YORK, April 18—The Cunard liner Carpathia, a ship of gloom, sorrow and succor, came into New York tonight with first news direct from the great White Star liner Titanic, which sank off the Grand Banks of Newfoundland early on Monday morning last.

The great liner went down with her band playing, taking with her to death all but 674 of her human cargo of 2388 souls.

To this awful death list six persons were added.

## STORY OF HEROISM

### Maj Butt Stopped Stampede By Shooting Down Cravens.

By JOHN W. CARBERRY.

NEW YORK, April 18—The tale of the sinking of the steamship Titanic is a story of heroism. There were brave men on board that ship, which with hull opened by the force of teh collision with the iceberg and practically broken in two by the subsequent explosion of the boilers, went down early Sunday morning with lights brightly burning and the band playing "Nearer My God To Thee."

From captain to millionaire passengers' rare courage and self-sacrifice were displayed, and only half a dozen cravens who attempted to precede the women into the lifeboats were shot. It is because of the bravery of those men of the Titanic that tonight at

# "We have been living together for many years. Where you go, I go."

—*Ida Straus to her husband, Isidor*

{"If any man jumps in the boat I'll shoot him like a dog." —Attributed to Fifth Officer Harold Lowe}

## Courage

Opposite Page:
*Boston Daily Globe*, Friday, April 19, 1912
*Only in recent years has it been proven that the starboard side of the ship was not "badly torn," as the* Daily Globe *reported. The news article contains other errors, as well, including the report—for which there is no evidence—that Captain Smith shot himself.*
The Mariners' Museum

Right:
Isidor and Ida Straus
*Isidor and Ida Straus, both in their sixties, were returning from a holiday on the French Riviera. After placing her maid, Ellen Bird, in Lifeboat 8 and handing her a blanket, Ida Straus stepped back to remain with her husband. Passengers saw them sitting on a deck bench with their arms around each other during that perilous night.*
The Mariners' Museum

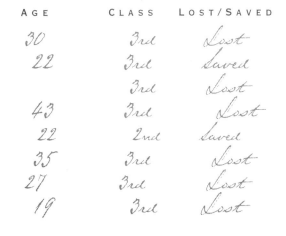

| Passenger | Age | Class | Lost/Saved |
|---|---|---|---|
| Miss Kate Connolly | 30 | 3rd | Lost |
| Miss Kate Connolly | 22 | 3rd | Saved |
| Mr. Patrick Connors | | 3rd | Lost |
| Mr. Jacob Cook | 43 | 3rd | Lost |
| Mrs. Selena Rogers Cook | 22 | 2nd | Saved |
| Mr. Bartol Cor | 35 | 3rd | Lost |
| Mr. Ivan Cor | 27 | 3rd | Lost |
| Mr. Ludovik Cor | 19 | 3rd | Lost |

| PASSENGER | AGE | CLASS | LOST/SAVED |
|---|---|---|---|
| Mrs. Walter H. (Irene Colvin) Corbett | 30 | 2nd | Lost |
| Mrs. Percy C. (Mary Phyllis Elizabeth Miller) Corey | | 2nd | Lost |
| Mr. Harry Corn | 30 | 3rd | Lost |
| Mrs. Robert Clifford (Malvina Helen Lamson) Cornell | 55 | 1st | Saved |
| Mr. Harry Cotterill | 20 | 2nd | Lost |
| Mrs. William (Minnie) Coutts | 36 | 3rd | Saved |
| Master Neville Coutts | 3 | 3rd | Saved |
| Master William Leslie Coutts | 9 | 3rd | Saved |

{The Countess of Rothes corresponded with Seaman Thomas Jones every Christmas until her death.}

## COURAGE

Right:
COUNTESS OF ROTHES
*The twenty-seven-year-old Scottish Countess of Rothes rowed all night without complaining, and once aboard the* Carpathia, *she devoted herself entirely to the care of the steerage women and children. When a steward said to her, "You have made yourself famous by rowing the boat," Lady Rothes replied, "I hope not. I have done nothing."*
Courtesy *Illustrated London News* Picture Library

Opposite Page:
LAP ROBE, RMS *TITANIC*, CA. 1911
*Selena Rogers Cook, a twenty-two-year-old newlywed, gave her blanket to the woman holding infant Frank Aks after he and his mother, Leah, were separated.*
Courtesy The Family of Frank Aks

**"WHEN I SAW THE WAY SHE [THE COUNTESS OF ROTHES] WAS CARRYING HERSELF AND HEARD THE QUIET DETERMINED WAY SHE SPOKE TO THE OTHERS, I KNEW SHE WAS MORE OF A MAN THAN ANY WE HAD ON BOARD."**

—*Seaman Thomas Jones, in charge of Lifeboat 8*

With her seemingly watertight design, the *Titanic* carried sixteen wooden lifeboats, to comply with the British Board of Trade regulations. Including her four collapsible lifeboats, the *Titanic* had lifesaving capacity for 1,178 people—fewer than half the 3,547 passengers she was designed to carry. Even so, she exceeded the lifeboat requirements of the day by 17 percent.

# DISGRACE

Boarding a lifeboat meant deliverance, but deliverance with its own peculiar horror. Fearing they would be swamped, those in the lifeboats refused to pick up the more than 1,000 people who were freezing in the water around them. Some lifeboat occupants did urge the others to try to save people struggling in the water, but their pleas were rejected.

Opposite Page:
SURPASSING THE GREATEST BUILDINGS AND MEMORIALS OF THE EARTH
Postcard, ca. 1911
Courtesy Independence Seaport Museum Library, Thayer Collection

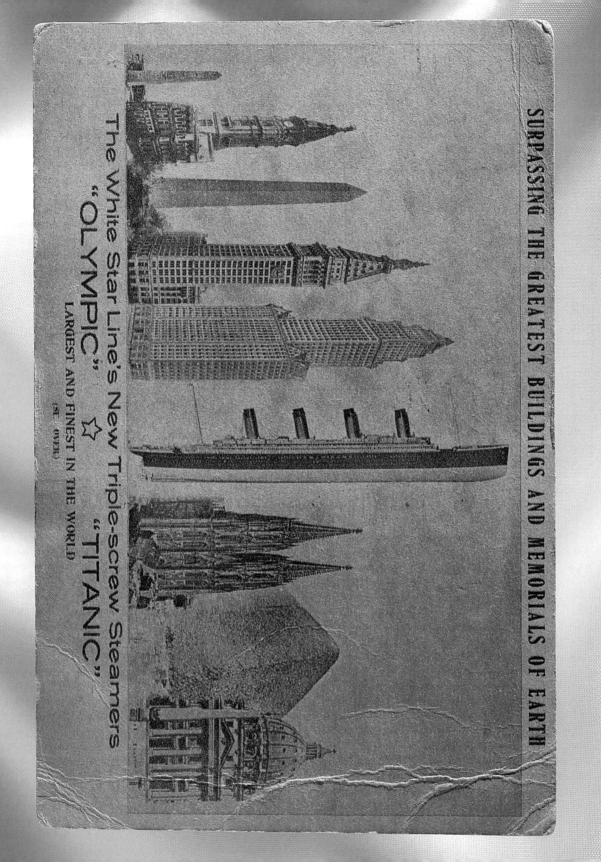

SURPASSING THE GREATEST BUILDINGS AND MEMORIALS OF EARTH
The White Star Line's New Triple-screw Steamers
"OLYMPIC" ☆ "TITANIC"
LARGEST AND FINEST IN THE WORLD
(SE OVER)

{For the rest of his life, Bruce Ismay did not allow the *Titanic* to be mentioned in his presence.}

**"I OUGHT TO HAVE GONE DOWN WITH THE SHIP. WOMEN AND CHILDREN DID. I SHOULD."**

*—Bruce Ismay at the inquiry*

## DISGRACE

Right:
JOSEPH BRUCE ISMAY
*As managing director of the White Star Line, Bruce Ismay helped mastermind the fabulous trinity—the* Olympic, *the* Titanic, *and the* Britannic*—and sailed on board the* Titanic *for her maiden voyage. Though Ismay was instrumental in loading the lifeboats, his reputation never recovered from the fact that he was among the few upper-class men to survive, and from the popular perception that he had cowardly used his position to get a place in a lifeboat.*
Courtesy *Illustrated London News* Picture Library

Opposite Page:
*TITANIC*, STARBOARD SIDE VIEW
*On* Titanic*'s starboard side, men were allowed to enter lifeboats. On the port side, men and older boys were turned away, sometimes by officers brandishing pistols.*
The Mariners' Museum

| PASSENGER | AGE | CLASS | LOST/SAVED |
|---|---|---|---|
| Mr. Daniel Coxon | 59 | 3rd | Lost |
| Mr. John Bertram Crafton | | 1st | Lost |
| Mr. Ernest James Crease | 19 | 3rd | Lost |
| Miss Laura Alice Cribb | 17 | 3rd | Saved |
| Mr. John Hatfield Cribb | 44 | 3rd | Lost |
| Capt. Edward Gifford Crosby | 70 | 1st | Lost |
| Mrs. Edward Gifford (Catherine Elizabeth Halstead) Crosby | 69 | 1st | Saved |
| Miss Harriet R. Crosby | 36 | 1st | Saved |

| PASSENGER | AGE | CLASS | LOST/SAVED |
|---|---|---|---|
| Mr. John Bradley Cumings | 39 | 1st | Lost |
| Mrs. John Bradley (Florence Briggs Thayer) Cumings | 38 | 1st | Saved |
| Mr. Tannous Daher | | 3rd | Lost |
| Mr. Charles Edward Dahl | 45 | 3rd | Saved |
| Miss Gerda Ulrika Dahlberg | 22 | 3rd | Lost |
| Mr. Branko Dakic | 19 | 3rd | Lost |
| Mr. Eugene Daly | 29 | 3rd | Saved |
| Miss Marcella Daly | 30 | 3rd | Saved |
| Mr. Peter Denis Daly | | 1st | Saved |
| Mr. Henry Damsgaard | 21 | 3rd | Lost |

{Only a few people were pulled from the freezing sea; of those, only a handful survived.}

## DISGRACE

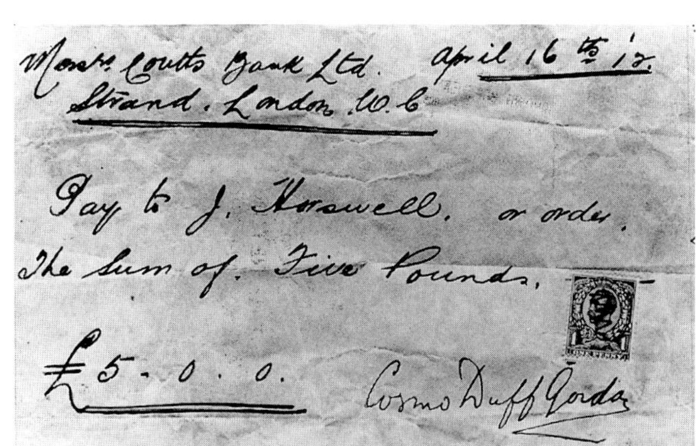

Messrs Coutts Bank Ltd. April 16th 12.
Strand. London. W.C.

Pay to J. Horswell. or order.
The sum of. Five Pounds.

£5-0-0. Cosmo Duff Gordon

Opposite Page:
LADY DUFF-GORDON
*The Duff-Gordons, self-absorbed Scottish aristocrats, both boarded Lifeboat 1. Though it could accommodate forty, the lifeboat was lowered with only twelve people aboard: seven crew members and five first-class passengers. Sir Cosmo tipped the lifeboat crew £5 apiece for their efforts.*
Courtesy Don Lynch Collection

Right:
DRAFT SIGNED BY SIR COSMO DUFF-GORDON
*Many suspected that Sir Cosmo Duff-Gordon had bribed the crew members of Lifeboat 1 to allow him to board with his wife. He explained at the inquiry that the £5 drafts he gave to the crewmen were to enable them to replace their sea kits, which were lost with the ship.*
Courtesy Brown Brothers, Sterling, Pennsylvania

**"I HAVE SAID THAT I DID NOT CONSIDER THE POSSIBILITY— OR RATHER I SHOULD SAY, THE POSSIBILITY OF BEING ABLE TO HELP ANYBODY NEVER OCCURRED TO ME AT ALL."**

*—Sir Cosmo Duff-Gordon*

{"No one came to tell us, no bell was rung, no horn was sounded."}

| PASSENGER | AGE | CLASS | LOST/SAVED |
|---|---|---|---|
| Mr. Ernst Gilbert Danborn | 34 | 3rd | Lost |
| Mrs. Ernst Gilbert (Anna Sigrid Maria Brogren) Danborn | 28 | 3rd | Lost |
| Master Gilbert Sigvard Emanuel Danborn | 4m | 3rd | Lost |
| Mr. Robert Williams Daniel | 27 | 1st | Saved |
| Mr. Yoto Danoff | 27 | 3rd | Lost |

Right:
THIRD-CLASS GENERAL ROOM
*Many third-class passengers found that the way to the upper decks—and the lifeboats—was barred. The third-class deck on the stern of the ship became a final refuge as the* Titanic*'s bow settled lower and lower.*
Courtesy Titanic Historical Society, Inc.

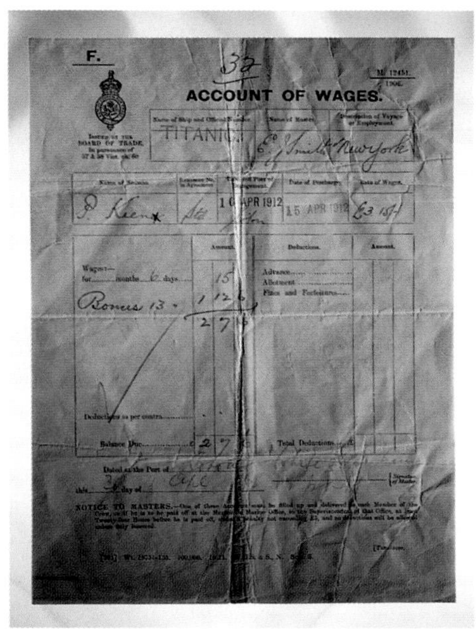

F.

ACCOUNT OF WAGES.

TITANIC

E. J. Smith New York

P. Keen

10 APR 1912

15 APR 1912

Bonus 13 -

## DISGRACE

Left:
ACCOUNT OF WAGES, STEWARD PERCY KEENE, APRIL 10–15, 1912
*According to mercantile law, Keene's wages stopped the moment the* Titanic *went under. However, Keene was ultimately granted six days' pay, plus a small bonus.*
Courtesy Stanley Lehrer Collection

Opposite Page:
CONTINUOUS CERTIFICATE OF DISCHARGE, STEWARD PERCY KEENE, 1912
Titanic *steward Percy Keene was abruptly discharged from duty on April 15, 1912, at latitude 41°15′N., longitude 50°14′W. The disaster was summed up in the terse phrase "Vessel lost." Keene returned to Southampton and was subsequently employed as a printer and steward aboard the White Star ship* Oceanic.
Courtesy Stanley Lehrer Collection

**"NOT A SINGLE WARNING WAS GIVEN IN THE PART OF THE SHIP IN WHICH I WAS. . . . WE COULD HAVE DIED LIKE RATS IN A TRAP FOR ALL THE WARNING WE RECEIVED."**

*—Mrs. George Stone, first-class passenger*

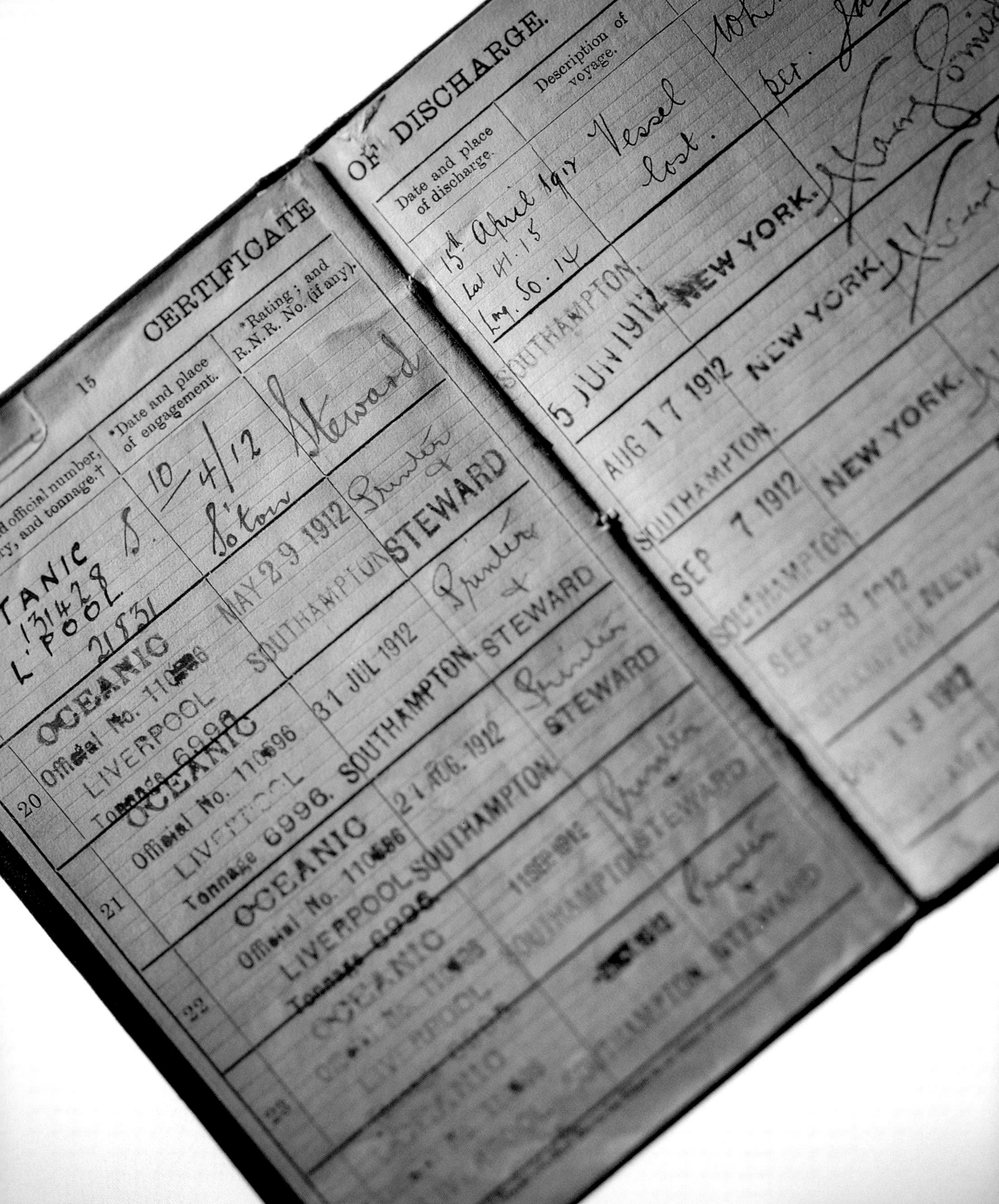

15

CERTIFICATE OF DISCHARGE.

| | ...d official number, ...y, and tonnage.† | *Date and place of engagement. | *Rating; and R.N.R. No. (if any). | Date and place of discharge. | Description of voyage. |
|---|---|---|---|---|---|
| | ...TANIC 131428 L'POOL 21831 | 10/4/12 S'ton | Steward | 15th April 1912 Lat 41.15 Long 50.14 | Vessel lost. |
| 20 | OCEANIC Official No. 110596 LIVERPOOL Tonnage 6996 | MAY 29 1912 SOUTHAMPTON | Printer & STEWARD | 5 JUN 1912 SOUTHAMPTON | NEW YORK. |
| 21 | OCEANIC Official No. 110596 LIVERPOOL Tonnage 6996. | 31 JUL 1912 SOUTHAMPTON. | Printer & STEWARD | AUG 17 1912 SOUTHAMPTON | NEW YORK. |
| 22 | OCEANIC Official No. 110596 LIVERPOOL Tonnage 6996 | 21 AUG 1912 SOUTHAMPTON | Printer & STEWARD | SEP 7 1912 SOUTHAMPTON | NEW YORK. |
| 23 | OCEANIC [illegible] LIVERPOOL | 11 SEP 1912 SOUTHAMPTON | Printer & STEWARD | SEP 28 1912 [illegible] | NEW [illegible] |
| | [illegible] | [illegible] SOUTHAMPTON | STEWARD | [illegible] | [illegible] |

# "[T]HE MEMORY OF GALLANT CAPTAIN SMITH OF THE TITANIC MUST BE DARKENED BY THE KNOWLEDGE OF THE ABSOLUTE FOOLHARDINESS OF HIS CONDUCT DURING THE CLOSING HOURS OF HIS LIFE."

—*The Plain Dealer* (Cleveland)

## DISGRACE

Opposite Page:
RICHMOND *TIMES-DISPATCH*, SUNDAY, APRIL 21, 1912
*Much of the inquiry that followed the disaster focused on Captain Smith's cancellation of a lifeboat drill the morning before the sinking, his decision to steam at full speed despite ice warnings, and his failure to raise a general alarm even when it became obvious the ship could not survive.*
The Mariners' Museum

Above:
FREDERICK FLEET WITH MEMBERS OF THE CREW DURING THE NEW YORK INQUIRY
*At the inquiry, lookout Frederick Fleet (third from left) reported that although he and the other lookout, George Symons, had asked for binoculars, none were provided. Straining to peer through the dark on the night of April 14, Fleet spotted the iceberg too late.*
Courtesy Tony Stone Images/Hulton Getty Picture Library

| PASSENGER | AGE | CLASS | LOST/SAVED |
|---|---|---|---|
| Mr. Anthony Abbing | 42 | 3rd | Lost |
| Master Eugene Joseph Abbott | 13 | 3rd | Lost |
| Mr. Rossmore Edward Abbott | 16 | 3rd | Lost |
| Mrs. Stanton (Rosa) Abbott | 35 | 3rd | Saved |

{Frederick Fleet survived only because a senior crewman ordered him to board a lifeboat and help row toward lights on the horizon—presumably those of the *Californian*.}

# The Times Dispatch

FOUNDED 1850. FOUNDED 1886. WHOLE NUMBER 18,962. RICHMOND, VA., SUNDAY, APRIL 21, 1912. THE WEATHER TO-DAY—FAIR. PRICE FIVE CENTS.


# arnings of Icebergs Ahead Allowed to Pass Unheeded, and Doomed Liner Titanic Is Pushed On at Highest Speed

## HOLDING UEST OVER S NOW LYING TTOM OF SEA

ommittee Tear-
eVeil That Still
uds Titanic
Mystery.

AL INQUIRY
TAKE PLACE

ifted to Washington,
Monday Passengers
bers of Crew Who
Stricken Liner Will
r Stories—J. Bruce
enied Refuge Abroad,
n Relate His Share in
toric Midnight Mad-

, April 20.—Leaving
tunned and aghast at
in a bare, surface in-
of the tragedy of the
Senate inquiry com-
ght shifted operations
gton. Monday the
nd of the government
thrusting aside the
ouding with mystery
se of the disaster.
face has barely been
the real investigation
come," said Senator
len Smith, of Michi-
an of the preliminary
he stepped aboard his
capital to-night.
icial inquiry at Wash-
nday morning will
dramatically hasty,
zied and sensational
ere, which, Senator
, have impeded the

eaving to-night the
but implacable force
nment was set in mo-
earching, thorough, if
quest, for an inquest
of a nation over the
i bodies lying two
the waves.

tnesses Summoned.

nesses, all snatched
by the rescue ship
to-night were sum-
ppear Monday before
Senate committee se-
robe the catastrophe.
Bruce Ismay, man-
or of the White Star
lowliest stoker of the
anic, the government
truth of the marine
Ismay, the object of
and vituperation as
scorched any public
etell his story. From
lips—whose owner
ge abroad—will again
s part in the midnight

engers, possibly in-
. John Jacob Astor,

### Committee of U. S. Senators Investigating Loss of Titanic

SENATOR DUNCAN U. FLETCHER — SENATOR WILLIAM ALDEN SMITH OF MICHIGAN, CHAIRMAN — SENATOR GEORGE C. PERKINS of CALIFORNIA

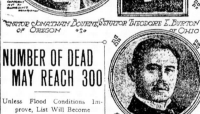

## NEBRASKA SWEPT BY PROGRESSIVES

Roosevelt Is Heavy Winner, Capturing Entire Delegation of Sixteen.

### CLARK LEADS DEMOCRATS

Wilson Runs Second to Speaker, and Governor Harmon Is Third.

Omaha, Neb., April 20.—Late returns to-night from the primary election in Nebraska confirm the early returns that the progressives have swept the State.

Roosevelt is a 3 to 1 winner for the Republicans. He captured the entire delegation of sixteen.

Clark, for the Democrats, won out in the State in nearly the same ratio as Roosevelt. He lost two delegates to Harmon in the Second District.

La Follette ran second to Roosevelt in the Republican column, and Taft made a poor third.

Wilson ran second to Clark for the Democrats, and Harmon was third.

For member of the national committee, R. B. Howell, progressive Republican, ran away from Victor Rosewater, present acting chairman of the committee.

P. L. Hall, of Lincoln, will be the Democratic national committeeman. George W. Norris and Norris Brown were running neck and neck for the Republican nomination for Senator. Norris, with half of the State heard from, seemed to have the edge.

Former Governor Shallenberger appeared to have defeated W. N. Thompson for the Democratic nomination for the senatorship.

Howard B. Aldridge, of Omaha, will contest the seat of Congressman Lobeck.

**Roosevelt Leads in Oregon.**

Portland Ore., April 20.—With the returns coming in slowly and still far from complete, Colonel Roosevelt tonight had a slight lead over Senator La Follette as Oregon's choice in the presidential preference primaries.

La Follette showed his greatest strength in the cities and towns in which he spoke during his campaign of the State. Roosevelt's strength centred chiefly in the rural districts. Taft ran third in all sections of the State.

Wilson is apparently the choice of the Democrats for President, though Champ Clark polled a heavy vote in the rural districts. Governor Harmon polled a nominal vote.

Senator Jonathan Bourne, Jr., was defeated decisively by Ben Selling.

Dr. Harry Lane defeated Pierce for the Democratic nomination for Senator.

**West Virginia for Colonel.**

Wheeling, W. Va., April 20.—Twenty-nine counties of West Virginia, voting to-day on delegates to the State con-

SENATOR JONATHAN BOURNE OF OREGON — SENATOR THEODORE E. BURTON OF OHIO — SENATOR FRANCIS G. NEWLANDS OF NEVADA

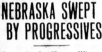

## NUMBER OF DEAD MAY REACH 300

Unless Flood Conditions Improve, List Will Become Much Larger.

### MORE BREAKS IN LEVEES

Government and State United in Efforts to Relieve Suffering.

New Orleans, April 20.—Three hundred persons are dead from the breaking of levees along the lower Mississippi River, and the number will be doubled before the end of the month unless the unexpected occurs. These are not actual figures, but are based upon an average given by men at Vicksburg, Jackson and Greenville, Miss.; Tallulah, Lake Providence and Baton Rouge, La., and at other strategic points in the valley. To-night the known death list stood at forty-one, but there are many sections that have not been explored, and where no attempt at rescue has been made. The consensus of opinion among the big planters of the inundated delta section is that the drowned to date there number between 200 and 400.

At one place last night fifteen negroes were drowned. This was near Benoit, Miss., when the levee broke at Beulah. In Mississippi and North Louisiana at least 50,000 are homeless.

Seven negroes were drowned at Lobdell last night. To-day reports of a break near Greenville, Miss., created a small panic in that vicinity, and despite repeated denials, the situation was known to be so grave that many residents of the section made all preparations to flee at a moment's notice.

SENATOR F. M. SIMMONS OF NORTH CAROLINA

## MAY SEND WARSHIP TO MEXICAN COAST

Will Enable Isolated Americans to Leave Disturbed Districts.

Washington, April 20.—President Taft probably will send a warship soon to the west coast of Mexico to enable Americans isolated in Sinaloa and other States to leave the disturbed districts. A State Department announcement to-night declared this action likely in view of the general anxiety for Americans in those localities.

State Department officials pointed out to-night that with the suspension of railroad communication and the interruption of telegraph service, American citizens on the west coast of Mexico, especially at Los Mochis, in Sinaloa, where there are many Americans, as well as in the vicinity of Mazatlan, are isolated. This fact, together with many reports of increased lawlessness on the west coast, is causing much anxiety to Americans in the region affected, and their friends in the United States.

## ISMAY REGAINING HIS COMPOSURE

Tilts His Head Back and Smiles Indulgent Little Smile.

### WORRIED ABOUT CLOTHING

He Was Able to Save Only One Suit When Titanic Went Down.

[Special to The Times-Dispatch.]

New York, April 20.—Joseph Bruce Ismay is going to Washington to-morrow. He will make no attempt to evade the Senate investigating committee's subpoena. He said as much this afternoon, leaning against a mantelshelf in the Waldorf-Astoria and smiling his peculiar and indulgent little smile.

"Really," he said, "we should have gone without a subpoena, so long as this matter is pending."

Ismay talks with head tilted back, viewing his listener as from a great height. His attitude is that of a man who had been used to looking down upon his listeners. He has passed his life among subordinates, has Ismay, from the days when he first went abroad with an English nurse until now, when he commands the fleets and the finances of the International Mercantile Marine, at a salary of £35,000 a year, and he displays the results of this training.

**Not a Club Man.**

He does not seek social contact with those whom he might perhaps regard as his equals, as indicated by the fact that despite his reputed wealth he is a member of but one club.

Ismay is not much of a talker, but he has grown more loquacious since he left his comfortable cabin aboard the Carpathia, politely edged his way

## KNOWN FIVE HOURS BEFORE COLLISION OF VESSEL'S DANGER

Hearing Before Senate Committee Confirms Fact That White Star Liner and All the Lives She Bore Were Sacrificed That Quick Run Might Be Recorded.

### ISMAY ADMITS SENDING MESSAGES FROM CARPATHIA

Grilled on Witness Stand, He Confesses That He Sought to Hold Liner Cedric That Rescued Members of Titanic's Crew Might Be Transferred and Rushed Back to England—Liner Frankfurt Heard Wireless Call for Aid, but Proceeded on Her Way—Operators Give Their Dramatic Versions of What Happened After Iceberg Was Struck.

(Special to The Times-Dispatch.)

New York, April 20.—Continued investigation into the Titanic disaster by the Senate subcommittee to-day served only further to confirm the fact that the great ship had been forced at top speed in the face of aerial warnings of icebergs ahead. The testimony of young Harold Bride, assistant Marconi operator aboard the ship, disclosed the warning of danger ahead, five hours before the collision, and the relay of this warning to the bridge, just as Second Officer Lightoller, the afternoon before, had fixed the speed of the ship.

Apparently that phase of the investigation stands settled to the satisfaction of Senator William Alden Smith and his colleagues, for to-day much of the time of the short session was taken up with other matters nearly as significant, which dwelt with the hours just before the impact, the last hours of the ship, and what came after those who lived were drifting until the coming of the Carpathia.

**Wireless Operators Tell Their Stories.**

It was the day of the wireless operator and of his experiences both in the doomed vessel and the rescuing one. The witnesses in their order were: Harold T. Cottam, operator of the Carpathia, and young Bride. Third Officer Herbert J. Pitman, of the Titanic, appeared for a minute on the stand just before adjournment was taken, but he answered one question only, as to the fate of the log. So far as he knew, he swore, that important volume is to-day at the bottom of the sea. The other significant facts established were: The C. Q. D. call went forth by command of Captain Smith. It reached the liner Frankfurt, of the North German Lloyd, which seemed to be nearest to the scene, but that vessel was never heard of afterward, which indicated that she did not appreciate the gravity of the situation aboard the Titanic.

**Dramatic Narrative of Young Bride.**

One witness and then another told of the rush of the Carpathia, the messages and the preparations; there were reports of the communication with other vessels, which were eager to aid, and, above all, stood out the bare, bald narrative of the boy Bride, of his experiences, which began two minutes after the impact and ended when he was dragged from under a capsized boat upon the bottom of it to wait for rescue; it told of a youngster of nineteen never thinking to leave his post until the captain ordered him to save himself; it settled accurately the final jump of Captain Smith without a life preserver from the bridge into the sea, and then his last desperate fight to save himself. There was nothing of the dramatic about the lad, but after it was over Senator Smith, who led him kindly for hours, confessed that he had not been able to see at times for the tears in his eyes.

Back of him came the keen, alert Cottam with his story of the messages, and finally with the denial that neither he nor any other

"It was the most awful thing that anyone could ever conceive." In eleven words, first-class survivor Marian Thayer captured the disbelief with which the *Titanic*'s owners, builders, passengers, crew, their loved ones, and a stunned world attempted to comprehend what had happened. So many gone so quickly. Some families

# TRAGEDY

waited agonizing days before the fate of their relatives was confirmed. Names were added to and taken off the survivor lists. So much pure, horrific tragedy and, in the end, the glorious ship so appallingly vulnerable to error and to chance. As the *Titanic*'s loss would prove, more than amazement or anger, it is our collective sense of tragedy that endures.

Opposite Page:
NEWSBOY IN LONDON
Courtesy Tony Stone Images/Hulton Getty Picture Library

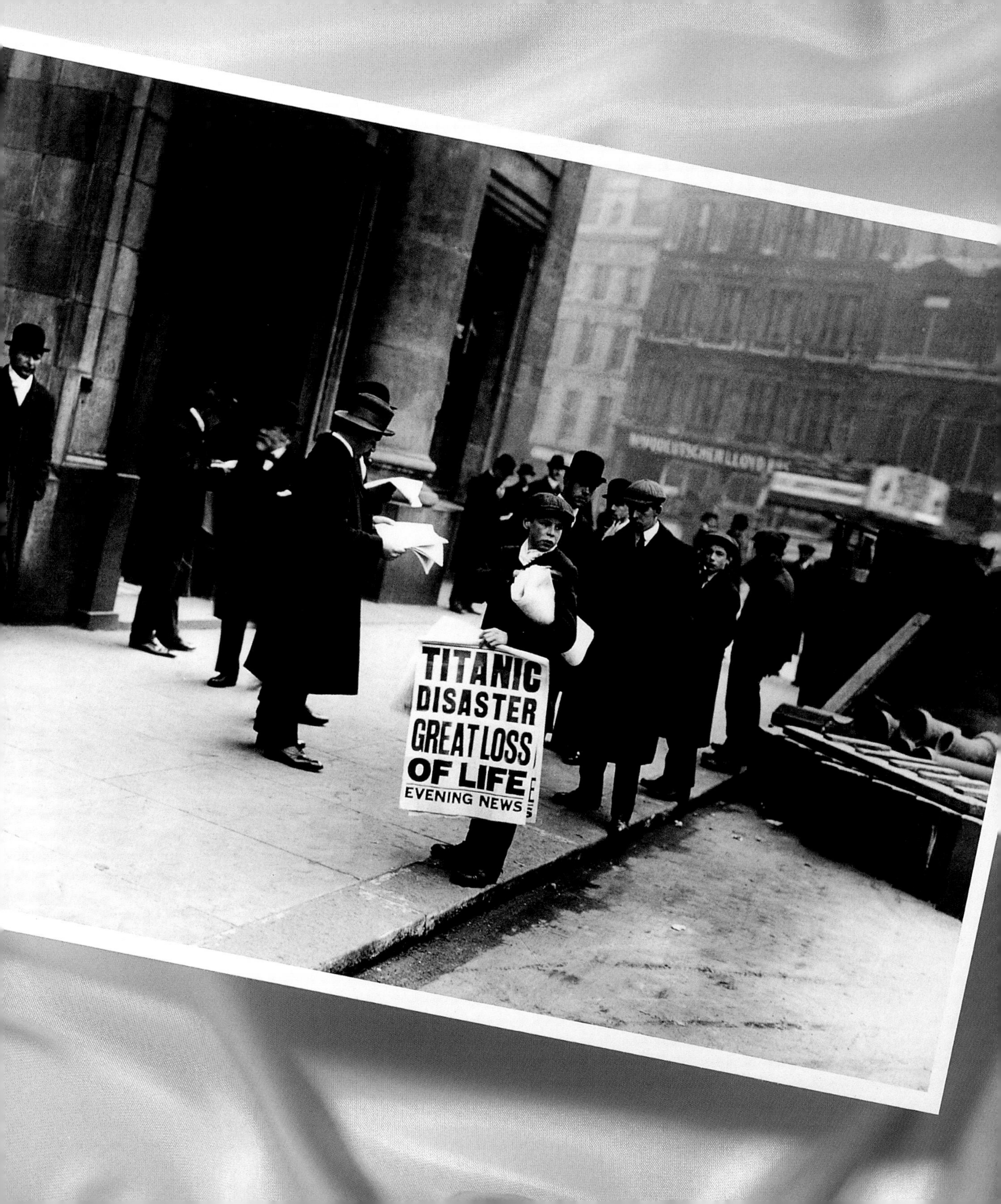
TITANIC
DISASTER
GREAT LOSS
OF LIFE
EVENING NEWS

## "I AM SAILING TODAY THURSDAY ON TITANIC ON HER MAIDEN TRIP, TO NEW YORK, HER FIRST TRIP ON THE ATLANTIC. GOODBYE. LOVE, P.D."

*—Third-class passenger Patrick Dooley*

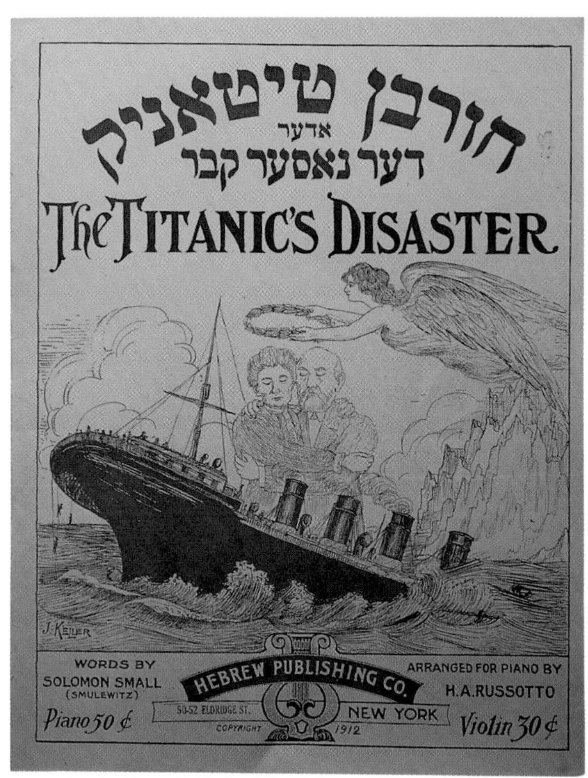


### Tragedy

Opposite Page:
*THE IRISH EMIGRANT*, CA. 1912
*Irish emigrant Patrick Dooley mailed this postcard to his beloved Mary from Queenstown on April 11, 1912. This was the last she heard from him, for he perished in the sinking.*
Courtesy Stanley Lehrer Collection

Left:
"THE *TITANIC*'S DISASTER," 1912
Sheet music, Hebrew Publishing Company
*Grief for the* Titanic *victims took many forms. Solomon Small and H. A. Russotto wrote this commemorative song with Yiddish lyrics. The cover includes a sketch of Ida and Isidor Straus embracing as the ship goes down.*
Courtesy Kenneth Schultz

| PASSENGER | AGE | CLASS | LOST/SAVED |
|---|---|---|---|
| Mr. Evan Davies | 22 | 3rd | Lost |
| Mr. John Davies | 21 | 3rd | Lost |
| Mr. Joseph Davies | 17 | 3rd | Lost |
| Mr. Alfred Davies | 24 | 3rd | Lost |
| Mrs. Agnes Davis | 49 | 2nd | Lost |
| Master John Morgan Davis | 8 | 2nd | Saved |

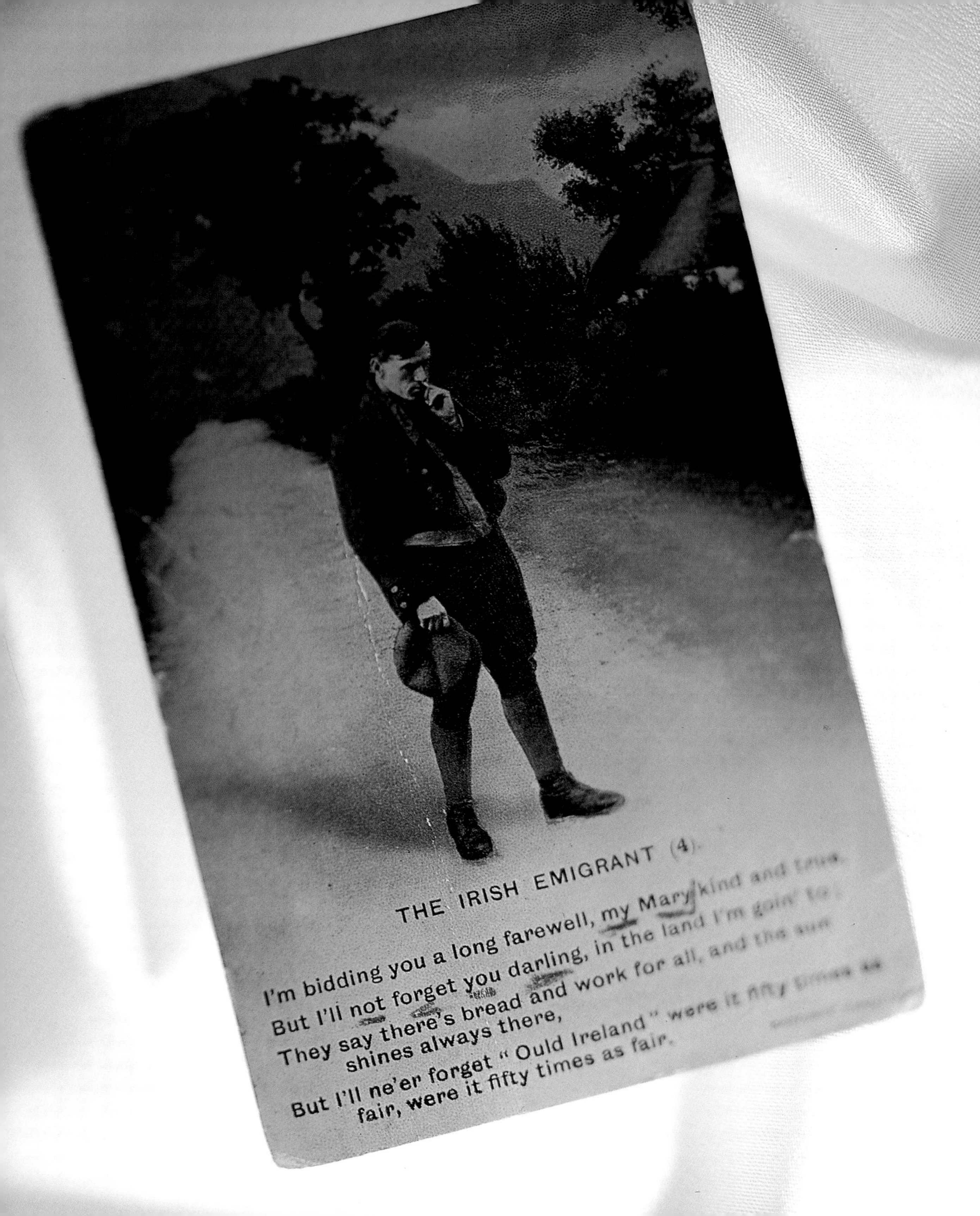

THE IRISH EMIGRANT (4).
I'm bidding you a long farewell, my Mary kind and true,
But I'll not forget you darling, in the land I'm goin' to;
They say there's bread and work for all, and the sun
shines always there,
But I'll ne'er forget "Ould Ireland" were it fifty times as
fair, were it fifty times as fair.

113

| Passenger | Age | Class | Lost/Saved |
|---|---|---|---|
| Miss Mary Davis | 28 | 2nd | Saved |
| Mr. Thomas Henry Davison | | 3rd | Lost |
| Mrs. Thomas Henry (Mary Finck) Davison | | 3rd | Saved |
| Mr. Jose Joaquim De Brito | | 2nd | Lost |
| Mr. William Joseph De Messemaeker | 36 | 3rd | Saved |

## Tragedy

Below:
JOHN AND ANNIE SAGE AND THEIR NINE CHILDREN IN FRONT OF THEIR HOME
*John and Annie Sage and their nine children, ages five to twenty-two, were traveling from Peterborough, England, to Jacksonville, Florida, to begin life on the family's new citrus farm. The entire family went down with the* Titanic.
Courtesy Haynes Publishing

Opposite Page:
MILLVINA DEAN WITH HER MOTHER AND BROTHER, CA. 1914
*At six weeks of age, Millvina Dean was the youngest person aboard the* Titanic. *She was traveling with her parents and older brother in third class. Her father was lost, along with nearly all the other men in steerage.*
Courtesy Southampton City Heritage Services

**ACCESS TO DECK AREAS WAS STRICTLY DICTATED BY CLASS— A FACT THAT BECAME TRAGICALLY CLEAR WHEN DISASTER STRUCK AND THIRD-CLASS PASSENGERS TRIED TO MAKE THEIR WAY TO THE LIFEBOATS.**

{*Titanic*'s third-class accommodations were spread out on four different decks. It was not uncommon for the journey to or from a third-class berth to take as long as an hour.}

{"[I]t was as though they lost their own willpower and expected God to do all the work for them."—a *Titanic* survivor}

## "TELL YOUR MOTHER THAT I LOVED HER DEARLY AND STILL DO."

*—Michel Navratil*

### TRAGEDY

Right:
FATHER THOMAS BYLES
*Like many of the heroes of the* Titanic, *Father Thomas went down with the ship. Hundreds of second- and third-class passengers formed a circle with the priest at the ship's stern and prayed, cried, sang, and begged God and Mary for help. They continued praying, and were given absolution, until the water was over their heads.*
Courtesy Titanic Historical Society, Inc.

Opposite Page:
MICHEL AND EDMOND NAVRATIL
*Among the survivors picked up by the rescue ship* Carpathia *were two small boys who spoke no English—Michel Jr. and Edmond Navratil. The rest of the world called them the* Titanic *orphans. Estranged from his wife, their father, Michel Navratil, had kidnapped the boys from Nice, France, and was taking them to America. The father perished. The boys eventually were reunited with their mother, Marcelle, who saw their picture in a newspaper.*
The Mariners' Museum

| PASSENGER | AGE | CLASS | LOST/SAVED |
|---|---|---|---|
| Mr. William Joseph De Messemaeker | 36 | 3rd | Saved |
| Mrs. William Joseph (Anna) De Messemaeker | 36 | 3rd | Saved |
| Mr. Theo De Mulder | 30 | 3rd | Saved |
| Madame Berthe De Villiers | | 1st | Saved |
| Madame Berthe De Villiers | | 1st | Saved |
| Mr. Percy Deacon | 18 | 2nd | Lost |
| Master Bertram Vere Dean | 1 | 3rd | Saved |
| Mrs. Bertram (Eva) Dean | 33 | 3rd | Saved |
| Mr. Bertram Dean | 26 | 3rd | Lost |
| Miss Elizabeth Gladys (Millvina) Dean | 2m | 3rd | Saved |
| Mrs. Sebastiano (Argenia Genovese) Del Carlo | 22 | 2nd | Saved |
| Mr. Sebastiano Del Carlo | 28 | 2nd | Lost |

Throughout the early morning of Monday, April 15, wireless stations along the eastern seaboard monitored the transmissions of rescue vessels steaming toward the site of the sinking. Hopes were raised with early reports that

# RESCUE

all had been saved. Three days later, when the *Carpathia* arrived in New York, landing cards were handed to rescued *Titanic* passengers. Each card listed the bearer simply as "ex *Titanic*."

Opposite Page:
CUNARD LINE LANDING OR CUSTOM CARD, 1912
*Landing card issued to first-class passenger Gilbert M. Tucker, Jr., aboard* Carpathia.
Courtesy Stanley Lehrer Collection

CUNARD LINE.

SECOND CABIN

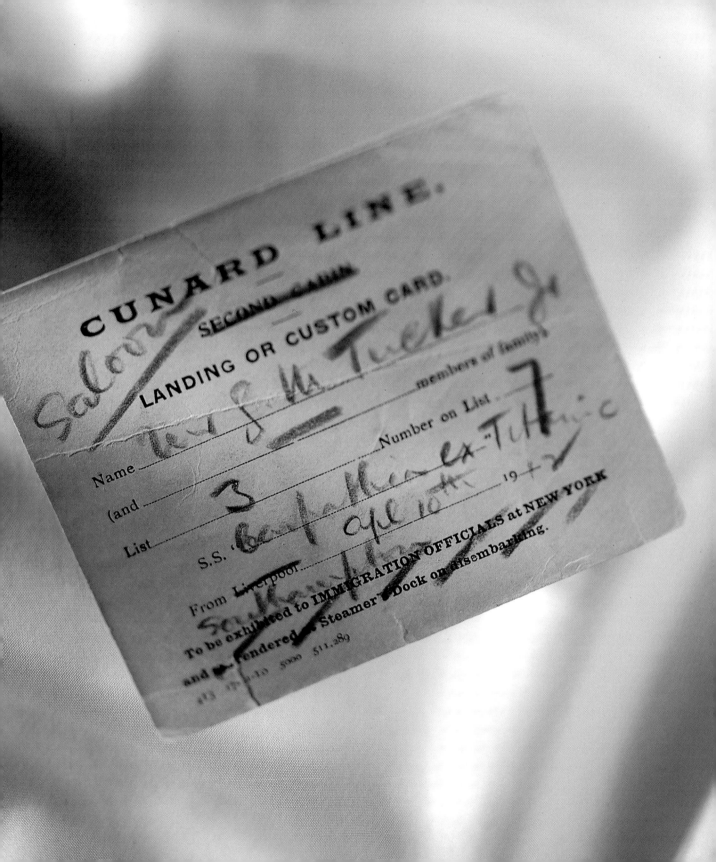

LANDING OR CUSTOM CARD.

Name ........................................ members of family's

(and ........................................ Number on List ..........

List ........................................

S.S. "........................................ 19....

From Liverpool.

To be exhibited to IMMIGRATION OFFICIALS at NEW YORK

and surrendered at Steamer's Dock on disembarking.

**Disgusted with Quartermaster Robert Hitchens's orders to sit passively and drift on the 28-degree water, Molly Brown took command of the boat.**

{With a capacity of 65, Lifeboat 6 was lowered with only thirty people, including two crew members assigned to work the boat.}

## Rescue

Opposite Page:
LIFEBOAT 6 APPROACHES THE *CARPATHIA* WITH MOLLY BROWN AND LOOKOUT FREDERICK FLEET ON BOARD.
*Lifeboat 6 was the second boat to be lowered, and it was not full. At this early stage in the disaster, passengers believed there was no danger and the lowering of boats was merely a safety precaution.*
Courtesy Don Lynch Collection

Left:
MARGARET "MOLLY" BROWN
*Forty-four-year-old Mrs. Margaret (Molly) Brown, an eccentric and high-spirited millionairess from Denver, was traveling on the* Titanic *without her husband. After boarding Lifeboat 6, she spurned a crewman's order to sit quietly. She then showed the women in the boat how to row and kept the terrified and freezing passengers active and hopeful.*
Courtesy Corbis-Bettmann

Right:
ANCIENT EGYPTIAN FIGURINE,
SHAWABTI OR USHABTI, CA. 700 B.C.
Faience with turquoise glaze
*As she left the* Titanic, *Molly Brown carried this statuette as a good-luck talisman. Prior to booking passage on the* Titanic, *she visited Egypt, where she met the Astors and joined them for sightseeing. Mrs. Brown brought aboard the* Titanic *three crates of ancient Egyptian models destined for the Denver Museum. She generously presented the talisman to Captain Rostron of the* Carpathia *to thank him for speeding to the aid of* Titanic *survivors.*
Courtesy Stanley Lehrer Collection

| PASSENGER | AGE | CLASS | LOST/SAVED |
|---|---|---|---|
| Mr. Regyo Delalic | 25 | 3rd | Lost |
| Mr. Herbert Denbury | 25 | 2nd | Lost |
| Mr. Mito Denkoff | | 3rd | Lost |
| Mr. Samuel Dennis | 23 | 3rd | Lost |
| Mr. William Dennis | 26 | 3rd | Lost |
| Miss Margaret Devaney | 19 | 3rd | Saved |

| PASSENGER | AGE | CLASS | LOST/SAVED |
|---|---|---|---|
| Mr. Frank Dewar | 65 | 3rd | Lost |
| Mr. William Dibden | 18 | 2nd | Lost |
| Mr. Elias Dibo | | 3rd | Lost |
| Mr. Albert Adrian Dick | 31 | 1st | Saved |
| Mrs. Albert Adrian (Vera Gillespie) Dick | 17 | 1st | Saved |
| Mr. Jovan Dimic | 42 | 3rd | Lost |
| Mr. Vattcho Dintcheff | 43 | 3rd | Lost |
| Dr. Washington Dodge | | 1st | Saved |
| Mrs. Washington (Ruth Vidaver) Dodge | | 1st | Saved |
| Master Washington Dodge | 4 | 1st | Saved |
| Mrs. Ada Doling | 32 | 2nd | Saved |
| Miss Elsie Doling | 18 | 2nd | Saved |

{The *Titanic* carried 3,560 life jackets and 49 life preservers. She had been certified to carry 3,547 passengers and crew.}

## RESCUE

Opposite Page:
LIFEBOAT FENDER WITH PLAQUE,
RMS *TITANIC*, CA. 1911
*One of the few surviving lifeboat fenders was recovered by a rescue ship. Affixed to the fender is a rare White Star Line metal lifeboat plaque. A metal plate bearing the name Liverpool reportedly was stolen from the fender many years ago.*
Courtesy Kenneth Schultz

Left:
"MUDDIE BOONS"
(MAID MARGARET BURNS)
WITH DOUGLAS AND
DAISY SPEDDEN, 1909
1998 Leighton H. Coleman III,
Spedden Collection


**"OH, MUDDIE,**

**LOOK AT THE BEAUTIFUL NORTH POLE WITH**

**NO SANTA CLAUS ON IT!"**

*—Six-year-old Douglas Spedden from the lifeboat as the sun rose*

{Only two of the honeymooning couples aboard the *Titanic* survived together.}

| Passenger | Age | Class | Lost/Saved |
|---|---|---|---|
| Mr. Patrick Dooley | 32 | 3rd | Lost |
| Mr. End Dorkings | | | Saved |
| Mr. Patrick Dooley | 32 | 3rd | Lost |
| Mr. Edward Arthur Dorkings | 19 | 3rd | Saved |
| Mrs. Frederick Charles (Suzette Baxter) Douglas | 27 | 1st | Saved |
| Mr. Walter Donald Douglas | 50 | 1st | Lost |

## Rescue

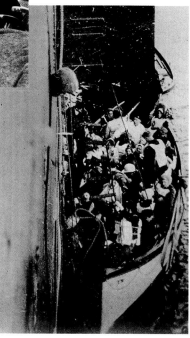

Above:
WEARY SURVIVORS REST AND TALK ON THE DECK OF THE *CARPATHIA*.
*Here, first-class honeymooners Dorothy and George Harder talk with Clara Hays, possibly consoling her on the loss of her husband, Charles.*
Courtesy *Illustrated London News* Picture Library

Left:
SURVIVORS IN LIFEBOAT ALONGSIDE THE *CARPATHIA*
Courtesy Brown Brothers, Sterling, Pennsylvania

Opposite Page:
CAPTAIN ARTHUR H. ROSTRON OF THE *CARPATHIA*
The Mariners' Museum

**"ALL SAFE ON CARPATHIA.**

**NOTIFY FAMILY AND FRIENDS."**

—*Radiotelegram sent by Frederic Spedden*

# CAPTAIN ROSTRON ASKED A CLERGYMAN ON BOARD [THE CARPATHIA] TO LEAD A SERVICE OF THANKSGIVING FOR THOSE SAVED, AND OF BURIAL FOR THOSE LOST.

{"I think I'll stick to the big ship, Billy, and take a chance." —First-class passenger George Widener}

Opposite Page:
WILLIAM RICHARDS
*Three-year-old William Rowe Richards was traveling second class with his mother, Emily, and his ten-month-old brother. He is seen here standing on a wicker chair dressed in a nightgown made for him from a blanket aboard the* Carpathia.
Courtesy Don Lynch Collection

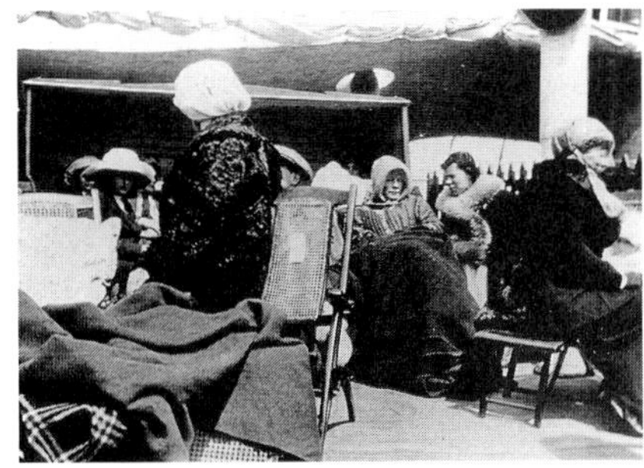

Left:
WOMEN SURVIVORS BUNDLED UP AGAINST THE COLD ON THE DECK OF THE *CARPATHIA*.
Courtesy Brown Brothers, Sterling, Pennsylvania

## RESCUE

Right:
THE *CARPATHIA* LEAVING NEW YORK HARBOR, FLAGS STILL AT HALF-MAST
*Her history-making rescue complete, the* Carpathia, *restocked with linens and supplies borrowed from another Cunard Line vessel, leaves her New York pier for the second time, bound for the Mediterranean.*
Courtesy Brown Brothers, Sterling, Pennsylvania

| PASSENGER | AGE | CLASS | LOST/SAVED |
|---|---|---|---|
| Mrs. Walter Donald (Mahala Dutton) Douglas | 48 | 1st | Saved |
| Mr. William James Douton | | 2nd | Lost |
| Miss Elizabeth Dowdell | 30 | 3rd | Saved |
| Miss Elizabeth Doyle | 24 | 3rd | Lost |
| Miss Jennie Drapkin | 23 | 3rd | Saved |
| Mr. Josef Drazonovic | | 3rd | Lost |

On the morning of April 15, headlines screamed the latest news. Frantic friends and families of passengers and crew waited outside the offices of the White Star Line. However, it was late in the day before the truth was known. Three days later, on the night of April 18, a Thursday, over 30,000 people

# DEATH

crowded the Cunard Pier as the *Carpathia* arrived in New York. Amid the furious flash of cameras and the shouted questions of reporters, the *Titanic*'s dazed survivors disembarked—new widows, fatherless children, bereft friends by the hundreds—all now touched by death.

Opposite Page:
*Chicago Daily Tribune*, April 18, 1912
Courtesy Collection of James and Felicia Kreuzer, New Wireless Pioneers

1528 X L Renaine R3. 18 12 HOPKINS

# Chicago Daily Tribune

THE WORLD'S GREATEST NEWSPAPER

THURSDAY, APRIL 18, 1912.—TWENTY-FOUR PAGES. PRICE ONE CENT IN CHICAGO AND SUBURBS. ELSEWHERE TWO CENTS.

# WORLD STILL REMAINS IN SUSPENSE, HOPING TO HEAR OF OTHER RESCUES; CARPATHIA MAY ARRIVE TONIGHT.

## ...OF THE NEWS

...APRIL 18, 1912.

**...R FORECAST.**

...ity—Cloudy and continued ...y fair; brisk to high north... diminishing and becoming

...ursday, preceded by rain or ...portion; Friday cloudy. ...6:35. Moonset, 8:22 p. m.

**...RE IN CHICAGO.** ...24 hours.]

...m. Wednesday...37
...m. Thursday...32

| | |
|---|---|
| ...m.......35 | 6 p. m.......36 |
| ...m.......36 | 7 p. m.......36 |
| ........36 | 8 p. m.......36 |
| ...m.......36 | 9 p. m.......35 |
| ...m.......36 | 10 p. m.......34 |
| ...m.......36 | 11 p. m.......34 |
| ...m.......37 | Midnight ....33 |
| ...m.......37 | 1 a. m.......32 |

...5; normal for the day, 46. ...1, 538. ...rs to 7 p. m., .58. Deficiency ...hes. ...les an hour at 3:14 p. m. ...a. m., 87%; 7 p. m., 94%. ...a. m., 30.01; 7 p. m., 29.76. ...nt weather report see page 17.

**...EX, 17. BARGAINS, 16**

**TITANIC.**

...in New York today or ...tanic survivors. Every ...ade to make reception ...rescued. Congress will ...place blame of disaster ...or legislation to prevent ...in future. Rulers of ...sages to President Taft ...over Titanic disaster. ...fulfills prophecy made ...y, 1910. Persistent ru... ...of the Titanic's sinking ...Marconi, angered by ...work of wireless oper... ...Director Ismay, saved ...ticized by Philadelphia ...F. H. Blackmarr on Car... ...E TRIBUNE first direct ...cago. **Pages 1-2-3-4.**

**...LITICAL.**

...s forty-eight delegates ...ns from congressional **Page 1.**

...reeted by large crowds **Page 8.**

...cts its Democratic dele... ...wood. **Page 7.**

**...OREIGN.**

...to demand of United ...ge. **Page 5.**

**...SHINGTON.**

...termine whether United ...will be elected by popu... **Page 6.**

...Lathrop appointed chief ...dren's bureau. **Page 9.**

**LOCAL.**

...cold, and wrapped in ...s result of advertise... **Page 13.**

...shark who settles when ...man is reporter. **Page 24.**

**...AND INDUSTRY.**

... **Page 15.**

...ancial. **Page 15.**

... **Page 17.**

**...PORTING.**

...k Curley names Las ...site and July 4 as date ...n battle. **Page 10.**

...ome season against Cincin... ...her permitting. **Page 11.**

...receive $9,200 in prizes ...tourney. **Page 11.**

**...F OCEAN STEAMSHIPS.**

| | Port. |
|---|---|
| ... | New York. |
| ... | Queenstown. |
| ...II | Southampton. |
| ...VICTORIA | Southampton. |
| ... | Liverpool. |
| ... | San Francisco. |
| ... | San Francisco. |
| ... | San Francisco. |
| ... | Victoria. |
| | Port. |
| ... | San Francisco. |
| ...N | San Francisco. |
| ... | London. |
| ... | New York. |
| ... | New York. |
| ... | New York. |
| ... | Madeira. |
| ... | Piraeus. |
| ... | Barcelona. |
| ... | Venice. |
| ... | Yokohama. |
| ... | Yokohama. |
| ... | Hongkong. |
| ... | Hongkong. |

## ...CE OF $2,000,000.

...nies in This Country ...Will Fight "Double ...ty Clause."

...17.—[Special.]—Accident ...s in this country and in ...to lose approximat...

## CONGRESS PLANS RIGID INQUIRY ON WRECK OF TITANIC

### Survivors and Line Officials Will Be Called to Explain Great Loss of Life.

### NEW LAWS WILL FOLLOW

### Legislation to Enforce Use of More Small Boats Proposed in Many Bills Offered.

### SEEK TO SAFEGUARD WIRELESS

Washington, D. C., April 17.—Congress acted swiftly today to determine who was to blame for the Titanic disaster and enact legislation to prevent similar disasters in the future.

The senate agreed to a resolution directing a thorough investigation by the commerce committee into the cause leading to the wreck, with particular reference to the inadequacy of life boats. This resolution was presented by Senator Smith of Michigan and was passed by unanimous consent in one hour and twenty minutes.

Representative Alexander of Missouri, chairman of the house committee on merchant marine and fisheries, announced today an investigation in which the survivors will be summoned to tell the facts concerning the inability of the steamship officials to save the lives of all the passengers on the giant liner.

**Will Summon Line Officials.**

The congressional investigations probably will result in the summoning of officials of the White Star line to state what precautions for safety are taken on the White Star liners.

"There could be no greater motive for stringent legislation than the fate of the host of passengers whom the life boats of the Titanic could not carry to safety," said Representative Alexander. "There could be no more pungent illustration of the necessity of of the scenes enacted on the wreck in the three hours that passed between the collision with the iceberg and the plunge of the hulk to the bottom."

Revenue cutter officials in Washington believe the disaster will result in insurance companies insisting upon steamships taking a more southerly course across the ocean. The investigations by insurance companies, maritime exchanges, and foreign maritime boards are expected to be thorough, but the congressional investigation, because of the power of congress to compel witnesses to testify, is expected to reveal many important facts.

**Text of Smith Resolution.**

The Smith resolution of inquiry is sweeping in its provisions. It is as follows:

Resolved, That the committee on commerce, or a subcommittee thereof, is hereby authorized and directed to investigate the causes leading to the wreck of the White Star liner Titanic, with its attendant loss of life, so shocking to the civilized world.

Resolved, Further, that said committee or subcommittee is hereby empowered to summon witness, send for persons and papers and to take such testimony as may be necessary to determine the responsibility therefor, with a view to such legislation as may be necessary to prevent, as far as possible, any repetition of such a disaster.

Resolved, Further, that the committee shall inquire particularly into the number of lifeboats, life rafts, and life preservers, and other equipment for the protection of the passengers and crew, the number of persons aboard the Titanic, whether passengers or crew, and whether adequate inspections had been made of

## RESCUE SHIP STILL SILENT AS TO WRECK

### Wireless Service Limited to Messages from Survivors.

### REFUSE CRUISER'S AID

### Small Hope Remains Fishing Boats Picked Up Some Victims.

### WORD FROM THE OLYMPIC

**BULLETIN.**

[BY CABLE TO THE CHICAGO TRIBUNE.]

Halifax, N. S., April 17.—The cable steamer Minia reports that she picked up a wireless dispatch stating that the Baltic [illegible] captain of the Minia says, however, that he was not in direct touch with the Baltic. He heard many conflicting wireless telegrams and cannot vouch for the accuracy of the statement that the Baltic rescued some of the passengers.

[The story told in the above bulletin is entirely improbable, for the Baltic has been heard from since the sinking of the Titanic and it reported no one on board from that vessel.—Ed. Tribune.]

New York, April 17.—[Special.]—Until the Cunard liner Carpathia, carrying the survivors of the Titanic wreck, reaches port here late Thursday night or Friday morning the details of the disaster will be unknown.

The Carpathia was in wireless communication with the station at Siasconsett, Mass., for several hours today, but the messages were confined to the names of survivors, which were forwarded to Washington, and personal messages from survivors to friends and relatives ashore.

**RELATIVES MUST WAIT.**

Electrical storms, a conflict of messages, the impossibility of any news trickling landward until the new list of survivors had been relayed to the government station at President Taft's orders—all these operated to sustain anxiety and aggravate suspense

## THE LAST BOAT.

[Copyright: 1912: By John T. McCutcheon.]

McCUTCHEON

Chester for information as to the circumstances of the collision and foundering, the Carpathia, for some reason that mystified those waiting for intelligence, was receiving messages but not answering them.

It is known that a wirless for J. Bruce Ismay, the managing director of the White Star line, congratulating him on his escape, was relayed through the station at Newport to the Carpathia.

**CAN GET NO NEWS.**

Hurrying toward the Carpathia at twenty-four knots speed, the chester used its powerful wireless all day. It asked for a full list of the survivors and for such inormation as would throw light on the disaster, but for hours the appeals were disregarded.

The wireless man at the Boston navy yard with his ear keen for Carpathia tidings

### *Third Cabin People Saved; on Carpathia.*

Portland, Me., April 17.—Names of third class passengers rescued from the wrecked steamship Titanic by the Carpathia were received by wireless tonight. The list, as far as it has been received, is:

| | |
|---|---|
| Adlerson, ——. | Mathjoax, Karl. |
| Angusen, Helena. | Malliedell, Bertha. |
| Dianodelmn, Delia. | Merrigan, Maggie. |
| Doyt, Agnes. | Maran, Bertha. |
| Eldegrek, Leonch. | Madsen, Kristof. |
| Hanwakan (?). | Moss, Albert. |
| Kirora, Krikorean. | McGovern, Mary. |
| Ludguis, Aing. | McDermott, Delia. |
| Murphy, Nora. | Marlkarl, ——. |
| Mullin, Katie. | McKaren, John. |
| McCarthy, Katie. | McKey, Ernest. |
| Messemockes, G. D. | McKey, Alice. |
| Messemockes, Annie. | McCormack, Thos. |
| Yusef, Madera. | Nickaren, John. |
| Moubarek, Bunos. | Nelson, Bertha. |

and one of the steamships which heard the Titanic's call for help, came today. The message suggested that the bodies of some of the Titanic's passengers were on the Californian. The message was as follows:

"On board the steamship Olympic, east bound, by wireless, Cape Race and land lines to New York, April 17.—

"The bodies of some, at least, of the victims of the lost Titanic will be brought, probably to Boston, on the Leyland liner Californian. Wireless advices reaching us from the scene of the disaster say that some have been recovered. They will be tenderly cared for, and we understand that they will be taken to port as soon as the Californian resumes its interrupted voyage, just when we do not know.

**GREAT SORROW ON OLYMPIC.**

"The Olympic is proceeding. It could do

{Before dawn, when the *Carpathia* reached the *Titanic's* last known position, she found floating wreckage and the lifeboats spread out over several miles.}

**DEATH FROM HYPOTHERMIA COMES GENTLY. . . .
MOST OF THE <u>TITANIC</u>'S LOST SOULS
SLIPPED INTO THEIR FINAL SLEEP
WITHIN SEVERAL MINUTES OF ENTERING THE FREEZING OCEAN.**

## DEATH

Right:
ROBERT DOUGLAS NORMAN
*Believing he could swim to safety, Scottish civil engineer R. D. Norman gave his life jacket to a woman and her child. His watch was recovered several days after the disaster and shows the time when he entered the icy water. It reads 3:06 (A.M.), the hour in the time zone through which the* Titanic *had passed during the day of April 14. Norman had not yet reset his watch one hour earlier, to 2:06 A.M.*
Courtesy National Maritime Museum, Greenwich, England

Opposite Page:
GOLD POCKET WATCH, OWNED BY ROBERT DOUGLAS NORMAN, CA. 1880
Courtesy National Maritime Museum, Greenwich, England

| PASSENGER | AGE | CLASS | LOST/SAVED |
|---|---|---|---|
| Master Marshall Brines Drew | 8 | 2nd | Saved |
| Mrs. James Vivian (Lulu Thorne Christian) Drew | 34 | 2nd | Saved |
| Mr. James Vivian Drew | 42 | 2nd | Lost |
| Miss Bridget Driscoll | 24 | 3rd | Saved |
| Sir Cosmo Edmund Duff Gordon | 49 | 1st | Saved |
| Lady Lucille Wallace Sutherland Duff Gordon | 48 | 1st | Saved |
| Mr. William Cothers Dulles | 39 | 1st | Lost |
| Mr. Joseph Duquemin | 24 | 3rd | Saved |
| Miss Florentina Duran y More | | 2nd | Saved |
| Miss Asuncion Duran y More | | 2nd | Saved |

| Passenger | Age | Class | Lost/Saved |
|---|---|---|---|
| Mr. Adolf Fredrik Dyker | 23 | 3rd | Lost |
| Mrs. Adolf Fredrik Dyker (Anna Elizabeth Judith Andersson) | 22 | 3rd | Lost |
| Mrs. Boulton (Olive Potter) Earnshaw | 23 | 1st | Saved |
| Mr. Joso Econovic | | 3rd | Lost |
| Mr. Gustaf Hjalmar Edvardsson | 18 | 3rd | Lost |
| Mr. George Floyd Eitemiller | 23 | 2nd | Lost |
| Mr. Hans Linus Eklund | 16 | 3rd | Lost |
| Mr. Johan Ekstrom | 45 | 3rd | Lost |
| Mr. Joseph Elias | | 3rd | Lost |

{"Here you are. You may need it." —Chief Officer Wilde to other officers as he passed out revolvers}

## Death

Opposite Page:
CHIEF OFFICER HENRY T. WILDE
*Several survivors said Wilde shot himself as the ship went down; others said he shot two men who were trying to enter lifeboats ahead of women and children.*
The Mariners' Museum

Above:
FAMILY AND FRIENDS CROWD THE WHITE STAR OFFICES IN SOUTHAMPTON, ENGLAND.
Courtesy Southampton City Heritage Services

**"PLEASE SEND FULL LIST TITANIC SURVIVORS STOP SEND A RUSH MESSAGE."**

—*From a wireless message sent to the* Carpathia *from the Marconi Company's Montreal office*

{The *Mackay-Bennett* crew recovered 306 bodies; 116 were buried at sea, and 190 were taken to Halifax for burial.}

**TO THE TOWN OF HALIFAX, NOVA SCOTIA, FELL THE TASK OF TENDING TO THE <u>TITANIC</u>'S DEAD. THE CABLE SHIP <u>MACKAY-BENNETT</u> WAS SENT OUT TO GATHER BODIES.**

## DEATH

Left:
THE *MACKAY-BENNETT*,
THE "FUNERAL SHIP" OUT OF HALIFAX
*The White Star Line chartered the* Mackay-Bennett *for a difficult assignment: searching the area where the* Titanic *had sunk and recovering the bodies of passengers and crew. A team of undertakers and a priest boarded the ship along with over one hundred coffins and tons of ice.*
The Mariners' Museum

Opposite Page:
LETTER FROM HELEN OSTBY TO HOPE CHAPIN
*When survivor Helen Ostby came aboard the* Carpathia, *she was taken in by Hope Chapin, who was setting off on a honeymoon with her husband. In this letter, Ostby writes, "The* Mackay-Bennett *ship found Father's body, which was a great relief."*
The Mariners' Museum, gift of Howard Chapin

| PASSENGER | AGE | CLASS | LOST/SAVED |
|---|---|---|---|
| Mr. Elias Elias | | 3rd | Lost |
| Mr. John Elias | | 3rd | Lost |
| Mr. James Elsbury | 47 | 3rd | Lost |
| Miss Virginia Ethel Emanuel | 5 | 3rd | Saved |
| Mr. Thomas Emmeth | | 3rd | Lost |

Providence

61 Cooke Street

Dear Hope,—

I have wanted to write for a long while but until lately my hand was too shaky — however I hope this reaches you over there.

I can never thank you and Howard enough for all you did for us on the Carpathia — you may say there was not much to do;

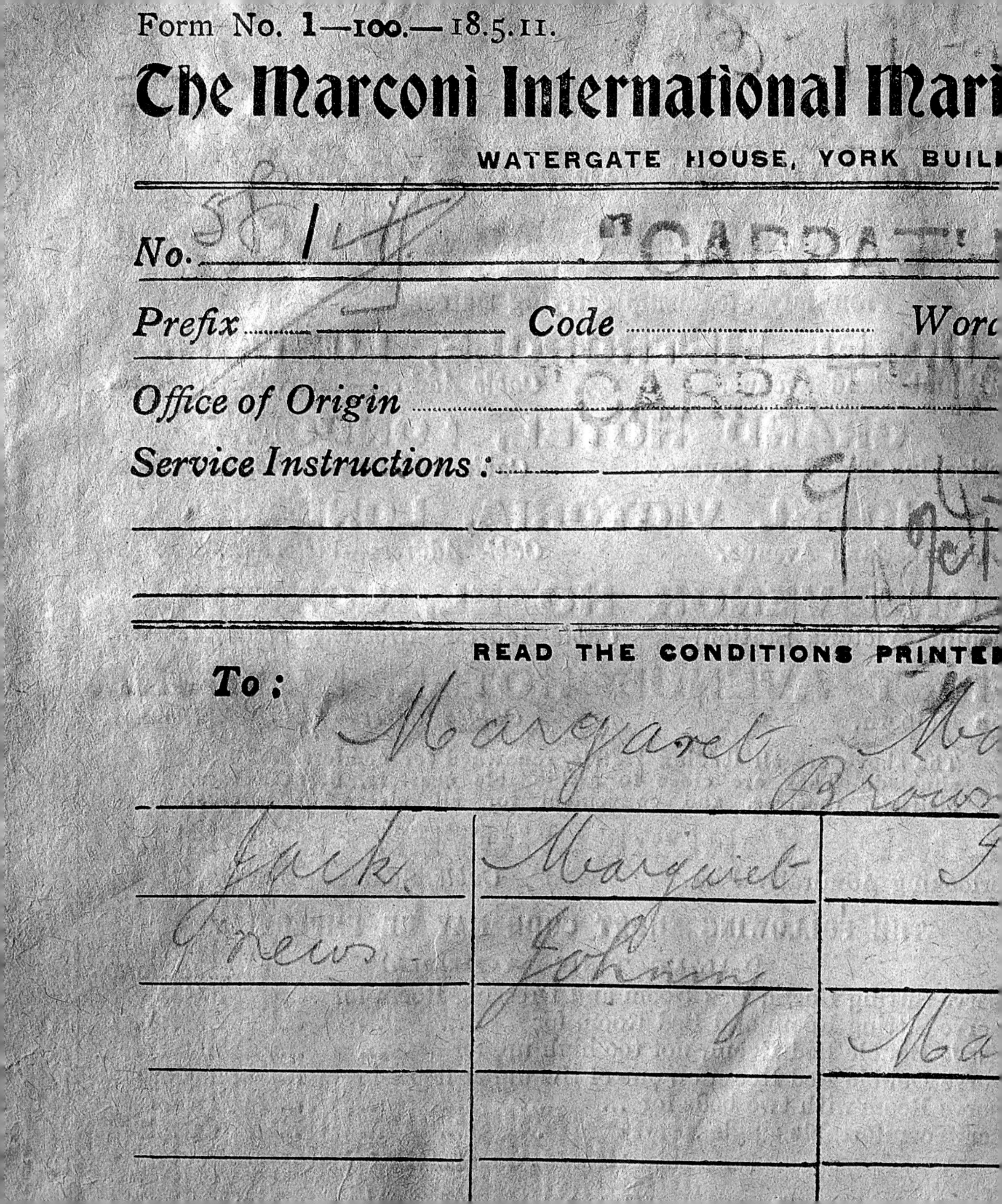

Form No. 1—100.—18.5.11.

# The Marconi International Mari

WATERGATE HOUSE, YORK BUIL

*No.* 58/14 CARPATH

*Prefix* ............ *Code* ............ *Word*

*Office of Origin* ............ CARPATH

*Service Instructions:* ............

READ THE CONDITIONS PRINTE

**To:** Margaret Ma
Brow

| Jack | Margaret | |
|---|---|---|
| news | Johnny | |
| | | Ma |

*Sent date* ______________

# ...ommunication Company, Ltd.

...DELPHI, LONDON, W.C.

...ICE ______________ 19 12

**CHARGES TO PAY.**

| | | |
|---|---|---|
| Marconi Charge ... | 16 | 8 |
| Other Line Charge... | 14 | 7 |
| Delivery Charge ... | | |
| Total . . £ | 1. 11 | 3 |

| Office sent to | Time sent | By whom sent |
|---|---|---|
| MSA | 2 50 m. | |

...E BACK OF THE FORM.

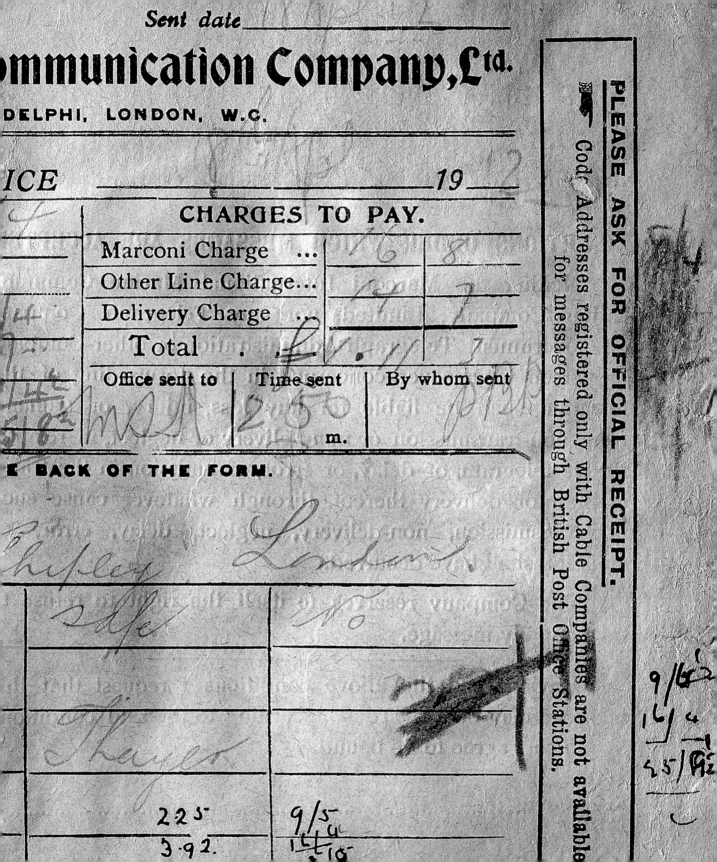

London

Shipley

No

Thayer

225 9/5

3.92 1/4 10

**PLEASE ASK FOR OFFICIAL RECEIPT.**

☞ Code Addresses registered only with Cable Companies are not available for messages through British Post Office Stations.

Built to crown an epoch, the *Titanic* was lost on the sixth day of her maiden voyage. Her immediate aftermath was heartbreak. With time and a huge public outcry, however, another legacy emerged—greater safety at sea. Shipping lanes were shifted to avoid the greatest danger of ice, and regulations governing passenger safety were expanded. Not the least of these was the requirement that every passenger

# AFTERMATH

and crew member be assigned a specific place in a lifeboat. In response to popular demand, the International Convention for the Safety of Life at Sea convened in 1913 and has reconvened periodically throughout the century. In addition, new regulations were instituted requiring that ship radios be operated twenty-four hours a day and the formation of an International Ice Patrol.

Opposite Page:
WHITE STAR LINE—TYPES OF WORLD FAMOUS LINERS
*The* Titanic *is conspicuously absent from this colorful lithograph, which was printed soon after the disaster.*
The Mariners' Museum

Previous Pages:
MARCONIGRAM SENT FROM THE *CARPATHIA* TO NEW YORK, APRIL 15, 1912:
"Jack, Margaret safe. No news Johnny. Marian Thayer."
Courtesy Collection of James and Felicia Kreuzer, New Wireless Pioneers

WHITE STAR LINE

TYPES OF WORLD
FAMOUS LINERS

THE LIVERPOOL PRINTING & STATIONERY COMPANY, LIMITED.

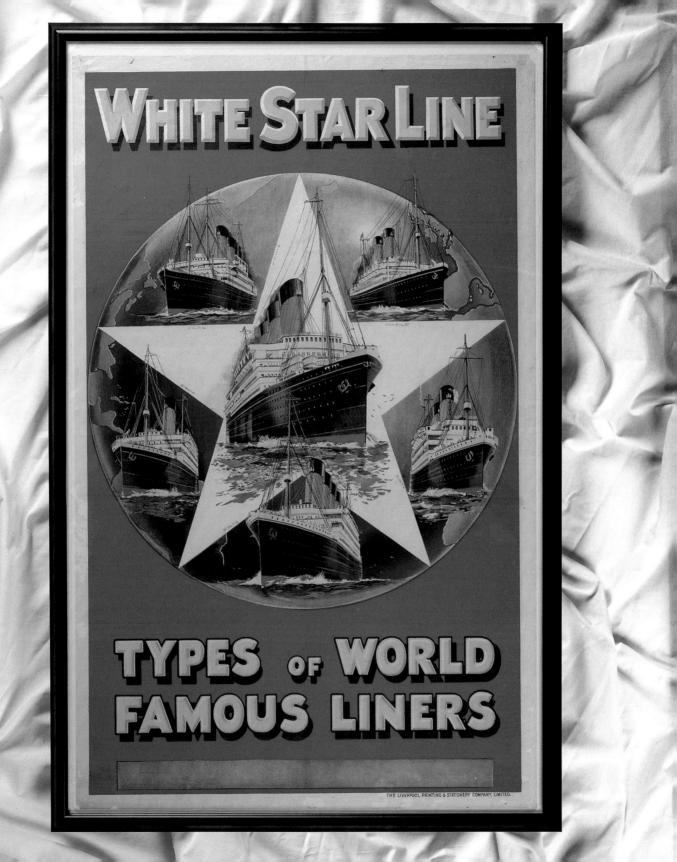

**"WE . . . BEG TO ADVISE YOU THAT YOUR CLAIM HAS BEEN PLACED ON FILE AND WILL RECEIVE THE MOST CAREFUL CONSIDERATION."**

*—Letter from White Star Line official to Leah Aks*

# AFTERMATH

MOE LEVY
J.L. MITCHELL

LEVY & MITCHELL
Attorneys at Law
NATIONAL BANK OF COMMERCE BLDG.
Norfolk, Va.

April 5th, 1916.

Messrs. House, Grossman and Vorhaus,
New York, N.Y.

Gentlemen:-

IN RE: AKS VS. TITANIC. Beg to acknowledge receipt of yours of the 4th inst., enclosing check for $81.67 in settlement of collection in the above matter less two-thirds of the fee.

Thanking you for your prompt attention in connection with this matter, we beg to remain,

Yours very truly,

Levy & Mitchell

L/G.

Above:
LETTER FROM LEVY AND MITCHELL, ATTORNEYS-AT-LAW, TO MESSRS. HOUSE, GROSSMAN, AND VORHAUS, APRIL 16, 1916
*Four years after the* Titanic *disaster, Leah Aks received $81.67 for the property she had lost. First-class passenger Charlotte Drake Cardeza, by contrast, was compensated with more than $177,000 for her losses.*
Courtesy The Family of Frank P. Aks

Opposite Page:
LETTER FROM T. T. KEILY, WHITE STAR LINE, TO MRS. LEAH AKS, ACKNOWLEDGING RECEIPT OF HER CLAIM FOR LOSSES ON THE *TITANIC*, MAY 29, 1912
Courtesy The Family of Frank P. Aks

{The Aks family settled in Norfolk, Virginia, and had two more children. They named their only daughter Carpathia.}

| PASSENGER | AGE | CLASS | LOST/SAVED |
|---|---|---|---|
| Mr. Ingvar Enander | 21 | 2nd | Lost |
| Miss Caroline Louise Endres | | 1st | Saved |
| Miss Elizabeth Mussey Eustis | 53 | 1st | Saved |
| Miss Edith Corse Evans | 36 | 1st | Lost |
| Mr. Thomas James Everett | | 3rd | Lost |

30 JAMES STREET
LIVERPOOL

CANUTE ROAD
SOUTHAMPTON

1 COCKSPUR ST., S. W.
38 LEADENHALL ST., E. C.
LONDON

WHITE STAR LINE

9 BROADWAY

TELEGRAPHIC ADDRESS
"ISMAY"

Third Class DEPARTMENT

NEW YORK, May 29-12.

Mrs. Leah Akz,
c/o Harry Greene,
131 College Place,
Norfolk, Va.

Dear Madam:-

N. B.—PASSAGES ARE ONLY BOOKED SUBJECT TO ALL THE TERMS AND CONDITIONS APPEARING ON THE PASSAGE TICKETS.

We acknowledge the receipt of yours of 1st inst. and in reply beg to advise that your claim has been placed on file and will receive the most careful consideration. We are quite sure that you will appreciate that since this terrible disaster the Line has not been able to complete the necessary investigation but that all claims will be carefully examined and replies sent after an opportunity for investigation has been afforded.

Yours very truly,
WHITE STAR LINE.
Per [signature]

TTK/JR.

Henry will meet you and take you where you want to go also Ma B.

It didn't seem as if I could go home from Rochester and not see you.

I also got two new waists.

I have read papers; trying to get some hope, but all fail now I shall pray for the body. He was so good to me.

Well, Lis, take good care of yourself.

Milton sends a good hug and kiss

Tell your mother that mother left some things there and if she will send them C.O.D. by Express.

Try and get Ual to write how you are. It would be some comfort to hear from you

With Love

F

141

| PASSENGER | AGE | CLASS | LOST/SAVED |
|---|---|---|---|
| Mr. Arne Jonas Fahlstrom | 19 | 3rd | Lost |
| Mr. James Farrell | | 3rd | Lost |
| Mrs. Lizzie Faunthorpe | | 2nd | Saved |
| Mr. Harry Faunthorpe | | 2nd | Lost |
| Mr. Charles Fillbrook | | 2nd | Saved |
| Mr. Luigi Finoli | | 3rd | Lost |

## AFTERMATH

Opposite Page:
LETTER FROM AN UNIDENTIFIED SURVIVOR TO FELLOW SURVIVOR LILLIAN BENTHAM, APRIL 24, 1912
Courtesy Craig A. Sopin Collection

Left:
SECOND OFFICER CHARLES LIGHTOLLER WITH THIRD OFFICER HERBERT JOHN PITTMAN
*Second Officer Lightoller (with pipe) responded to more than 1,600 questions at the American inquiry. He is seen here talking with Third Officer Pittman just after their return to England on the* Adriatic.
Courtesy Hulton Getty Picture Library

**"I HAVE READ THE PAPERS TRYING TO GET SOME HOPE, BUT ALL FAIL NOW. I SHALL PRAY FOR THE BODY. HE WAS SO GOOD TO ME."**

*—Passage in a letter from a* Titanic *survivor writing about the loss of her husband*

{"Not only the *Titanic* herself but the confidence of an age was shattered by the collision with an iceberg." —Gillian Hutchinson, *The Wreck of the* Titanic}

{The American inquiry lasted more than a month—from April 19 to May 25, 1912.}

| PASSENGER | AGE | CLASS | LOST/SAVED |
|---|---|---|---|
| Mr. Eberrhard Telander Fischer | | 3rd | Lost |
| Mrs. Alfred (Antoinette) Flegenheim | | 1st | Saved |
| Mr. John Flynn | | 3rd | Lost |
| Mr. John Irving Flynn | | 1st | Saved |
| Mr. James Flynn | | 3rd | Lost |
| Mr. William Foley | | 3rd | Lost |
| Mr. Joseph Foley | | 3rd | Lost |
| Mr. Choong Foo | | 3rd | Lost |
| Mr. Neil Watson Ford | 16 | 3rd | Lost |
| Mr. Arthur Ford | | 3rd | Lost |

## AFTERMATH

Opposite Page:
"WRECK OF THE *TITANIC*,"
WILLIAM BALTZELL, 1912
Sheet music
The Mariners' Museum,
gift of Frances Matthews

Left:
THE *TITANIC* INQUIRY, LONDON
Courtesy *Illustrated London News*
Picture Library

In the United States, Senator William Alden Smith led an inquiry into the tragedy. Many hoped that the ensuing British investigation would clear up the large number of remaining questions, but those hopes were dashed when it became apparent that the aim of the British inquiry was not to probe but to sanitize the disaster.

**STILL, MANY QUESTIONS ABOUT THE <u>TITANIC</u> DISASTER REMAINED UNANSWERED. . . .**

With love and best wishes
Alma

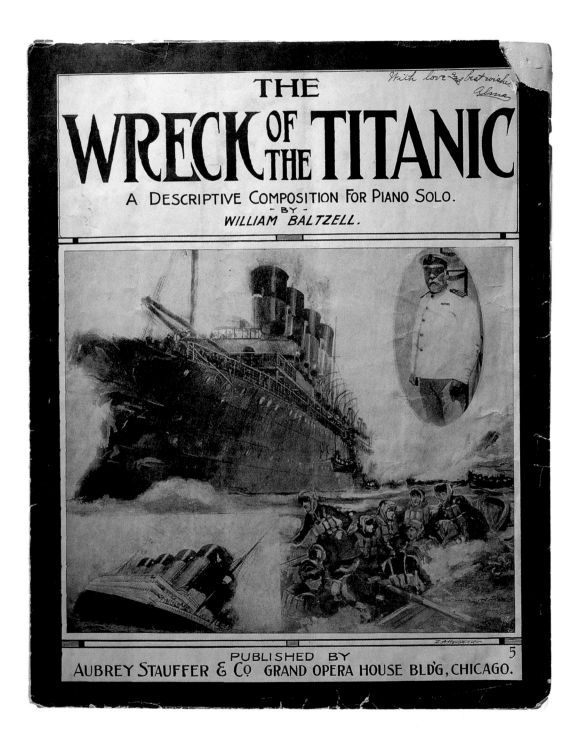

# THE WRECK OF THE TITANIC

A DESCRIPTIVE COMPOSITION FOR PIANO SOLO.

- BY -

*WILLIAM BALTZELL.*

Z. A. HENDRICK

PUBLISHED BY
AUBREY STAUFFER & Co. GRAND OPERA HOUSE BLD'G, CHICAGO.

5

257 Battic St
Elizabeth
New Jersey
U S

Thurs 16.1.19

My dear Lillian
In answer to your most wel-
come letter of last week was
so glad to have from you
but sorry to here you had
bean ill with your back. I
do hope you are all right
again. well dear as far my
self I dont get on like
I would like to but dear I
am so Broken hearted I can't
help it I do miss my dear
husband and Brothers and

dont forget to write
again to me dear
my cough is not
better yet

Miss

# "OH IT IS TERRIBLE POOR BERT . . . OH TO THINK THAT IT HAD TO BE AND EVERYBODY SEEMED SO HAPPY. I AM BROKENHEARTED OVER MY DEAR HUSBAND SUCH A GOOD FELLOW HE WAS."

*—Letter from Lillian Renouf to Miss Lillian Bentham*

{"All the values of life changed, and the daily incidents, which once seemed of such importance to us, dwindled into mere trivialities."
—Daisy Spedden in her diary a couple of years after the sinking}

## AFTERMATH

Below:
MARCONIGRAM SENT FROM THE *CARPATHIA* TO NEW YORK, APRIL 15, 1912
*In this message, passenger Dorothy Harder states that the* Titanic *sank, that she and George are safe, but that they "lost everything."*
Courtesy Craig A. Sopin Collection

Above:
THE MAY FAMILY
*Mrs. May, the widow of a* Titanic *crewman, is shown here with six of her eight children. Her husband and nineteen-year-old son, both firemen, died on the* Titanic. *On the extreme right is Mrs. May's widowed daughter-in-law, holding her twelve-week-old baby. Like many* Titanic *widows, Mrs. May was left with a large family to care for. On both sides of the Atlantic, many orphans' and widows' funds were established to help provide for the nearly 700 families of lost crew members.*
Courtesy Haynes Publishing

Opposite Page:
LETTER FROM LILLIAN RENOUF TO MISS LILLIAN BENTHAM, MAY 16, 1912
Courtesy Craig A. Sopin Collection

Form No. 1—100.—17.11.11. Sent date
The Marconi International Marine Communication Company, Ltd.
WATERGATE HOUSE, YORK BUILDINGS, ADELPHI, LONDON, W.C.
No. 3030 "CARPATHIA" OFFICE 19
Prefix Code Words 10
Office of Origin "CARPATHIA"
CHARGES TO PAY.
Marconi Charge
Other Line Charge 18/9
Delivery Charge
PLEASE ASK FOR O... Code Addresses registered for messages
On Board S. S. New York Harbor, 191
TO V. A. Harder
117 Eighth Ave. Brooklyn
Titanic sank George & I safe on Carpathia lost everything
Dorothy

Telegrams Promptly Forwarded from QUARANTINE, New York Harbor, to EUROPE and All Parts of the World. Tariff Same as from New York City.
THE COMPANY'S UNIFORMED COLLECTORS MEET ALL INCOMING STEAMERS AT NEW YORK, TO RECEIVE CABLEGRAMS AND TELEGRAMS. TELEGRAPH AND CABLE ADDRESSES REGISTERED AT TELEGRAPH OFFICES IN ANY PART OF THE WORLD ARE AVAILABLE BY THIS LINE.

# *TITANIC*
## *fortune & fate*

## THE MARINERS' MUSEUM
## JANUARY 24, 1998–NOVEMBER 1, 1998
## LENDERS TO THE EXHIBITION

### LENDERS OF OBJECTS ASSOCIATED WITH THE *TITANIC*

Mrs. Marie Aks
*Norfolk, Virginia*

The Family of Frank P. Aks
*Norfolk, Virginia*
*Baltimore, Maryland*

Bachman-May Collection
*Ocean Grove, New Jersey*

Carolyn K. Barry
*Suffolk, Virginia*

Jamie Corson
*Hampton, Virginia*

Ellis Island Immigration Museum, Statue of Liberty National Monument
*New York, New York*

Heather Friedle
*Newport News, Virginia*

Independence Seaport Museum Library, Thayer Collection
*Philadelphia, Pennsylvania*

Collection of James and Felicia Kreuzer, New Wireless Pioneers
*Elma, New York*

Stanley Lehrer Collection
*Valley Stream, New York*

Ken Marschall
*Redondo Beach, California*

The Miottel Collection
*San Francisco, California*

The National Maritime Museum
*Greenwich, England*

North Carolina Museum of History
*Raleigh, North Carolina*

James E. O'Neill, Jr.
*Peekskill, New York*

Dr. and Mrs. Harriet Powell
*Newport News, Virginia*

Joanne Rigby, JoAnne's This, That and the Other
*Poquoson, Virginia*

Mr. Richard L. Rowland and Dr. Karen M. LaParo
*Charlottesville, Virginia*

Mr. Kenneth Schultz
*Hoboken, New Jersey*

Mr. Craig A. Sopin
*Philadelphia, Pennsylvania*

Steiff USA
*New York, New York*

Twentieth Century Fox Film Corporation and Twentieth Century Fox Film Archives
*Beverly Hills, California*

Valentine Museum
*Richmond, Virginia*

## Lenders of Photographs Associated with the *Titanic*

The Family of Frank P. Aks
*Norfolk, Virginia*
*Baltimore, Maryland*

Archive Photos
*New York, New York*

Brown Brothers Collection
*Sterling, Pennsylvania*

Leighton H. Coleman, III
*Saint James, New York*

Corbis-Bettmann
*New York, New York*

Corbis Images
*Bellevue, Washington*

*Cork Examiner*
*Cork, Ireland*

Dr. Ronald C. Denney
*Kent, England*

John P. Eaton
*Cold Spring, New York*

Charles A. Haas
*Randolph, New Jersey*

Harvard University Archives
*Cambridge, Massachusetts*

Haynes Publishers
*Somerset, England*

*Illustrated London News* Picture Library
*London, England*

Independence Seaport Museum
*Philadelphia, Pennsylvania*

Stanley Lehrer Collection
*Valley Stream, New York*

Library of Congress
*Washington, D.C.*

Don Lynch Collection
*Los Angeles, California*

Madison Press
*Toronto, Ontario*

Marconi Museum
*Essex, England*

Ken Marschall Collection
*For prints and posters of Ken Marschall* Titanic *artwork, contact:*
*Trans-Atlantic Designs*
*P.O. Box 539, Redondo Beach, CA 90277. E-mail TADesigns@aol.com*

McCord Museum of Canadian History
*Montreal, Quebec*

Merseyside Maritime Museum
*Liverpool, England*

National Maritime Museum
*Greenwich, England*

New York Public Library
*New York, New York*

Jeremy Nightingale Collection
*Kent, England*

Sheridan House
*Dobbs Ferry, New York*

Southampton City Heritage Collection
*Southampton, England*

Steamship Historical Society Collection
University of Baltimore Library
*Baltimore, Maryland*

Tony Stone Images/
Hulton Getty Picture Library
*Chicago, Illinois*

Titanic Historical Society, Inc.
*Indian Orchard, Massachusetts*

University of Pennsylvania Archives
*Philadelphia, Pennsylvania*

Ulster Folk and Transport Museum
*County Down, Northern Ireland*

Neland Whiting
*Beach Haven, New Jersey*

# *Titanic* Passengers

| Name | Age | Class | Lost/Saved |
|---|---|---|---|
| Mr. Anthony Abbing | 42 | 3rd | Lost |
| Master Eugene Joseph Abbott | 13 | 3rd | Lost |
| Mr. Rossmore Edward Abbott | 16 | 3rd | Lost |
| Mrs. Stanton Abbott (Rosa) | 35 | 3rd | Saved |
| Miss Anna Karen Abelseth | 16 | 3rd | Saved |
| Mr. Olaus Abelseth | 25 | 3rd | Saved |
| Mr. Samuel Abelson | 30 | 2nd | Lost |
| Mrs. Samuel Abelson (Anna) | 28 | 2nd | Saved |
| Mrs. Joseph Abraham (Sophie Easu) | 18 | 2nd | Saved |
| Mr. August Abrahamsson | 20 | 3rd | Saved |
| Mr. Mauritz Nills Martin Adahl | 30 | 3rd | Lost |
| Mr. John Adams | 26 | 3rd | Lost |
| Mrs. Johanna Persdotter Ahlin | 40 | 3rd | Lost |
| Mr. Ali Ahmed | 24 | 3rd | Lost |
| Mr. Isak Aijo-Nirva | 41 | 3rd | Lost |
| Master Philip Aks (Frank) | 10m* | 3rd | Saved |
| Mrs. Sam Aks (Leah Rosen) | 18 | 3rd | Saved |
| Mr. Charles Augustus Aldworth | 30 | 2nd | Lost |
| Mr. William Alexander | 23 | 3rd | Lost |
| Mr. Ilmari Rudolf Alhomaki | 20 | 3rd | Lost |
| Mr. William Ali | 25 | 3rd | Lost |
| Miss Elisabeth Walton Allen | 29 | 1st | Saved |
| Mr. William Henry Allen | 35 | 3rd | Lost |
| Miss Helen Loraine Allison | 2 | 1st | Lost |
| Mr. Hudson Joshua C. Allison | 30 | 1st | Lost |
| Mrs. Hudson J. C. Allison (Bessie Waldo Daniels) | 25 | 1st | Lost |
| Master Hudson Trevor Allison | 11m | 1st | Saved |
| Mr. Owen George Allum | 18 | 3rd | Lost |
| Mr. Albert Karvin Andersen | 32 | 3rd | Lost |
| Mr. Thor Olsvigen Andersen | 20 | 3rd | Lost |
| Mr. Harry Anderson | 47 | 1st | Saved |
| Mr. Anders Johan Andersson | 39 | 3rd | Lost |
| Mrs. Anders Andersson (Alfrida K. Brogren) | 39 | 3rd | Lost |
| Miss Ebba Iris Andersson | 6 | 3rd | Lost |
| Miss Ellis Anna Maria Andersson | 2 | 3rd | Lost |
| Miss Erna Andersson | 17 | 3rd | Saved |
| Miss Ida Augusta M. Andersson | 38 | 3rd | Lost |
| Miss Ingeborg Constancia Andersson | 9 | 3rd | Lost |
| Mr. Johan Samuel Andersson | 26 | 3rd | Lost |
| Miss Sigrid Elizabeth Andersson | 11 | 3rd | Lost |
| Master Sigvard Harald Elias Andersson | 4 | 3rd | Lost |
| Mr. Paul Edvin Andreasson | 20 | 3rd | Lost |
| Mr. Edgar Samuel Andrew | 18 | 2nd | Lost |
| Mr. Frank Andrew | | 2nd | Lost |
| Miss Kornelia Theodosia Andrews | 63 | 1st | Saved |
| Mr. Thomas Andrews, Jr. | 39 | 1st | Lost |
| Mr. Minko Angheloff | 26 | 3rd | Lost |
| Mr. William A. Angle | 34 | 2nd | Lost |
| Mrs. William A. Angle (Florence) | 32 | 2nd | Saved |
| Mrs. Edward Dale Appleton (Charlotte Lamson) | 58 | 1st | Saved |
| Mr. Josef Arnold | 25 | 3rd | Lost |
| Mrs. Josef Arnold (Josephine Frank) | 18 | 3rd | Lost |
| Mr. Ernst Axel Algot Aronsson | 24 | 3rd | Lost |

**m=months*

# *Titanic* Passengers

| Name | Age | Class | Lost/Saved |
|---|---|---|---|
| Mr. Ramon Artagaveytia | | 1st | Lost |
| Mr. John Ashby | 57 | 2nd | Lost |
| Mr. Adola Asim | 35 | 3rd | Lost |
| Mr. Carl Oscar Asplund | 40 | 3rd | Lost |
| Mrs. Carl Oscar Asplund (Selma Augusta Johansson) | 38 | 3rd | Saved |
| Master Carl Edgar Asplund | 5 | 3rd | Lost |
| Master Clarence Gustaf Hugo Asplund | 9 | 3rd | Lost |
| Master Edwin Rojj Felix Asplund | 3 | 3rd | Saved |
| Master Filip Oscar Asplund | 13 | 3rd | Lost |
| Mr. John Charles Asplund | 23 | 3rd | Saved |
| Miss Lillian Gertrud Asplund | 5 | 3rd | Saved |
| Lady Cynthia Asquith | | 1st | Saved |
| Mr. Gerios Assaf | | 3rd | Lost |
| Mrs. Mariana Assaf | 45 | 3rd | Saved |
| Mr. Ali Assam | 23 | 3rd | Lost |
| Col. John Jacob Astor | 47 | 1st | Lost |
| Mrs. John Jacob Astor (Madeline Talmadge Force) | 19 | 1st | Saved |
| Mr. Solomon Attala (Kalil) | 27 | 3rd | Lost |
| Miss Malaka Attalah | 17 | 3rd | Lost |
| Mrs. Leontine Pauline Aubert | | 1st | Saved |
| Mr. Albert Augustsson | 23 | 3rd | Lost |
| Mr. Rafoul Baccos | 20 | 3rd | Lost |
| Mr. Karl Alfred Backstrom | 32 | 3rd | Lost |
| Mrs. Karl Alfred Backstrom (Maria Mathilda Gustafsson) | 33 | 3rd | Saved |
| Miss Eugenie Baclini | 3 | 3rd | Saved |
| Miss Helene Baclini | | 3rd | Saved |
| Miss Maria Baclini | | 3rd | Saved |
| Mrs. Solomon Baclini (Latifa) | 24 | 3rd | Saved |
| Miss Emily Louisa Badman | 18 | 3rd | Saved |
| Mr. Mohammed Badt | 40 | 3rd | Lost |
| Mr. Percy Andrew Bailey | 18 | 2nd | Lost |
| Mr. Charles R. Baimbrigge | 23 | 2nd | Lost |
| Mr. Cerin Balkic | 26 | 3rd | Lost |
| Mrs. Ada E. Hall Balls | 36 | 2nd | Lost |
| Mr. Frederick J. Banfield | 28 | 2nd | Lost |
| Miss Ayout Banoura | 15 | 3rd | Lost |
| Mrs. Catherine Barbara | 45 | 3rd | Lost |
| Miss Saude Barbara | 18 | 3rd | Lost |
| Mr. Algernon H. Barkworth | | 1st | Saved |
| Miss Julia Barry | 27 | 3rd | Lost |
| Mr. David Barton | 22 | 3rd | Lost |
| Rev. Robert James Bateman | 51 | 2nd | Lost |
| Mr. John D. Baumann | | 1st | Lost |
| Mrs. James Baxter (Helene De Laudeniere Chaput) | 50 | 1st | Saved |
| Mr. Quigg Edmond Baxter | 24 | 1st | Lost |
| Mr. Edward Beane | 32 | 2nd | Lost |
| Mrs. Edward Beane (Ethel Clarke) | 19 | 2nd | Lost |
| Mr. Thomson Beattie | 36 | 1st | Lost |
| Mr. Henry James Beauchamp | 28 | 2nd | Lost |
| Mr. William Thomas Beaven | 19 | 3rd | Lost |
| Mrs. Allen Oliver Becker (Nellie E. Baumgardner) | 36 | 2nd | Saved |
| Miss Marion Louise Becker | 4 | 2nd | Saved |
| Master Richard F. Becker | 1 | 2nd | Saved |

# *Titanic* Passengers

| Name | Age | Class | Lost/Saved |
|---|---|---|---|
| Miss Ruth Elizabeth Becker | 12 | 2nd | Saved |
| Mr. Richard Leonard Beckwith | 37 | 1st | Saved |
| Mrs. Richard Beckwith (Sally Monypeny) | 47 | 1st | Saved |
| Mr. Lawrence Beesley | 34 | 2nd | Saved |
| Mr. Karl Howell Behr | 26 | 1st | Saved |
| Mr. John Viktor Bengtsson | 26 | 3rd | Lost |
| Miss Lillian W. Bentham | 19 | 2nd | Saved |
| Mr. Karl Ivar Sven Berglund | 22 | 3rd | Lost |
| Mr. William S. Berriman | 23 | 2nd | Lost |
| Mr. Tannous Betros | 20 | 3rd | Lost |
| Miss Bertha Bett | 17 | 2nd | Saved |
| Mr. Lee Bing | 32 | 3rd | Saved |
| Mr. Hans Birkeland | 21 | 3rd | Lost |
| Mr. Jakob Birnbaum | 25 | 1st | Lost |
| Mr. Dickinson H. Bishop | 25 | 1st | Saved |
| Mrs. Dickinson H. Bishop (Helen Walton) | 19 | 1st | Saved |
| Mr. Ernst Herbert Bjorklund | 18 | 3rd | Lost |
| Mr. Mauritz Hakan Bjornstrom | 28 | 1st | Saved |
| Mr. Stephen Weart Blackwell | 45 | 1st | Lost |
| Mr. Henry Blank | 39 | 1st | Saved |
| Miss Caroline Bonnell | 29 | 1st | Saved |
| Miss Elizabeth Bonnell | 58 | 1st | Saved |
| Miss Margaret Boone (Muddy) | | 1st | Saved |
| Mr. John James Borebank | | 1st | Lost |
| Mr. Guentcho Bostandyeff | 26 | 3rd | Lost |
| Mr. William Hull Botsford | 26 | 2nd | Lost |
| Master Akar Boulos | 6 | 3rd | Lost |
| Mr. Hanna Boulos | | 3rd | Lost |
| Mrs. Joseph Boulos (Sultana) | | 3rd | Lost |
| Miss Laura Boulos | 9 | 3rd | Lost |
| Mr. John Bourke | 40 | 3rd | Lost |
| Mrs. John Bourke (Catherine) | 32 | 3rd | Lost |
| Miss Mary Bourke | | 3rd | Lost |
| Mr. David Bowen | 26 | 3rd | Lost |
| Miss Grace Scott Bowen | 45 | 1st | Saved |
| Mr. Soloman Bowenur | | 2nd | Lost |
| Miss Elsie Edith Bowerman | 22 | 1st | Saved |
| Mrs. James H. Bracken | 27 | 2nd | Lost |
| Miss Bridget Delia Bradley | 26 | 3rd | Lost |
| Mr. James Bertram Brady | 40 | 1st | Lost |
| Miss Elin Ester Maria Braf | 20 | 3rd | Lost |
| Mr. Youssef Brahim | | 3rd | Lost |
| Mr. Emil Brandeis | 48 | 1st | Lost |
| Mr. Lewis Richard Braund | 29 | 3rd | Lost |
| Mr. Owen Harris Braund | 22 | 3rd | Lost |
| Mr. George Arthur Brayton | | 1st | Saved |
| Dr. Arthur Jackson Brewe | | 1st | Lost |
| Mr. Karl Rudolf Brobeck | 22 | 3rd | Lost |
| Mr. William Alfred Brocklebank | 35 | 3rd | Lost |
| Miss Edith E. Brown | 15 | 2nd | Saved |
| Mrs. James Joseph Brown (Margaret "Molly" Tobin) | 44 | 1st | Saved |
| Mr. John Murray Brown (Caroline Lane Lamson) | 59 | 1st | Saved |
| Miss Mildred Brown | 24 | 2nd | Saved |

# *Titanic* Passengers

| Name | Age | Class | Lost/Saved |
|---|---|---|---|
| Mr. Thomas William Brown | 45 | 2nd | Lost |
| Mrs. Thomas William Brown (Elizabeth C.) | 40 | 2nd | Saved |
| Miss Dagmar Bryhl | 20 | 2nd | Saved |
| Mr. Kurt Arnold G. Bryhl | 25 | 2nd | Lost |
| Mr. Daniel Buckley | 21 | 3rd | Saved |
| Miss Katherine Buckley | 20 | 3rd | Lost |
| Mrs. William Robert Bucknell (Emma Eliza Ward) | 60 | 1st | Saved |
| Mr. Jeremiah Burke | 19 | 3rd | Lost |
| Miss Mary Delia Burns | 18 | 3rd | Lost |
| Miss Kate Buss | 36 | 2nd | Saved |
| Mr. Reginald Fenton Butler | 25 | 2nd | Lost |
| Maj. Archibald Willingham Butt | 45 | 1st | Lost |
| Rev. Thomas Roussel D. Byles | | 2nd | Lost |
| Mrs. Carolina Bystrom | | 2nd | Lost |
| Mr. Grego Cacic | 18 | 3rd | Lost |
| Mr. Luka Cacic | 38 | 3rd | Lost |
| Mr. Manda Cacic | | 3rd | Lost |
| Mr. Maria Cacic | 30 | 3rd | Lost |
| Mr. Edward P. Calderhead | | 1st | Saved |
| Mr. Albert Francis Caldwell | 26 | 2nd | Saved |
| Mrs. Albert Francis Caldwell (Sylvia Mae Harbaugh) | 26 | 2nd | Saved |
| Master Alden Gates Caldwell | 10m | 2nd | Saved |
| Mr. Peter Calic | 17 | 3rd | Lost |
| Miss Clear Cameron | 31 | 2nd | Saved |
| Miss Mary Canavan | 21 | 3rd | Lost |
| Mr. Patrick Canavan | 21 | 3rd | Lost |
| Mrs. Edward Candee (Helen Churchill Hungerford) | 53 | 1st | Saved |
| Mr. Ernest Cann | 21 | 3rd | Lost |
| Mr. Joseph Caram (Kareem) | | 3rd | Lost |
| Mrs. Joseph Caram (Kareem) (Maria Elias) | | 3rd | Lost |
| Mr. William Carbines | 19 | 2nd | Lost |
| Mrs. James Warburton M. Cardeza (Charlotte Wardle Drake) | 58 | 1st | Saved |
| Mr. Thomas Drake M. Cardeza | 36 | 1st | Saved |
| Mr. August Sigfrid Carlsson | 28 | 3rd | Lost |
| Mr. Carl Robert Carlsson | 24 | 3rd | Lost |
| Mr. Frans Olof Carlsson | 33 | 1st | Lost |
| Mr. Julius Carlsson | 33 | 3rd | Lost |
| Miss Helen Carr | 16 | 3rd | Saved |
| Miss Jeannie Carr | 37 | 3rd | Lost |
| Mr. Francisco Carrau | | 1st | Lost |
| Mr. Jose Pedro Carrau | | 1st | Lost |
| Rev. Ernest Courtenay Carter | 54 | 2nd | Lost |
| Mrs. Ernest Courtenay Carter (Lilian Hughes) | 44 | 2nd | Lost |
| Miss Lucile Polk Carter | 14 | 1st | Saved |
| Mr. William Ernest Carter | 36 | 1st | Saved |
| Mrs. William Ernest Carter (Lucile Polk) | 36 | 1st | Saved |
| Master William Thorton Carter II | 11 | 1st | Saved |
| Mr. Alfred John Carver | 28 | 3rd | Lost |
| Mr. Howard Brown Case | 49 | 1st | Lost |
| Mrs. Henry Arthur Cassebeer, Jr. (Genevieve Fosdick) | | 1st | Saved |
| Mr. Nassef Belmenly Cassem | | 3rd | Saved |
| Mr. Tyrell William Cavendish | 36 | 1st | Lost |
| Mrs. Tyrell William Cavendish (Julia Florence Siegel) | | 1st | Saved |

# *TITANIC* PASSENGERS

| NAME | AGE | CLASS | LOST/SAVED |
|---|---|---|---|
| Mr. Francesco Celotti | 24 | 3rd | Lost |
| Mr. Herbert Fuller Chaffee | 46 | 1st | Lost |
| Mrs. Herbert Fuller Chaffee (Carrie Toogood) | 47 | 1st | Saved |
| Mr. Norman Campbell Chambers | 27 | 1st | Saved |
| Mrs. Norman Campbell Chambers (Bertha Griggs) | 31 | 1st | Saved |
| Mr. Charles H. Chapman | 52 | 2nd | Lost |
| Mr. John Henry Chapman | 30 | 2nd | Lost |
| Mrs. John Henry Chapman (Elizabeth Lawry) | 28 | 2nd | Lost |
| Mr. David Chartens | 21 | 3rd | Lost |
| Mr. Emir Farres Chebab | | 3rd | Lost |
| Miss Gladys Cherry | | 1st | Saved |
| Mr. Paul Chevre | | 1st | Saved |
| Mrs. Edith Martha Chibnall | | 1st | Saved |
| Mr. Chang Chip | 32 | 3rd | Lost |
| Mr. Roderick Robert Chisholm | | 1st | Lost |
| Mr. Emil Christmann | 29 | 3rd | Lost |
| Mrs. Alice Frances Christy | | 2nd | Saved |
| Miss Julie Christy | | 2nd | Saved |
| Mr. Apostolos Chronopoulos | 26 | 3rd | Lost |
| Mr. Demetrios Chronopoulos | 18 | 3rd | Lost |
| Mr. Walter Miller Clark | 27 | 1st | Lost |
| Mrs. Walter Miller Clark (Virginia McDowell) | 26 | 1st | Saved |
| Mr. Charles V. Clarke | 29 | 2nd | Lost |
| Mrs. Charles V. Clarke (Ada Maria) | 28 | 2nd | Saved |
| Mr. George Quincy Clifford | | 1st | Lost |
| Mr. Domingos Fernandes Coelho | 20 | 3rd | Lost |
| Mr. Gershon (Gus) Cohen | 19 | 3rd | Saved |
| Mr. Patrick Colbert | 24 | 3rd | Lost |
| Mr. Fotio Coleff | 24 | 3rd | Lost |
| Mr. Peyo Coleff | 36 | 3rd | Lost |
| Mr. Reginald Charles Coleridge | 29 | 2nd | Lost |
| Mr. Erik Collander | 27 | 2nd | Lost |
| Mr. Sidney C. Stuart Collett | 24 | 2nd | Saved |
| Mr. Edward Pomeroy Colley | | 1st | Lost |
| Mr. Harvey Collyer | 35 | 2nd | Lost |
| Mrs. Harvey Collyer (Charlotte Tate) | 31 | 2nd | Saved |
| Miss Marjory Collyer | 8 | 2nd | Saved |
| Mr. Alexander Taylor Compton, Jr. | 37 | 1st | Lost |
| Mrs. Alexander Taylor Compton (Mary Eliza Ingersoll) | 64 | 1st | Saved |
| Miss Sara Rebecca Compton | 39 | 1st | Saved |
| Mr. Thomas Henry Conlin | 31 | 3rd | Lost |
| Mr. Michael Connaghton | 31 | 3rd | Lost |
| Miss Kate Connolly | 30 | 3rd | Lost |
| Miss Kate Connolly | 22 | 3rd | Saved |
| Mr. Patrick Connors | | 3rd | Lost |
| Mr. Jacob Cook | 43 | 3rd | Lost |
| Mrs. Selena Rogers Cook | 22 | 2nd | Saved |
| Mr. Bartol Cor | 35 | 3rd | Lost |
| Mr. Ivan Cor | 27 | 3rd | Lost |
| Mr. Ludovik Cor | 19 | 3rd | Lost |
| Mrs. Walter H. Corbett (Irene Colvin) | 30 | 2nd | Lost |
| Mrs. Percy C. Corey (Mary Phyllis Elizabeth Miller) | | 2nd | Lost |
| Mr. Harry Corn | 30 | 3rd | Lost |

# *Titanic* Passengers

| Name | Age | Class | Lost/Saved |
|---|---|---|---|
| Mrs. Robert Clifford Cornell (Malvina Helen Lamson) | 55 | 1st | Saved |
| Mr. Harry Cotterill | 20 | 2nd | Lost |
| Master Neville Coutts | 3 | 3rd | Saved |
| Mrs. William Coutts (Minnie) | 36 | 3rd | Saved |
| Master William Leslie Coutts | 9 | 3rd | Saved |
| Mr. Daniel Coxon | 59 | 3rd | Lost |
| Mr. John Bertram Crafton | | 1st | Lost |
| Mr. Ernest James Crease | 19 | 3rd | Lost |
| Mr. John Hatfield Cribb | 44 | 3rd | Lost |
| Miss Laura Alice Cribb | 17 | 3rd | Saved |
| Capt. Edward Gifford Crosby | 70 | 1st | Lost |
| Mrs. Edward Gifford Crosby (Catherine Elizabeth Halstead) | 69 | 1st | Saved |
| Miss Harriet R. Crosby | 36 | 1st | Saved |
| Mr. John Bradley Cumings | 39 | 1st | Lost |
| Mrs. John Bradley Cumings (Florence Briggs Thayer) | 38 | 1st | Saved |
| Mr. Tannous Daher | | 3rd | Lost |
| Mr. Charles Edward Dahl | 45 | 3rd | Saved |
| Miss Gerda Ulrika Dahlberg | 22 | 3rd | Lost |
| Mr. Branko Dakie | 19 | 3rd | Lost |
| Mr. Eugene Daly | 29 | 3rd | Saved |
| Miss Marcella Daly | 30 | 3rd | Saved |
| Mr. Peter Denis Daly | | 1st | Saved |
| Mr. Ernst Gilbert Danborn | 34 | 3rd | Lost |
| Mrs. Ernst Gilbert Danborn (Anna Sigrid Maria Brogren) | 28 | 3rd | Lost |
| Master Gilbert Sigvard Emanuel Danborn | 4m | 3rd | Lost |
| Mr. Robert Williams Daniel | 27 | 1st | Saved |
| Mr. Yoto Danoff | 27 | 3rd | Lost |
| Mr. Khristo Dantchoff | 25 | 3rd | Lost |
| Mr. Thornton Davidson | 31 | 1st | Lost |
| Mrs. Thornton Davidson (Orian Hays) | 27 | 1st | Saved |
| Mr. Alfred Davies | 24 | 3rd | Lost |
| Mr. Charles Henry Davies | 21 | 2nd | Lost |
| Mr. Evan Davies | 22 | 3rd | Lost |
| Mr. John Davies | 21 | 3rd | Lost |
| Mr. Joseph Davies | 17 | 3rd | Lost |
| Mrs. Agnes Davis | 49 | 2nd | Lost |
| Master John Morgan Davis | 8 | 2nd | Saved |
| Miss Mary Davis | 28 | 2nd | Saved |
| Mr. Thomas Henry Davison | | 3rd | Lost |
| Mrs. Thomas Henry Davison (Mary Finck) | | 3rd | Saved |
| Mr. Jose Joaquim De Brito | | 2nd | Lost |
| Mr. William Joseph De Messemaeker | 36 | 3rd | Saved |
| Mrs. William Joseph De Messemaeker (Anna) | 36 | 3rd | Saved |
| Mr. Theo De Mulder | 30 | 3rd | Saved |
| Madame Berthe De Villiers | | 1st | Saved |
| Mr. Percy Deacon | 18 | 2nd | Lost |
| Mr. Bertram Dean | 26 | 3rd | Lost |
| Mrs. Bertram Dean (Eva) | 33 | 3rd | Saved |
| Master Bertram Vere Dean | 1 | 3rd | Saved |
| Miss Elizabeth Gladys Dean (Millvina) | 2m | 3rd | Saved |
| Mr. Sebastiano Del Carlo | 28 | 2nd | Lost |
| Mrs. Sebastiano Del Carlo (Argenia Genovese) | 22 | 2nd | Saved |
| Mr. Regyo Delalic | 25 | 3rd | Lost |

# *Titanic* Passengers

| Name | Age | Class | Lost/Saved |
|---|---|---|---|
| Mr. Herbert Denbury | 25 | 2nd | Lost |
| Mr. Mito Denkoff | | 3rd | Lost |
| Mr. Samuel Dennis | 23 | 3rd | Lost |
| Mr. William Dennis | 26 | 3rd | Lost |
| Miss Margaret Devaney | 19 | 3rd | Saved |
| Mr. Frank Dewar | 65 | 3rd | Lost |
| Mr. William Dibden | 18 | 2nd | Lost |
| Mr. Elias Dibo | | 3rd | Lost |
| Mr. Albert Adrian Dick | 31 | 1st | Saved |
| Mrs. Albert Adrian Dick (Vera Gillespie) | 17 | 1st | Saved |
| Mr. Jovan Dimic | 42 | 3rd | Lost |
| Mr. Valtcho Dintcheff | 43 | 3rd | Lost |
| Dr. Washington Dodge | | 1st | Saved |
| Mrs. Washington Dodge (Ruth Vidaver) | | 1st | Saved |
| Master Washington Dodge | 4 | 1st | Saved |
| Mrs. Ada Doling | 32 | 2nd | Saved |
| Miss Elsie Doling | 18 | 2nd | Saved |
| Mr. Patrick Dooley | 32 | 3rd | Lost |
| Mr. Edward Arthur Dorkings | 19 | 3rd | Saved |
| Mrs. Frederick Charles Douglas (Suzette Baxter) | 27 | 1st | Saved |
| Mr. Walter Donald Douglas | 50 | 1st | Lost |
| Mrs. Walter Donald Douglas (Mahala Dutton) | 48 | 1st | Saved |
| Mr. William James Douton | | 2nd | Lost |
| Miss Elizabeth Dowdell | 30 | 3rd | Saved |
| Miss Elizabeth Doyle | 24 | 3rd | Lost |
| Miss Jennie Drapkin | 23 | 3rd | Saved |
| Mr. Josef Drazonovic | | 3rd | Lost |
| Mr. James Vivian Drew | 42 | 2nd | Lost |
| Mrs. James Vivian Drew (Lulu Thorne Christian) | 34 | 2nd | Saved |
| Master Marshall Brines Drew | 8 | 2nd | Saved |
| Miss Bridget Driscoll | 24 | 3rd | Saved |
| Sir Cosmo Edmund Duff Gordon | 49 | 1st | Saved |
| Lady Lucille Wallace Sutherland Duff Gordon | 48 | 1st | Saved |
| Mr. William Cothers Dulles | 39 | 1st | Lost |
| Mr. Joseph Duquemin | 24 | 3rd | Saved |
| Miss Asuncion Duran y More | | 2nd | Saved |
| Miss Florentina Duran y More | | 2nd | Saved |
| Mr. Adolf Fredrik Dyker | 23 | 3rd | Lost |
| Mrs. Adolf Fredrik Dyker (Anna Elizabeth Judith Andersson) | 22 | 3rd | Lost |
| Mrs. Boulton Earnshaw (Olive Potter) | 23 | 1st | Saved |
| Mr. Joso Econovic | | 3rd | Lost |
| Mr. Gustaf Hjalmar Edvardsson | 18 | 3rd | Lost |
| Mr. George Floyd Eitemiller | 23 | 2nd | Lost |
| Mr. Hans Linus Eklund | 16 | 3rd | Lost |
| Mr. Johan Ekstrom | 45 | 3rd | Lost |
| Mr. Elias Elias | | 3rd | Lost |
| Mr. John Elias | | 3rd | Lost |
| Mr. Joseph Elias | | 3rd | Lost |
| Mr. James Elsbury | 47 | 3rd | Lost |
| Miss Virginia Ethel Emanuel | 5 | 3rd | Saved |
| Mr. Thomas Emmeth | | 3rd | Lost |
| Mr. Ingvar Enander | 21 | 2nd | Lost |
| Miss Caroline Louise Endres | | 1st | Saved |

# *Titanic* Passengers

| Name | Age | Class | Lost/Saved |
|---|---|---|---|
| Miss Elizabeth Mussey Eustis | 53 | 1st | Saved |
| Miss Edith Corse Evans | 36 | 1st | Lost |
| Mr. Thomas James Everett | | 3rd | Lost |
| Mr. Arne Jonas Fahlstrom | 19 | 3rd | Lost |
| Mr. James Farrell | | 3rd | Lost |
| Mr. Harry Faunthorpe | | 2nd | Lost |
| Mrs. Lizzie Faunthorpe | | 2nd | Saved |
| Mr. Charles Fillbrook | | 2nd | Saved |
| Mr. Luigi Finoli | | 3rd | Lost |
| Mr. Eberhard Telander Fischer | | 3rd | Lost |
| Mrs. Alfred Flegenheim (Antoinette) | | 1st | Saved |
| Mr. James Flynn | | 3rd | Lost |
| Mr. John Flynn | | 3rd | Lost |
| Mr. John Irving Flynn | | 1st | Saved |
| Mr. Joseph Foley | | 3rd | Lost |
| Mr. William Foley | | 3rd | Lost |
| Mr. Choong Foo | | 3rd | Lost |
| Mr. Arthur Ford | | 3rd | Lost |
| Miss Doolina Margaret Ford | 21 | 3rd | Lost |
| Mr. Edward Watson Ford | 18 | 3rd | Lost |
| Mrs. Edward Ford (Margaret Ann) | 48 | 3rd | Lost |
| Miss Maggie Ford | 9 | 3rd | Lost |
| Mr. Neil Watson Ford | 16 | 3rd | Lost |
| Mr. Benjamin Laventall Foreman | 30 | 1st | Lost |
| Miss Alice Elizabeth Fortune | 24 | 1st | Saved |
| Mr. Charles Alexander Fortune | 19 | 1st | Lost |
| Miss Ethel Flora Fortune | 28 | 1st | Saved |
| Miss Mabel Fortune | 23 | 1st | Saved |
| Mr. Mark Fortune | 64 | 1st | Lost |
| Mrs. Mark Fortune (Mary McDougald) | 60 | 1st | Saved |
| Mr. Patrick Fox | | 3rd | Lost |
| Mr. Stanley Fox | | 2nd | Lost |
| Mr. Charles Franklin | | 3rd | Lost |
| Mr. Thomas Parnham Franklin | | 1st | Lost |
| Dr. Henry William Frauenthal | 49 | 1st | Saved |
| Mrs. Henry William Frauenthal (Clara Heinsheimer) | | 1st | Saved |
| Mr. Isaac Gerald Frauenthal | 44 | 1st | Saved |
| Miss Marguerite Frolicher | 22 | 1st | Saved |
| Mr. Maxmillian Frolicher-Stehli | 60 | 1st | Saved |
| Mrs. Maxmillian Frolicher-Stehli (Margaretha E. Stehli) | 48 | 1st | Saved |
| Miss Annie C. Funk | 38 | 2nd | Lost |
| Mr. Jacques Futrelle | 37 | 1st | Lost |
| Mrs. Jacques Futrelle (May Peel) | 35 | 1st | Saved |
| Mr. Joseph J. Fynney | 35 | 2nd | Lost |
| Mr. Harry Gale | 35 | 2nd | Lost |
| Mr. Shadrach Gale | 38 | 2nd | Lost |
| Mr. Martin Gallagher | 25 | 3rd | Lost |
| Mr. John Garfirth | | 3rd | Lost |
| Miss Ethel Garside | 24 | 2nd | Saved |
| Mr. Alfred Gaskell | 16 | 2nd | Lost |
| Mr. Lawrence Gavey | 26 | 2nd | Lost |
| Mr. Arthur H. Gee | 47 | 1st | Lost |
| Mrs. Shahini Weappi George | | 3rd | Saved |

# *Titanic* Passengers

| Name | Age | Class | Lost/Saved |
|---|---|---|---|
| Miss Dorothy Gibson | 22 | 1st | Saved |
| Mrs. Leonard Gibson (Pauline C. Boeson) | 45 | 1st | Saved |
| Mr. William Gilbert | 45 | 2nd | Lost |
| Mr. Edgar Giles | 24 | 2nd | Lost |
| Mr. Frederick Giles | 21 | 2nd | Lost |
| Mr. Ralph Giles | 22 | 2nd | Lost |
| Mr. Leslie Gilinski | 22 | 3rd | Lost |
| Mr. John Gill | | 2nd | Lost |
| Mr. William Gillespie | 34 | 2nd | Lost |
| Miss Katie Gilnagh | 16 | 3rd | Saved |
| Mr. Hans Christensen Givard | 30 | 2nd | Lost |
| Miss Mary Agatha Glynn | | 3rd | Saved |
| Mr. Samuel L. Goldenberg | 49 | 1st | Saved |
| Mrs. Samuel L. Goldenberg (Edwiga Grabowsko) | | 1st | Saved |
| Mr. George B. Goldschmidt | 71 | 1st | Lost |
| Mr. Frank John Goldsmith | 33 | 3rd | Lost |
| Mrs. Frank John Goldsmith (Emily A. Brown) | | 3rd | Lost |
| Master Frank John William Goldsmith | 9 | 3rd | Lost |
| Mr. Nathan Goldsmith | 41 | 3rd | Lost |
| Mr. Manuel Estanslas Goncalves | 38 | 3rd | Lost |
| Mr. Charles E. Goodwin | 14 | 3rd | Lost |
| Mr. Frederick Goodwin | 40 | 3rd | Lost |
| Mrs. Frederick Goodwin (Augusta) | 43 | 3rd | Lost |
| Master Harold V. Goodwin | 9 | 3rd | Lost |
| Miss Jessie A. Goodwin | 10 | 3rd | Lost |
| Miss Lillian A. Goodwin | 16 | 3rd | Lost |
| Master Sidney L. Goodwin | 6 | 3rd | Lost |
| Master William F. Goodwin | 11 | 3rd | Lost |
| Col. Archibald Gracie IV | 54 | 1st | Saved |
| Mr. George Edward Graham | 38 | 1st | Lost |
| Miss Margaret Edith Graham | 19 | 1st | Saved |
| Mrs. William Thompson Graham (Edith Junkins) | 58 | 1st | Saved |
| Mr. George Green | 40 | 3rd | Lost |
| Mr. Samuel Greenberg | | 2nd | Lost |
| Mrs. Leo David Greenfield (Blanche Stouse) | 45 | 1st | Saved |
| Mr. William Bertram Greenfield | 23 | 1st | Saved |
| Mr. Daniel Danielsen Gronnestad | 32 | 3rd | Lost |
| Mr. Robert Guest | | 3rd | Lost |
| Mr. Benjamin Guggenheim | 46 | 1st | Lost |
| Mr. Alfred Ossian Gustafsson | 20 | 3rd | Lost |
| Mr. Anders Vilhelm Gustafsson | 37 | 3rd | Lost |
| Mr. Johan Birger Gustafsson | 28 | 3rd | Lost |
| Mr. Karl Gideon Gustafsson | 19 | 3rd | Lost |
| Miss Aloisia Haas | 24 | 3rd | Lost |
| Miss Kate Hagardon | 17 | 3rd | Lost |
| Mr. Ingvald Olsen Hagland | 28 | 3rd | Lost |
| Mr. Konrad Mathias R. Hagland | 19 | 3rd | Lost |
| Mr. Pekka Pietari Hakkarainen | 28 | 3rd | Lost |
| Mrs. Pekka Pietari Hakkarainen (Elin Dolk) | 24 | 3rd | Saved |
| Mr. Reginald Hale | 30 | 2nd | Lost |
| Master Viljo Hamalainen | 1 | 2nd | Saved |
| Mrs. William Hamalainen (Anna) | 23 | 2nd | Saved |
| Mr. Henrik Juul Hansen | 26 | 3rd | Lost |

# *TITANIC* PASSENGERS

| NAME | AGE | CLASS | LOST/SAVED |
|---|---|---|---|
| Mr. Henry Damsgaard Hansen | 21 | 3rd | Lost |
| Mr. Peter Claus Hansen | 41 | 3rd | Lost |
| Mrs. Peter Claus Hansen (Jennie L. Howard) | 45 | 3rd | Saved |
| Mr. William Harbeck | 44 | 2nd | Lost |
| Mr. George Achilles Harder | 25 | 1st | Saved |
| Mrs. George Achilles Harder (Dorothy Annan) | 21 | 1st | Saved |
| Miss Alice Harknett | 21 | 3rd | Lost |
| Mr. Abraham Harmer | 25 | 3rd | Lost |
| Mr. Henry Sleeper Harper | 48 | 1st | Saved |
| Mrs. Henry Sleeper Harper (Myra Haxtun) | 49 | 1st | Saved |
| Rev. John Harper | 28 | 2nd | Lost |
| Miss Nina Harper | 6 | 2nd | Saved |
| Mr. George Harris | 30 | 2nd | Saved |
| Mr. Henry Harris | 45 | 1st | Lost |
| Mrs. Henry Birkhardt Harris (Irene Wallach) | 36 | 1st | Saved |
| Mr. Walter Harris | | 2nd | Lost |
| Mr. William Henry Harrison | | 1st | Lost |
| Mr. Benjamin Hart | 43 | 2nd | Lost |
| Mrs. Benjamin Hart (Esther) | 45 | 2nd | Saved |
| Miss Eva M. Hart | 7 | 2nd | Saved |
| Mr. Henry Hart | 28 | 3rd | Lost |
| Mr. M. Houssein Hassan | | 3rd | Lost |
| Mr. Harry Haven (Homer) | 35 | 1st | Saved |
| Mr. Walter James Hawksford | | 1st | Saved |
| Mr. Charles Melville Hays | 55 | 1st | Lost |
| Mrs. Charles Melville Hays (Clara Jennings Gregg) | 52 | 1st | Saved |
| Miss Margaret Beckstein Hays | 24 | 1st | Saved |
| Mr. Christopher Head | | 1st | Lost |
| Miss Nora Healy | | 3rd | Saved |
| Mr. Oscar Hedman | 27 | 3rd | Saved |
| Mr. Ling Hee | | 3rd | Saved |
| Miss Nora Hegarty | 18 | 3rd | Lost |
| Miss Laina Heikkinen | 26 | 3rd | Saved |
| Miss Wendla Maria Heininen | 23 | 3rd | Lost |
| Miss Hilda Maria Hellstrom | 22 | 3rd | Saved |
| Miss Nora Hemming | 21 | 3rd | Lost |
| Mr. Ignaz Hendekovic | | 3rd | Lost |
| Miss Delia Henery | 23 | 3rd | Lost |
| Miss Jenny Lovisa Henriksson | 28 | 3rd | Lost |
| Miss Alice Herman | 24 | 2nd | Saved |
| Miss Kate Herman | 24 | 2nd | Saved |
| Mr. Samuel Herman | 49 | 2nd | Lost |
| Mrs. Samuel Herman (Jane Laver) | 48 | 2nd | Saved |
| Mrs. Mary D. Hewlett | | 2nd | Saved |
| Mr. Leonard Mark Hickman | 34 | 2nd | Lost |
| Mr. Lewis Hickman | 32 | 2nd | Lost |
| Mr. Stanley George Hickman | 21 | 2nd | Lost |
| Mr. Herbert Henry Hilliard | | 1st | Lost |
| Miss Marta Hiltunen | 18 | 2nd | Lost |
| Mr. William Edward Hipkins | | 1st | Lost |
| Miss Jean Gertrude Hippach | 16 | 1st | Saved |
| Mrs. Louis Albert Hippach (Ida Sophia Fischer) | 44 | 1st | Saved |
| Mrs. Alexander Hirvonen (Helga E.) | 22 | 3rd | Saved |

# *Titanic* Passengers

| Name | Age | Class | Lost/Saved |
|---|---|---|---|
| Miss Hildur E. Hirvonen | 2 | 3rd | Saved |
| Mrs. Elizabeth Hocking | 53 | 2nd | Saved |
| Miss Ellen Hocking (Nellie) | 21 | 2nd | Saved |
| Mr. George Hocking | 23 | 2nd | Lost |
| Mr. Samuel James Hocking | | 2nd | Lost |
| Mr. Henry Price Hodges | | 2nd | Lost |
| Mrs. John C. Hogeboom (Anna Andrews) | 51 | 1st | Saved |
| Mr. Stephen Hold | 42 | 2nd | Lost |
| Mrs. Stephen Hold (Annie Margaret) | 36 | 2nd | Saved |
| Mr. John Fredrik A. Holm | 43 | 3rd | Lost |
| Mr. Johan Martin Holthen | 28 | 3rd | Lost |
| Mr. Alexander Oskar Holverson | 42 | 1st | Lost |
| Mrs. Alexander Oskar Holverson (Mary Aline Towner) | | 1st | Saved |
| Miss Eluna Honkanen | 27 | 3rd | Saved |
| Mr. Ambrose Hood, Jr. | 21 | 2nd | Lost |
| Mr. John Horgan | | 3rd | Lost |
| Mr. Masafumi Hosono | 41 | 2nd | Saved |
| Mr. Benjamin Howard | | 2nd | Lost |
| Mrs. Benjamin Howard (Ellen Truelove) | | 2nd | Lost |
| Miss Mary Howard | | 3rd | Saved |
| Mr. Frederick Mayfield Hoyt | 38 | 1st | Saved |
| Mrs. Frederick Mayfield Hoyt (Jane Ann Forby) | 35 | 1st | Saved |
| Mr. William F. Hoyt | | 1st | Lost |
| Mr. Adolf Mathias Humblen | 42 | 3rd | Lost |
| Mr. George Henry Hunt | 33 | 2nd | Lost |
| Mr. Abraham Hyman | 34 | 3rd | Saved |
| Mr. Ylio Ilieff | | 3rd | Lost |
| Miss Ida Livija Ilmakangas | 27 | 3rd | Lost |
| Miss Pieta Sofia Ilmakangas | 25 | 3rd | Lost |
| Miss Ann Eliza Isham | 50 | 1st | Lost |
| Mr. Joseph Bruce Ismay | 49 | 1st | Saved |
| Mr. Konio Ivanoff | | 3rd | Lost |
| Mr. Sidney Samuel Jacobsohn | | 2nd | Lost |
| Mrs. Sidney Samuel Jacobsohn (Amy Frances Christy) | | 2nd | Saved |
| Mr. Carl Olof Jansson | 21 | 3rd | Saved |
| Mr. Jose Netto Jardin | 21 | 3rd | Lost |
| Mr. John Denzil Jarvis | | 2nd | Lost |
| Mr. Clifford Jefferys | | 2nd | Lost |
| Mr. Ernest Jefferys | | 2nd | Lost |
| Mr. Stephen Curnow Jenkin | | 2nd | Lost |
| Miss Carla Christine Jensen | 19 | 3rd | Saved |
| Mr. Hans Peder Jensen | 20 | 3rd | Lost |
| Mr. Niels Peder Jensen | 48 | 3rd | Lost |
| Mr. Svend Lauritz Jensen | 17 | 3rd | Lost |
| Miss Annie Jermyn | 22 | 3rd | Saved |
| Mrs. Amin S. Jerwan (Marie Thuillard) | 23 | 2nd | Saved |
| Mr. Bernt Johannesen | 32 | 3rd | Saved |
| Mr. Erik Johansson | 22 | 3rd | Lost |
| Mr. Jakob Alfred Johansson | 34 | 3rd | Lost |
| Mr. Karl Johansson | 31 | 3rd | Lost |
| Mr. Nils Johansson | 29 | 3rd | Lost |
| Mr. Oskar L. Johansson | 26 | 3rd | Saved |
| Mr. Alfred Johnson | 49 | 3rd | Lost |

# *TITANIC* PASSENGERS

| NAME | AGE | CLASS | LOST/SAVED |
|---|---|---|---|
| Miss Eleanor Ileen Johnson | 1 | 3rd | Saved |
| Master Harold Theodor Johnson | 4 | 3rd | Saved |
| Mr. Malkolm Joackim Johnson | 33 | 3rd | Lost |
| Mrs. Oscar Johnson (Alice Berg) | 27 | 3rd | Saved |
| Mr. William Cahoone Johnson, Jr. | 19 | 3rd | Lost |
| Mr. Andrew G. Johnston | 34 | 3rd | Lost |
| Mrs. Andrew G. Johnston (Elizabeth [Lily]) | 34 | 3rd | Lost |
| Miss Catherine H. Johnston (Carrie) | 8 | 3rd | Lost |
| Master William A. Johnston | 9 | 3rd | Lost |
| Mr. Charles Cresson Jones | 46 | 1st | Lost |
| Mr. Lazor Jonkoff | | 3rd | Lost |
| Mr. Nils Hilding Jonosson | 27 | 3rd | Lost |
| Mr. Carl Jonsson | 27 | 3rd | Saved |
| Mr. Henry Forbes Julian | | 1st | Lost |
| Miss Aina Maria Jussila | 21 | 3rd | Lost |
| Mr. Erik Jussila | 32 | 3rd | Saved |
| Miss Katriina Jussila | 20 | 3rd | Lost |
| Mr. Nikolai Erland Kallio | 17 | 3rd | Lost |
| Mr. Johannes K. Halverson Kalvig | 21 | 3rd | Lost |
| Mr. Sinai Kantor | 34 | 2nd | Lost |
| Mrs. Sinai Kantor (Miriam Sternim) | | 2nd | Saved |
| Mr. Milan Karajic | 30 | 3rd | Lost |
| Mr. Einar Gervasius Karlsson | 21 | 3rd | Saved |
| Mr. Julius Konrad Eugen Karlsson | 33 | 3rd | Lost |
| Mr. Nils August Karlsson | 22 | 3rd | Lost |
| Mrs. J. Frank Karnes (Claire Bennett) | 22 | 2nd | Lost |
| Miss Anna Karun | 4 | 3rd | Saved |
| Mr. Franz Karun | 39 | 3rd | Saved |
| Mr. Fared Kassem | | 3rd | Lost |
| Mr. Andrew Keane | 20 | 3rd | Lost |
| Mr. Daniel Keane | | 2nd | Lost |
| Miss Nora A. Keane | | 2nd | Saved |
| Mr. Arthur Keefe | | 3rd | Lost |
| Mr. Tido Kekie | 38 | 3rd | Lost |
| Miss Annie Kate Kelly | | 3rd | Saved |
| Mrs. Florence Kelly (Fannie) | 45 | 2nd | Saved |
| Mr. James Kelly | | 3rd | Lost |
| Mr. James Kelly | | 3rd | Lost |
| Miss Mary Kelly | 21 | 3rd | Saved |
| Mr. John Kennedy | 24 | 3rd | Saved |
| Mr. Edward Kent | 58 | 1st | Lost |
| Mr. Frederick R. Kenyon | 41 | 1st | Lost |
| Mrs. Frederick R. Kenyon (Marion) | | 1st | Saved |
| Mr. Betros Khalil | 25 | 3rd | Lost |
| Mrs. Betros Khalil (Zahie) | 20 | 3rd | Lost |
| Mr. Saad Khalil | | 3rd | Lost |
| Mr. John Kiernan | 25 | 3rd | Lost |
| Mr. Philip Kiernan | 19 | 3rd | Lost |
| Mr. Thomas Kilgannon | 21 | 3rd | Lost |
| Mr. Edwin Nelson Kimball, Jr. | 42 | 1st | Saved |
| Mrs. Edwin Nelson Kimball, Jr. (Gertrude Parsons) | 40 | 1st | Saved |
| Mr. Anton Kink | 29 | 3rd | Saved |
| Mrs. Anton Kink (Louise Heilmann) | 26 | 3rd | Saved |

# *Titanic* Passengers

| Name | Age | Class | Lost/Saved |
|---|---|---|---|
| Miss Louise Gretchen Kink | 4 | 3rd | Saved |
| Miss Maria Kink | 22 | 3rd | Lost |
| Mr. Vincenz Kink | 27 | 3rd | Lost |
| Rev. Charles Leonard Kirkland | | 2nd | Lost |
| Mr. Herman Klaber | | 1st | Lost |
| Miss Gertrud Emilia Klasen | 1 | 3rd | Lost |
| Mrs. Hulda Kristina Klasen | 36 | 3rd | Lost |
| Mr. Klas Albin Klasen | 18 | 3rd | Lost |
| Mr. Theodor Kraeff | | 3rd | Lost |
| Mr. Neshan Krekorian | 25 | 3rd | Saved |
| Mr. Johan Henrik J. Kvillner | 31 | 2nd | Lost |
| Mr. Sarkis Lahowd | 30 | 3rd | Lost |
| Rev. William Lahtinen | 30 | 2nd | Lost |
| Mrs. William Lahtinen (Anna Sylvan) | 26 | 2nd | Lost |
| Miss Kristina Sofia Laitinen | 37 | 3rd | Lost |
| Mr. Kristo Laleff | 23 | 3rd | Lost |
| Mr. Ali Lam | 38 | 3rd | Saved |
| Mr. Len Lam | 23 | 3rd | Lost |
| Mr. John James Lamb | | 2nd | Lost |
| Mrs. Amelia Lamore | | 2nd | Saved |
| Miss Aurora Adelia Landergren | 22 | 3rd | Saved |
| Mr. Patrick Lane | | 3rd | Lost |
| Mr. Fang Lang | 26 | 3rd | Saved |
| Mr. Joseph LaRoche | 26 | 2nd | Lost |
| Mrs. Joseph LaRoche (Juliette) | 22 | 2nd | Saved |
| Miss Louise LaRoche | 1 | 2nd | Saved |
| Miss Simonne LaRoche | 3 | 2nd | Saved |
| Mr. August Viktor Larsson | 29 | 3rd | Lost |
| Mr. Bengt Edvin Larsson | 29 | 3rd | Lost |
| Mr. Edvard Larsson-Rondbert | 22 | 3rd | Lost |
| Dr. Alice Farnham Leader | | 1st | Saved |
| Mr. Fahim Leeni | | 3rd | Saved |
| Mrs. Frank Lefebre (Frances) | 39 | 3rd | Lost |
| Master Henry Lefebre | 4 | 3rd | Lost |
| Miss Ida Lefebre | 2 | 3rd | Lost |
| Miss Jeannie Lefebre | 6 | 3rd | Lost |
| Miss Mathilde Lefebre | 11 | 3rd | Lost |
| Miss Bertha Lehmann | | 2nd | Saved |
| Mr. Antti Gustaf Leinonen | 32 | 3rd | Lost |
| Miss Jessie Leitch | | 2nd | Saved |
| Mr. Peter L. Lemberopolous | 30 | 3rd | Lost |
| Mr. Denis Lemon | 21 | 3rd | Lost |
| Miss Mary Lemon | 20 | 3rd | Lost |
| Mr. Lionel Leonard | 36 | 3rd | Lost |
| Mr. James Lester | | 3rd | Lost |
| Mr. Rene Jacques Levy | | 2nd | Lost |
| Mr. Ervin G. Lewy | | 2nd | Lost |
| Mr. Robert William Leyson | | 2nd | Lost |
| Miss Agda V. Lindahl | 25 | 3rd | Lost |
| Mr. Erik Gustaf Lindberg-Lind | 42 | 1st | Lost |
| Miss Augusta Charlotta Lindblom | 45 | 3rd | Lost |
| Mr. Edvard Bengtsson Lindell | 36 | 3rd | Lost |
| Mrs. Edvard Bengtsson Lindell (Elin Gerda) | 30 | 3rd | Lost |

# *Titanic* Passengers

| Name | Age | Class | Lost/Saved |
|---|---|---|---|
| Mr. Eino William Lindqvist | 20 | 3rd | Saved |
| Mrs. Carl Johan Lindstrom (Sigrid Posse) | 55 | 1st | Saved |
| Mr. Michael Linehan | 21 | 3rd | Lost |
| Mrs. Ernest H. Lines (Elizabeth Lindsey James) | 50 | 1st | Saved |
| Miss Mary Conover Lines | 16 | 1st | Saved |
| Mr. Lee Ling | 28 | 3rd | Lost |
| Mr. John Lingan | | 2nd | Lost |
| Mr. Simon Lithman | 20 | 3rd | Lost |
| Mr. William Arthur Lobb | 30 | 3rd | Lost |
| Mrs. William Arthur Lobb (Cordelia Stanlicke) | 26 | 3rd | Lost |
| Mr. Edward Lockyer | 21 | 3rd | Lost |
| Mr. Milton Clyde Long | 29 | 1st | Lost |
| Miss Gretchen Fiske Longley | 21 | 1st | Saved |
| Mr. Joseph Holland Loring | 30 | 1st | Lost |
| Mr. Charles Alexander Louch | | 2nd | Lost |
| Mrs. Charles Alexander Louch (Alice Adelaide) | | 2nd | Saved |
| Mr. John Lovell | 20 | 3rd | Lost |
| Mr. Nicola Lulich | 27 | 3rd | Saved |
| Mr. John Lundahl | 51 | 3rd | Lost |
| Miss Olga Elida Lundin | 23 | 3rd | Saved |
| Mr. Thure Edvin Lundstrom | 32 | 3rd | Saved |
| Mr. Stanko Lyntakoff | 44 | 3rd | Lost |
| Mrs. Mary Mack | 57 | 2nd | Lost |
| Mr. George William MacKay | 20 | 3rd | Lost |
| Miss Margaret Madigan | 21 | 3rd | Saved |
| Miss Georgette Alexandra Madill | 15 | 1st | Saved |
| Mr. Frithiof Madsen | 22 | 3rd | Saved |
| Mr. Matti Alexanteri Maenpaa | 22 | 3rd | Lost |
| Mr. John Edward Maguire | 30 | 1st | Lost |
| Miss Delia Mahon | | 3rd | Lost |
| Mr. Simon Maisner | 34 | 3rd | Lost |
| Mr. Kalle Edvard Makinen | 29 | 3rd | Lost |
| Mr. Noel Malachard | | 2nd | Lost |
| Mr. Albert Mallet | | 2nd | Lost |
| Mrs. Albert Mallet (Antoinette) | | 2nd | Saved |
| Master Andre Mallet | 2 | 2nd | Saved |
| Mr. Hanna Mamee | | 3rd | Saved |
| Mr. Leon Mampe | 20 | 3rd | Lost |
| Miss Mary Mangan | | 3rd | Lost |
| Mr. Serafino Emilio Mangiavacchi | | 2nd | Lost |
| Miss Margaret Mannion | 24 | 3rd | Saved |
| Mr. Hanna Mansour | 22 | 3rd | Lost |
| Rev. Joseph Mantvila | 27 | 2nd | Lost |
| Mr. Sarkis Mardirosian | 25 | 3rd | Lost |
| Mr. Pierre Marechal | | 1st | Saved |
| Mr. Dmitri Marinko | 23 | 3rd | Lost |
| Mr. Johann Markim | | 3rd | Lost |
| Mr. Marin Markoff | 35 | 3rd | Lost |
| Mrs. Kate Louise Marshall | 19 | 2nd | Saved |
| Mr. Nicola Martinoff | | 3rd | Lost |
| Mr. Daniel Warner Marvin | | 1st | Lost |
| Mrs. Daniel Warner Marvin (Mary Graham Farquarson) | | 1st | Saved |
| Mrs. Fatima Masselmany | 17 | 3rd | Saved |

# *Titanic* Passengers

| Name | Age | Class | Lost/Saved |
|---|---|---|---|
| Mr. William John Matthews | 30 | 2nd | Lost |
| Mr. Frank H. Maybery | 20 | 2nd | Lost |
| Mr. Thomas Francis McCaffry | 46 | 1st | Lost |
| Miss Katie McCarthy | 24 | 3rd | Saved |
| Mr. Timothy J. McCarthy | 54 | 1st | Lost |
| Mr. Thomas J. McCormack | 19 | 3rd | Saved |
| Miss Agnes McCoy | 28 | 3rd | Saved |
| Miss Alice McCoy | 22 | 3rd | Saved |
| Mr. Bernard McCoy | 21 | 3rd | Saved |
| Mr. Arthur Gordon McCrae | | 2nd | Lost |
| Mr. James Matthew McCrie | | 2nd | Lost |
| Miss Delia McDermott | | 3rd | Saved |
| Mr. Michael McElroy | | 3rd | Lost |
| Mr. James R. McGough | 36 | 1st | Saved |
| Mrs. Hugh McGovern (Mary) | | 3rd | Saved |
| Miss Annie McGowan | 15 | 3rd | Saved |
| Miss Katherine McGowan | 36 | 3rd | Lost |
| Mr. Peter D. McKane | 46 | 2nd | Lost |
| Mr. Martin McMahon | 20 | 3rd | Lost |
| Mr. Neal McNamee | 24 | 3rd | Lost |
| Mrs. Neal McNamee (Eileen) | 19 | 3rd | Lost |
| Mrs. Marion Ogden Meanwell | | 3rd | Lost |
| Mr. John Mechan | 22 | 3rd | Lost |
| Mrs. Thomas Meek (Annie L.) | | 3rd | Lost |
| Mr. Philemon Melkebuk | | 3rd | Lost |
| Mrs. Elizabeth Ann Mellenger | 41 | 2nd | Saved |
| Miss Madeleine Violet Mellenger | 13 | 2nd | Saved |
| Mr. William John Mellor | 19 | 2nd | Saved |
| Mr. Alfonso Meo | 48 | 3rd | Lost |
| Mr. August Meyer | 30 | 2nd | Lost |
| Mr. Edgar Joseph Meyer | 28 | 1st | Lost |
| Mrs. Edgar Joseph Meyer (Leila Saks) | | 1st | Saved |
| Mr. Karl Albert Midtsjo | 21 | 3rd | Saved |
| Mr. Stoytcho Mihoff | 28 | 3rd | Lost |
| Mr. Frank Miles | | 3rd | Lost |
| Mr. Francis Davis Millet | 65 | 1st | Lost |
| Mr. Jacob Christian Milling | 48 | 2nd | Lost |
| Miss Daisy E. Minahan | 33 | 1st | Saved |
| Dr. William Edward Minahan | 44 | 1st | Lost |
| Mrs. William Edward Minahan (Lillian E. Thorpe) | 37 | 1st | Saved |
| Mr. Ivan Mineff | 24 | 3rd | Lost |
| Mr. Lazar Minkoff | 21 | 3rd | Lost |
| Mr. Dika Mirko | 17 | 3rd | Lost |
| Mr. Henry Mitchell | 71 | 2nd | Lost |
| Mr. Mito Mitkoff | 23 | 3rd | Lost |
| Mr. Philip E. Mock | | 1st | Saved |
| Miss Helen Mary Mocklare | 23 | 3rd | Saved |
| Mr. Sigurd H. Moen | 25 | 3rd | Lost |
| Mr. Harry Markland Molson | 55 | 1st | Lost |
| Mrs. Bella Moor | 27 | 3rd | Saved |
| Master Mayer Moor | 6 | 3rd | Saved |
| Mr. Clarence Bloomfield Moore | 47 | 1st | Lost |
| Mr. Leonard Charles Moore | 19 | 3rd | Lost |

# *Titanic* Passengers

| Name | Age | Class | Lost/Saved |
|---|---|---|---|
| Miss Bertha Moran | 28 | 3rd | Saved |
| Mr. Daniel J. Moran | 27 | 3rd | Lost |
| Mr. James Moran | 22 | 3rd | Lost |
| Dr. Ernest Morawick | | 2nd | Lost |
| Mr. Henry Samuel Morley | 39 | 3rd | Lost |
| Mr. William Morley | | 2nd | Lost |
| Mr. Thomas Rowan Morrow | 30 | 3rd | Lost |
| Mr. Albert Johan Moss | 29 | 3rd | Saved |
| Mrs. George Moubarek (Amenia) | 26 | 3rd | Saved |
| Master George Moubarek | 7 | 3rd | Saved |
| Mr. Hanna John Moubarek | | 3rd | Saved |
| Master William George Moubarek | 3 | 3rd | Saved |
| Mrs. Mantoura Baloics Moussa | | 3rd | Saved |
| Mr. Rahamin Moutal | 35 | 3rd | Lost |
| Mr. Thomas C. Mudd | | 2nd | Lost |
| Miss Katie Mullins | 19 | 3rd | Saved |
| Miss Bertha E. Mulvihill | | 3rd | Saved |
| Mr. Joseph Murdlin | | 3rd | Lost |
| Miss Katherine Murphy | | 3rd | Saved |
| Miss Margaret Murphy | | 3rd | Saved |
| Miss Nora Murphy | 28 | 3rd | Saved |
| Mr. Peter Fabian Oliver Myhrman | 18 | 3rd | Lost |
| Mr. Thomas Francis Myles | 64 | 2nd | Lost |
| Miss Maria Nackid | 1 | 3rd | Saved |
| Mr. Said Nackid | 20 | 3rd | Saved |
| Mrs. Said Nackid (Mary Mowad) | 19 | 3rd | Saved |
| Mr. Toufik Nahil | | 3rd | Lost |
| Mr. Penko Naidenoff | 22 | 3rd | Lost |
| Miss Adele Kiamie Najib | | 3rd | Saved |
| Mr. William Henry Nancarrow | | 3rd | Lost |
| Mr. Minko Nankoff | 32 | 3rd | Lost |
| Mr. Mustafa Nasr | | 3rd | Lost |
| Mr. Nicholas Nasser | | 2nd | Lost |
| Mrs. Nicholas Nasser (Adele) | 19 | 2nd | Saved |
| Mr. Saade Jean Nassr | | 3rd | Lost |
| Mr. Charles H. Natsch | 36 | 1st | Lost |
| Miss Hannah Naughton | 21 | 3rd | Lost |
| Master Edmond Roger Navratil | 2 | 2nd | Saved |
| Mr. Michel Navratil | 32 | 2nd | Lost |
| Master Michel M. Navratil | 3 | 2nd | Saved |
| Mr. Robert Nemaugh | 26 | 3rd | Lost |
| Mr. Christo Nenkoff | 22 | 3rd | Lost |
| Mr. Israel Nesson | 26 | 2nd | Lost |
| Mr. Arthur Webster Newell | 58 | 1st | Lost |
| Miss Madeleine Newell | 31 | 1st | Saved |
| Miss Marjorie Newell | 23 | 1st | Saved |
| Miss Helen Monypeny Newsom | 19 | 1st | Saved |
| Mr. Joseph Charles Nicholls | 19 | 2nd | Lost |
| Mr. Arthur Ernest Nicholson | 64 | 1st | Lost |
| Master Elias Nicola-Yarred | 12 | 3rd | Saved |
| Miss Jamila Nicola-Yarred | 14 | 3rd | Saved |
| Miss Manta Josefina Nieminen | 29 | 3rd | Lost |
| Mr. Samuel Niklasson | 28 | 3rd | Lost |

# *Titanic* Passengers

| Name | Age | Class | Lost/Saved |
|---|---|---|---|
| Mr. August Ferdinand Nilsson | 21 | 3rd | Lost |
| Miss Bertha Olivia Nilsson | 18 | 3rd | Saved |
| Miss Helmina Josefina Nilsson | 26 | 3rd | Saved |
| Mr. Johan Niskanen | 39 | 3rd | Lost |
| Mr. Robert Douglas Norman | | 2nd | Lost |
| Mr. Richard Cater Nosworthy | | 3rd | Lost |
| Mr. Alfred Nourney (Baron von Drachstedt) | 20 | 1/2 | Saved |
| Mr. Mansour Novel | | 3rd | Lost |
| Mrs. Elizabeth Ramell Nye | 29 | 2nd | Saved |
| Miss Anna Nysten | 22 | 3rd | Saved |
| Mr. Johan H. Nysveen | 61 | 3rd | Lost |
| Mr. Denis O'Brien | 21 | 3rd | Lost |
| Mr. Thomas O'Brien | 27 | 3rd | Lost |
| Mrs. Thomas O'Brien (Hannah Godfrey) | 26 | 3rd | Saved |
| Mr. Patrick D. O'Connell | 17 | 3rd | Lost |
| Mr. Maurice O'Connor | | 3rd | Lost |
| Mr. Patrick O'Connor | 24 | 3rd | Lost |
| Miss Nellie O'Dwyer | 23 | 3rd | Saved |
| Mr. Patrick O'Keefe | 22 | 3rd | Saved |
| Miss Norah O'Leary | 17 | 3rd | Saved |
| Miss Bridget O'Neill | | 3rd | Lost |
| Miss Bridget O'Sullivan | 22 | 3rd | Lost |
| Mr. Nils Martin Odahl | 23 | 3rd | Lost |
| Miss Velin Ohman | 22 | 3rd | Saved |
| Master Arthur Olsen | 9 | 3rd | Saved |
| Mr. Charlie Olsen (Carl) | 50 | 3rd | Lost |
| Mr. Henry Margido Olsen | 28 | 3rd | Lost |
| Mr. Ole M. Olsen | 27 | 3rd | Lost |
| Miss Elida Olsson | 31 | 3rd | Lost |
| Mr. Nils Johan Olsson | 28 | 3rd | Lost |
| Mr. Oscar Johansson Olsson | 32 | 3rd | Saved |
| Mr. A. Fernand Omont | | 1st | Saved |
| Mr. Jeko Oreskovic | 23 | 3rd | Lost |
| Mr. Luka Oreskovic | 20 | 3rd | Lost |
| Mr. Maria Oreskovic | 20 | 3rd | Lost |
| Mr. Olof Elon Osen | 16 | 3rd | Lost |
| Miss Maria Osman | 31 | 3rd | Saved |
| Mr. Engelhart Cornelius Ostby | 64 | 1st | Lost |
| Miss Helen Raghnild Ostby | 22 | 1st | Saved |
| Mr. Richard Otter | 39 | 2nd | Lost |
| Mr. Servando Ovies y Rodriguez | | 1st | Lost |
| Mr. Percy Thomas Oxenham | 22 | 2nd | Saved |
| Mr. Julian Padro y Manent | | 2nd | Lost |
| Dr. Alfred Pain | 24 | 2nd | Lost |
| Mr. Emilio Pallas y Castello | | 2nd | Saved |
| Mr. Ernesti Arvid Panula | 16 | 3rd | Lost |
| Mr. Jaakko Arnold Panula | 14 | 3rd | Lost |
| Mrs. John Panula (Maria Emilia) | 41 | 3rd | Lost |
| Master Juha Niilo Panula | 7 | 3rd | Lost |
| Master Urho Abraham Panula | 2 | 3rd | Lost |
| Master William Panula | 1 | 3rd | Lost |
| Mr. Clifford R. Parker | 28 | 2nd | Lost |
| Mr. William Henry Marsh Parr | | 1st | Lost |

# *Titanic* Passengers

| Name | Age | Class | Lost/Saved |
|---|---|---|---|
| Mrs. Lutie Davis Parrish | 50 | 2nd | Saved |
| Mr. Austin Partner | | 1st | Lost |
| Mr. Jakob Pasic | 21 | 3rd | Lost |
| Mr. Uscher Paulner | | 3rd | Lost |
| Master Gosta Leonard Paulsson | 2 | 3rd | Lost |
| Mrs. Nils Paulsson (Alma Cornelia Berglund) | 29 | 3rd | Lost |
| Master Paul Folke Paulsson | 6 | 3rd | Lost |
| Miss Stina Viola Paulsson | 3 | 3rd | Lost |
| Miss Torborg Danira Paulsson | 8 | 3rd | Lost |
| Mr. Stefo Pavlovic | 32 | 3rd | Lost |
| Mr. Vivian Ponsonby Payne | 22 | 1st | Lost |
| Master Alfred Edward Peacock | 9m | 3rd | Lost |
| Mrs. Benjamin Peacock (Edith Nile) | 26 | 3rd | Lost |
| Miss Treasteall Peacock | 3 | 3rd | Lost |
| Mr. Ernest Pearce | 32 | 3rd | Lost |
| Mr. Thomas Pears | | 1st | Lost |
| Mrs. Thomas Pears (Edith) | | 1st | Saved |
| Mr. Mate Pecruic | 17 | 3rd | Lost |
| Mr. Tome Pecruic | 24 | 3rd | Lost |
| Mr. Olaf Pedersen | 29 | 3rd | Lost |
| Mr. Joseph Peduzzi | 24 | 3rd | Lost |
| Mr. Edvard Pekoniemi | 21 | 3rd | Lost |
| Mr. Nikolai Johannes Peltomaki | 25 | 3rd | Lost |
| Mr. Victor de Satode Penasco | 18 | 1st | Lost |
| Mrs. Victor de Satode Penasco (Josefa de Sota) | 17 | 1st | Saved |
| Mr. Frederick Pengelly | 20 | 2nd | Lost |
| Mr. John Henry Perkin | 22 | 3rd | Lost |
| Mr. Rene Pernot | | 2nd | Lost |
| Mr. Ernst Ulrik Persson | 25 | 3rd | Saved |
| Rev. Joseph M. Peruschitz | 40 | 2nd | Lost |
| Mrs. Catherine Peter (Joseph) | 24 | 3rd | Saved |
| Miss Mary Peter (Joseph) | 1 | 3rd | Saved |
| Master Michael J. Peter (Joseph) | 4 | 3rd | Saved |
| Miss Katie Peters | 26 | 3rd | Lost |
| Mr. Marius Petersen | 24 | 3rd | Lost |
| Miss Matilda Petranec | 31 | 3rd | Lost |
| Mr. Nedeca Petroff | 19 | 3rd | Lost |
| Mr. Pentcho Petroff | 29 | 3rd | Lost |
| Miss Ellen Natalia Pettersson | 18 | 3rd | Lost |
| Mr. Johan Emil Pettersson | 25 | 3rd | Lost |
| Major Arthur Godfren Peuchen | 52 | 1st | Saved |
| Miss Alice Phillips | 42 | 2nd | Saved |
| Mr. Robert Phillips | 21 | 2nd | Lost |
| Mr. Berk Pickard | 32 | 3rd | Saved |
| Miss Rosa Pinsky | 32 | 2nd | Saved |
| Mr. Vasil Plotcharsky | 27 | 3rd | Lost |
| Mr. Martin Ponesell | 34 | 2nd | Lost |
| Mr. Emilio Portaluppi | | 2nd | Saved |
| Mr. Walter Chamberlain Porter | 46 | 1st | Lost |
| Mr. George Potchett | 19 | 3rd | Lost |
| Mrs. Thomas Potter (Lily Alexenia Wilson), Jr. | 56 | 1st | Saved |
| Mr. Frank Pulbaum | | 2nd | Lost |
| Mrs. Frederick C. Quick (Jane Richards) | 33 | 2nd | Saved |

# *Titanic* Passengers

| Name | Age | Class | Lost/Saved |
|---|---|---|---|
| Miss Phyllis May Quick | 2 | 2nd | Saved |
| Miss Winifred Vera Quick | 8 | 2nd | Saved |
| Mr. Alexander Radeff | 27 | 3rd | Lost |
| Mr. Razi Raibid | | 3rd | Lost |
| Mr. James George Reed | 19 | 3rd | Lost |
| Mr. David Reeves | 36 | 2nd | Lost |
| Mr. Peter Henry Renouf | 34 | 2nd | Lost |
| Mrs. Peter Henry Renouf (Lillian Jefferys) | 30 | 2nd | Saved |
| Mr. John George Reuchlin | | 1st | Lost |
| Mrs. Encarnacion Reynaldo | 28 | 2nd | Saved |
| Mr. Harold Reynolds | 21 | 3rd | Lost |
| Mr. George Lucien Rheims | | 1st | Saved |
| Master Albert Rice | 10 | 3rd | Lost |
| Master Arthur Rice | 4 | 3rd | Lost |
| Master Eric Rice | 7 | 3rd | Lost |
| Master Eugene Rice | 2 | 3rd | Lost |
| Master George Rice | 9 | 3rd | Lost |
| Mrs. William Rice (Margaret Norton) | 39 | 3rd | Lost |
| Mr. Emil Richard | 23 | 2nd | Lost |
| Master George Sidney Richards | 10m | 2nd | Saved |
| Mrs. Sidney Richards (Emily Hocking) | 25 | 2nd | Saved |
| Master William Rowe Richards | 3 | 2nd | Saved |
| Miss Sanni Riihiivuori | 21 | 3rd | Lost |
| Mr. Matti Rintamaki | | 3rd | Lost |
| Miss Hannah Riordan | 20 | 3rd | Saved |
| Miss Lucy Risdale | 50 | 2nd | Saved |
| Mr. Samuel Risien | 68 | 3rd | Lost |
| Mrs. Samuel Risien (Emma) | 58 | 3rd | Lost |
| Mrs. Edward Scott Robert (Elisabeth Walton McMillan) | 43 | 1st | Saved |
| Mr. Alexander A. Robins | 50 | 3rd | Lost |
| Mrs. Alexander A. Robins (Charity Laury) | 47 | 3rd | Lost |
| Mr. Washington Augustus Roebling, II | 31 | 1st | Lost |
| Mr. Harry Rogers | | 2nd | Lost |
| Mr. William John Rogers | 29 | 3rd | Lost |
| Mr. Charles Hallis Romaine | | 1st | Saved |
| Mr. Karl Kristian Rommetvedt | 49 | 3rd | Lost |
| Mr. Hugh R. Rood | | 1st | Lost |
| Miss Salli Helena Rosblom | 2 | 3rd | Lost |
| Mr. Viktor Rickard Rosblom | 18 | 3rd | Lost |
| Mrs. Viktor Rosblom (Helena Wilhelmina) | 41 | 3rd | Lost |
| Miss Edith Louise Rosenbaum | 33 | 1st | Saved |
| Mr. John Hugo Ross | | 1st | Lost |
| Miss Sarah Roth | 26 | 3rd | Saved |
| Countess Rothes (Noel Lucy Martha Dyer-Edwardes) | 27 | 1st | Saved |
| Mr. Martin Rothschild | 55 | 1st | Lost |
| Mrs. Martin Rothschild (Elizabeth L. Barrett) | 54 | 1st | Saved |
| Mr. Richard Henry Rouse | 50 | 3rd | Lost |
| Mr. Alfred G. Rowe | | 1st | Lost |
| Miss Emily Rugg | 21 | 2nd | Saved |
| Mr. Alfred George John Rush | 16 | 3rd | Lost |
| Mr. Edward Ryan | | 3rd | Saved |
| Mr. Patrick Ryan | | 3rd | Lost |
| Mr. Arthur Larned Ryerson | 61 | 1st | Lost |

# *Titanic* Passengers

| Name | Age | Class | Lost/Saved |
|---|---|---|---|
| Mrs. Arthur Larned Ryerson (Emily Marie Borie) | 48 | 1st | Saved |
| Miss Emily Borie Ryerson | 18 | 1st | Saved |
| Master John Borie Ryerson | 13 | 1st | Saved |
| Miss Suzette Parker Ryerson | 21 | 1st | Saved |
| Mr. Amin Saad | | 3rd | Lost |
| Mr. Adolphe Saalfeld | | 1st | Saved |
| Mr. Matthew Sadlier | 20 | 3rd | Lost |
| Mr. Harry Sadowitz | 16 | 3rd | Lost |
| Miss Ada Sage | 9 | 3rd | Lost |
| Miss Constance Sage | 7 | 3rd | Lost |
| Miss Dorothy Sage | 13 | 3rd | Lost |
| Mr. Douglas Sage | 18 | 3rd | Lost |
| Mr. Frederick Sage | 16 | 3rd | Lost |
| Mr. George Sage | 19 | 3rd | Lost |
| Mr. John George Sage | 44 | 3rd | Lost |
| Mrs. John George Sage (Annie) | 44 | 3rd | Lost |
| Miss Stella Sage | 20 | 3rd | Lost |
| Master Thomas Sage | 4 | 3rd | Lost |
| Master William Sage | 11 | 3rd | Lost |
| Mr. Karl Johan Salander | 24 | 3rd | Lost |
| Miss Anna Saljelsvik | 23 | 3rd | Saved |
| Mr. Abraham L. Salomon | | 1st | Saved |
| Mr. Johan Werner Salonen | 39 | 3rd | Lost |
| Mr. Elias Samaan | | 3rd | Lost |
| Mr. Hanna Samaan | | 3rd | Lost |
| Mr. Joussef Samaan | | 3rd | Lost |
| Miss Beatrice Irene Sandstrom | 1 | 3rd | Saved |
| Mrs. Hjalmar Sandstrom (Agnes Charlotta Bengtsson) | 24 | 3rd | Saved |
| Miss Marguerite Rut Sandstrom | 4 | 3rd | Saved |
| Mr. Simon Sivertsen Sather | | 3rd | Lost |
| Mr. William Henry Saundercock | 20 | 3rd | Lost |
| Mr. Frederick Sawyer | 23 | 3rd | Lost |
| Mr. James Scanlan | | 3rd | Lost |
| Mrs. Paul Schabert (Emma Mock) | | 1st | Saved |
| Mr. Tudor Sdycoff | 42 | 3rd | Lost |
| Mr. Charles Frederick Sedgwick | | 2nd | Lost |
| Master Betros Seman | 9 | 3rd | Lost |
| Mr. Maurice Serota | | 3rd | Lost |
| Mr. Frederic Kimber Seward | 34 | 1st | Saved |
| Mr. Percival Sharp | | 2nd | Lost |
| Mr. Patrick Shaughnesay | | 3rd | Lost |
| Mr. Daher (Docart) Shedid (Sitik) | 19 | 3rd | Lost |
| Mr. Jean Sheerlinck | 29 | 3rd | Saved |
| Mr. Frederick B. Shellard | | 3rd | Lost |
| Mrs. William Shelley (Imanita) | 25 | 2nd | Saved |
| Miss Ellen Shine | 20 | 3rd | Saved |
| Mr. Charles Shorney | 22 | 3rd | Lost |
| Miss Elizabeth W. Shutes | 40 | 1st | Saved |
| Miss Lyyli Silven | 18 | 2nd | Saved |
| Mr. Spencer Victor Silverthorne | 36 | 1st | Saved |
| Mr. William Baird Silvey | 50 | 1st | Lost |
| Mrs. William Baird Silvey (Alice Munger) | 39 | 1st | Saved |
| Mr. John Simmons | 39 | 3rd | Lost |

# *Titanic* Passengers

| Name | Age | Class | Lost/Saved |
|---|---|---|---|
| Col. Alfons Simonius-Blumer | 54 | 1st | Saved |
| Miss Maude Sincock | 20 | 2nd | Saved |
| Mr. Arsun Sirayanian | | 3rd | Lost |
| Miss Anna Siukonnen | 30 | 2nd | Saved |
| Mr. Husen Sivic | 40 | 3rd | Lost |
| Mr. Antti Sivola | 21 | 3rd | Lost |
| Miss Anna Sofia Sjoblom | 18 | 3rd | Saved |
| Mr. Ernst Adolf Sjostedt | 59 | 2nd | Lost |
| Mr. John Henry Skinner | 32 | 3rd | Lost |
| Master Harald Skoog | 4 | 3rd | Lost |
| Master Karl Skoog | 10 | 3rd | Lost |
| Miss Mabel Skoog | 9 | 3rd | Lost |
| Miss Margit Skoog | 2 | 3rd | Lost |
| Mr. William Skoog | 40 | 3rd | Lost |
| Mrs. William Skoog (Ana Bernhardina Karlsson) | 43 | 3rd | Lost |
| Mr. Petco Slabenoff | 42 | 3rd | Lost |
| Miss Hilda Mary Slayter | 30 | 2nd | Saved |
| Mr. Richard James Slemen | 35 | 2nd | Lost |
| Mr. Selman Slocovski | 31 | 3rd | Lost |
| Mr. William Thomson Sloper | 28 | 1st | Saved |
| Mr. John Montgomery Smart | 56 | 1st | Lost |
| Mr. Mile Smiljanovic | 37 | 3rd | Lost |
| Mr. Augustus Smith (Schmidt) | 22 | 2nd | Lost |
| Mr. James Clinch Smith | 56 | 1st | Lost |
| Mr. Lucien Philip Smith | 24 | 1st | Lost |
| Mrs. Lucien Philip Smith (Mary Eloise Hughes) | 18 | 1st | Saved |
| Miss Marion Smith | | 2nd | Saved |
| Mr. Richard William Smith | | 1st | Lost |
| Miss Julia Smyth | 20 | 3rd | Saved |
| Mr. John Pillsbury Snyder | 24 | 1st | Saved |
| Mrs. John Pillsbury Snyder (Nelle Stevenson) | 23 | 1st | Saved |
| Mr. Hayden Sobey | 25 | 2nd | Lost |
| Mr. Peter Andreas Soholt | 19 | 3rd | Lost |
| Mrs. Lena Jacobsen Solvang | 63 | 3rd | Lost |
| Mr. Francis William Somerton | 31 | 3rd | Lost |
| Mr. Jules Sop | 25 | 3rd | Lost |
| Mr. Woolf Spector | 23 | 3rd | Lost |
| Mr. Frederic Oakley Spedden | 45 | 1st | Saved |
| Mrs. Frederic Oakley Spedden (Margaretta Corning Stone) | 40 | 1st | Saved |
| Master Robert Douglas Spedden | 6 | 1st | Saved |
| Mr. William Augustus Spencer | 57 | 1st | Lost |
| Mrs. William Augustus Spencer (Marie Eugenie) | | 1st | Saved |
| Dr. Max Staehlin | 32 | 1st | Saved |
| Mr. Ivan Staneff | 23 | 3rd | Lost |
| Mr. Jovan Stankovic | | 3rd | Lost |
| Miss Amy Elsie Stanley | 24 | 3rd | Saved |
| Mr. Edward Roland Stanley | 21 | 3rd | Lost |
| Mr. Samuel Ward Stanton | 41 | 2nd | Lost |
| Mr. William Thomas Stead | 62 | 1st | Lost |
| Mr. Charles Emil Henry Stengel | 54 | 1st | Saved |
| Mrs. Charles Emil Henry Stengel (Annie May Morris) | 43 | 1st | Saved |
| Mrs. Walter Bertram Stephenson (Martha Eustis) | 52 | 1st | Saved |
| Mr. Albert A. Stewart | | 1st | Lost |

# *Titanic* Passengers

| Name | Age | Class | Lost/Saved |
|---|---|---|---|
| Mr. Philip Joseph Stokes | 25 | 2nd | Lost |
| Mrs. George Nelson Stone (Martha E.) | 63 | 1st | Saved |
| Mr. Thomas Storey | 51 | 3rd | Lost |
| Mr. Ilia Stoyehoff | 19 | 3rd | Lost |
| Miss Ida Sofia Strandberg | 22 | 3rd | Lost |
| Mr. Juho Stranden | 31 | 3rd | Saved |
| Mr. Isidor Straus | 67 | 1st | Lost |
| Mrs. Isidor Straus (Ida Blun) | 63 | 1st | Lost |
| Mr. Ivan Strilic | | 3rd | Lost |
| Miss Selma Matilda Strom | 2 | 3rd | Lost |
| Mrs. Wilhelm Strom (Elna Matilda Persson) | 29 | 3rd | Lost |
| Mr. Victor Francis Sunderland | 19 | 3rd | Saved |
| Mr. Johan Julian Sundman | 44 | 3rd | Saved |
| Mr. Henry Sutehall, Jr. | 26 | 3rd | Lost |
| Mr. Frederick Sutton | 61 | 1st | Lost |
| Mr. Johan Svensson | 74 | 3rd | Lost |
| Mr. Johan Cervin Svensson | 14 | 3rd | Saved |
| Mr. Olof Svensson | 24 | 3rd | Lost |
| Mr. George Swane | 26 | 2nd | Lost |
| Mr. George Sweet | 14 | 2nd | Lost |
| Mrs. Frederick Joel Swift (Margaret Welles Barron) | 46 | 1st | Saved |
| Mr. Thomas Tannous | | 3rd | Lost |
| Mr. Emil Taussig | 52 | 1st | Lost |
| Mrs. Emil Taussig (Tillie Mandelbaum) | 39 | 1st | Saved |
| Miss Ruth Taussig | 18 | 1st | Saved |
| Mr. Elmer Zebley Taylor | 48 | 1st | Saved |
| Mrs. Elmer Zebley Taylor (Juliet Cummins Wright) | | 1st | Saved |
| Mr. Gunnar Isidor Tenglin | 25 | 3rd | Saved |
| Mr. John Borland Thayer | 49 | 1st | Lost |
| Mrs. John Borland Thayer (Marian Longstreth Morris) | 39 | 1st | Saved |
| Mr. John Borland Thayer, Jr. | 17 | 1st | Saved |
| Mr. Thomas Leonard Theobald | 34 | 3rd | Lost |
| Mrs. Alexander Thomas (Thelma) | 16 | 3rd | Saved |
| Master Assed Alexander Thomas | 5m | 3rd | Saved |
| Mr. Charles Thomas | | 3rd | Lost |
| Mr. John Thomas | | | |
| Mr. John Thomas, Jr. | 15 | 3rd | Lost |
| Mr. Alexander Thomson | 36 | 3rd | Lost |
| Mr. George Thorne | 46 | 1st | Lost |
| Mrs. Gertrude Maybelle Thorne | | 1st | Saved |
| Mr. Percival Thorneycroft | 36 | 3rd | Lost |
| Mrs. Percival Thorneycroft (Florence Kate White) | 32 | 3rd | Saved |
| Mr. Juho Tikkanen | 32 | 3rd | Lost |
| Mr. Roger Tobin | | 3rd | Lost |
| Mr. Lalio Todoroff | 23 | 3rd | Lost |
| Mr. Ernest William Toerber | 41 | 3rd | Lost |
| Mr. Ernest Portage Tomlin | 22 | 3rd | Lost |
| Miss Ellen Toomey | 50 | 2nd | Saved |
| Mr. Assad Torfa | 20 | 3rd | Lost |
| Mr. William Henry Tornquist | 25 | 3rd | Saved |
| Mrs. Darwin Touma (Thomas) (Anna Razi) | 27 | 3rd | Saved |
| Master George Touma (Thomas) | 7 | 3rd | Saved |
| Miss Hanna Touma (Thomas) | 9 | 3rd | Saved |

# *TITANIC* PASSENGERS

| NAME | AGE | CLASS | LOST/SAVED |
|---|---|---|---|
| Mr. Moses Aaron Troupiansky | 22 | 2nd | Lost |
| Mrs. William H. Trout (Jessie L.) | | 2nd | Saved |
| Miss Edwina Celia Troutt | 27 | 2nd | Saved |
| Mr. Gilbert Milligan Tucker, Jr. | 31 | 1st | Saved |
| Mr. Stefan Turcin | 36 | 3rd | Lost |
| Miss Anna Sofia Turja | 18 | 3rd | Saved |
| Mrs. Hedvig Turkula | 65 | 3rd | Saved |
| Mr. William John Turpin | 29 | 2nd | Lost |
| Mrs. William John Turpin (Dorothy Ann Wonnacott) | 27 | 2nd | Lost |
| Mr. Manuel E. Uruchurtu | | 1st | Lost |
| Mr. Joso Uzelas | 17 | 3rd | Lost |
| Mr. Austin Blyler Van Billiard | 35 | 3rd | Lost |
| Master James William Van Billiard | 10 | 3rd | Lost |
| Master Walter John Van Billiard | 9 | 3rd | Lost |
| Mr. John Joseph Van de Velde | 36 | 3rd | Lost |
| Mr. Nestor Van de Walle | 28 | 3rd | Lost |
| Miss Augusta Van der Planke | 18 | 3rd | Lost |
| Mr. Jules Van der Planke | 31 | 3rd | Lost |
| Mrs. Jules Van der Planke (Emilie) | 31 | 3rd | Lost |
| Mr. Leon Van der Planke | 16 | 3rd | Lost |
| Mr. Leo Peter Van der Steen | 28 | 3rd | Lost |
| Mr. Wyckoff Van Derhoef | 61 | 1st | Lost |
| Miss Catharine Van Impe | 10 | 3rd | Lost |
| Mr. Jean Baptiste Van Impe | 36 | 3rd | Lost |
| Mrs. Jean Baptiste Van Impe (Rosalie Govaert) | 30 | 3rd | Lost |
| Mr. David Vartunian | | 3rd | Saved |
| Mr. Catevelas Vassilios | 18 | 3rd | Lost |
| Mr. James Veale | 30 | 2nd | Lost |
| Mr. Olof Edvin Vendel | 20 | 3rd | Lost |
| Mr. Victor Vereruysse | 47 | 3rd | Lost |
| Miss Hulda Amanda Vestrom | 14 | 3rd | Lost |
| Mr. Jenko Vonk | 21 | 3rd | Lost |
| Mr. Achille Waelens | 22 | 2/3rd | Lost |
| Miss Nellie Walcroft | 35 | 2nd | Saved |
| Mr. William Anderson Walker | 47 | 1st | Lost |
| Mr. Frederick Ware | 34 | 3rd | Lost |
| Mr. John James Ware | 30 | 2nd | Lost |
| Mrs. John James Ware (Florence Louise Long) | 28 | 2nd | Saved |
| Mr. William J. Ware | 23 | 2nd | Lost |
| Mr. Charles William Warren | 30 | 3rd | Lost |
| Mr. Frank Manley Warren | 64 | 1st | Lost |
| Mrs. Frank Manley Warren (Anna S. Atkinson) | 60 | 1st | Saved |
| Miss Bertha Watt | 12 | 2nd | Saved |
| Mrs. James Watt (Bessie Inglis Milne) | 40 | 2nd | Saved |
| Mr. Yousif Wazli | | 3rd | Lost |
| Mr. James Webber | 66 | 3rd | Lost |
| Miss Susan Webber | 36 | 2nd | Saved |
| Col. John Weir | 60 | 1st | Lost |
| Mr. Leopold Weisz | 28 | 2nd | Lost |
| Mrs. Leopold Weisz (Mathilde) | 32 | 2nd | Saved |
| Mrs. Arthur H. Wells (Addie Trevaskis) | 29 | 2nd | Saved |
| Miss Joan Wells | 4 | 2nd | Saved |
| Master Ralph Lester Wells | 2 | 2nd | Saved |

# *Titanic* Passengers

| Name | Age | Class | Lost/Saved |
|---|---|---|---|
| Mr. August Edvard Wennerstrom | 26 | 3rd | Saved |
| Mr. Linhart Wenzel | | 3rd | Lost |
| Miss Barbara J. West | | 2nd | Saved |
| Miss Constance Miriam West | | 2nd | Saved |
| Mr. Edwy Arthur West | 36 | 2nd | Lost |
| Mrs. Edwy Arthur West (Ada Mary) | 33 | 2nd | Saved |
| Mr. Edward Wheadon | | 2nd | Lost |
| Mr. Edwin Wheeler | | 2nd | Lost |
| Mrs. Stuart J. White (Ella Holmes) | 55 | 1st | Saved |
| Mr. Percival Wayland White | 54 | 1st | Lost |
| Mr. Richard Frasar White | 21 | 1st | Lost |
| Mr. George Dennick Wick | 57 | 1st | Lost |
| Mrs. George Dennick Wick (Mary Hitchcock) | 45 | 1st | Saved |
| Miss Mary Natalie Wick | 31 | 1st | Saved |
| Mr. Charles Peter Widegren | 51 | 3rd | Lost |
| Mr. George Dunton Widener | 50 | 1st | Lost |
| Mrs. George Dunton Widener (Eleanor Elkins) | 50 | 1st | Saved |
| Mr. Harry Elkins Widener | 27 | 1st | Lost |
| Mr. Jacob Alfred Wiklund | 18 | 3rd | Lost |
| Mr. Karl Johan Wiklund | 21 | 3rd | Lost |
| Mr. Charles Wilhelms | 32 | 2nd | Saved |
| Mrs. Ellen Wilkes | 45 | 3rd | Saved |
| Mrs. Elizabeth Anne Wilkinson | | 2nd | Saved |
| Miss Constance Willard | 20 | 1st | Saved |
| Mr. Aaron Willer | | 3rd | Lost |
| Mr. Edward Willey | 18 | 3rd | Lost |
| Mr. Charles Duane Williams | 51 | 1st | Lost |
| Mr. Charles Eugene Williams | | 2nd | Saved |
| Mr. Fletcher Lambert Williams | | 1st | Lost |
| Mr. Howard Hugh Williams | 28 | 3rd | Lost |
| Mr. Leslie Williams | | 3rd | Lost |
| Mr. Richard Norris Williams, II | 21 | 1st | Saved |
| Mr. Einar Windelov | 21 | 3rd | Lost |
| Mr. Albert Wirz | 27 | 3rd | Lost |
| Mr. Phillippe Wiseman | 54 | 3rd | Lost |
| Mr. Camille Wittenrongel | 36 | 3rd | Lost |
| Mr. Hugh Woolner | | 1st | Saved |
| Mr. George Wright | | 1st | Lost |
| Miss Marion Wright | 26 | 2nd | Saved |
| Mr. Ivan Yalsevac | | 3rd | Lost |
| Mr. Antoni Yasbeck | 27 | 3rd | Lost |
| Mrs. Antoni Yasbeck (Celiney Alexander) | 15 | 3rd | Saved |
| Miss Marie Grice Young | 36 | 1st | Saved |
| Mr. Gerios Youssef | | 3rd | Lost |
| Miss Henriette Yrois | | 2nd | Lost |
| Miss Hileni Zabour | | 3rd | Lost |
| Miss Tamini Zabour | | 3rd | Lost |
| Mr. Artun Zakarian | | 3rd | Lost |
| Mr. Maprieder Zakarian | | 3rd | Lost |
| Mr. Rene Zievens | 24 | 3rd | Lost |
| Mr. Leo Zimerman | | 3rd | Lost |

# *Titanic* Crew

| Name | Occupation | Lost/Saved |
|---|---|---|
| E. Abbott | Pantryman | Lost |
| C. Abraham | Fireman | Lost |
| R. Adams | Fireman | Lost |
| P. Ahier | Saloon Steward | Lost |
| J. Akerman | Assistant Pantryman | Lost |
| A. Akermann | Steward | Lost |
| F. Allan | Lift Attendant | Lost |
| R. Allan | Bedroom Steward | Lost |
| B. Allaria | Assistant Waiter | Lost |
| E. Allen | Trimmer | Saved |
| E. Allen | Scullion | Lost |
| H. Allen | Fireman | Lost |
| A. S. Allsop | Junior Electrician | Lost |
| F. Allsop | Saloon Steward | Lost |
| J. Anderson | Assistant Boatswain | Saved |
| W. Anderson | Bedroom Steward | Lost |
| C. Andrews | Assistant Steward | Saved |
| E. Archer | Assistant Boatswain | Saved |
| A. Ashcroft | Clerk | Lost |
| H. Ashe | G. H. Steward | Lost |
| G. Aspelagi | Assistant Plateman | Lost |
| J. Avery | Trimmer | Saved |
| E. Ayling | Assistant Vegetable Cook | Lost |
| C. Back | Assistant Attendant | Lost |
| A. Baggott | Saloon Steward | Lost |
| E. Bagley | Saloon Steward | Lost |
| G. Bailey | Saloon Steward | Lost |
| G. W. Bailey | Fireman | Lost |
| W. Bailey | Master-at-Arms | Saved |
| Rich Baines | Greaser | Lost |
| Percy Ball | Plate Washer | Saved |
| W. Ball | Fireman | Lost |
| Banfi | Waiter | Lost |
| J. Bannon | Greaser | Lost |
| A. Barker | Assistant Baker | Lost |
| E. Barker | Saloon Steward | Lost |
| R. Barker | Second Purser | Lost |
| T. Barker | Assistant Butcher | Lost |
| C. Barlow | Fireman | Lost |
| G. Barlow | Bedroom Steward | Lost |
| Chas. Barnes | Fireman | Lost |
| J. Barnes | Fireman | Lost |
| W. Barnes | Assistant Baker | Lost |
| A. Barrett | Bell Boy | Lost |
| F. Barrett | Leading Fireman | Saved |
| F. W. Barrett | Fireman | Lost |
| A. Barringer | Saloon Steward | Lost |
| H. Barrow | Assistant Butcher | Lost |
| W. Barrows | Saloon Steward | Lost |
| S. Barton | Steward | Lost |
| G. Basilico | Waiter | Lost |
| F. Baxter | Linen Keeper | Lost |
| H. R. Baxter | Steward | Lost |
| L. Bazzi | Waiter | Lost |
| F. Beattie | Greaser | Lost |
| G. Beauchamp | Fireman | Saved |

# *Titanic* Crew

| Name | Occupation | Lost/Saved |
|---|---|---|
| W. Bedford | Assistant Cook | Lost |
| G. Beedem | Bedroom Steward | Lost |
| W. Beere | Kitchen Porter | Lost |
| J. Bell | Chief Engineer | Lost |
| T. Bendell | Fireman | Lost |
| T. Benhem | Saloon Steward | Saved |
| G. Bennett | Fireman | Lost |
| Mrs. Bennett | Stewardess | Saved |
| E. Benville | Fireman | Lost |
| B. Bernardi | Assistant Waiter | Lost |
| Florentini Berthold | Assistant Scullery Man | Lost |
| E. Bessant | Baggage Master | Lost |
| W. Bessant | Fireman | Lost |
| E. Best | Saloon Steward | Lost |
| D. Beux | Assistant Waiter | Lost |
| J. Bevis | Trimmer | Lost |
| C. Biddlecombe | Fireman | Lost |
| G. Bietrix | Sauce Cook | Lost |
| E. Biggs | Fireman | Lost |
| J. Billows | Trimmer | Lost |
| W. Binstead | Trimmer | Saved |
| W. Bishop | Bedroom Steward | Lost |
| A. Black | Fireman | Lost |
| D. Black | Fireman | Lost |
| H. Blackman | Fireman | Lost |
| P. Blake | Trimmer | Saved |
| S. Blake | Mess Steward | Lost |
| T. Blake | Fireman | Lost |
| J. Blaney | Fireman | Lost |
| E. Blann | Fireman | Lost |
| Miss Bliss | Stewardess | Saved |
| J. Blumet | Plateman | Lost |
| G. Bochet | Second Waiter | Lost |
| J. Bochetez | Assistant Chef | Lost |
| L. Bogie | Bedroom Steward | Lost |
| H. Bolhens | Larder Cook | Lost |
| W. Bond | Bedroom Steward | Lost |
| W. Boothby | Bedroom Steward | Lost |
| W. Boston | Assistant Deck Steward | Lost |
| W. Bott | Greaser | Lost |
| E. Boughton | Saloon Steward | Lost |
| Miss Bowker | Cashier | Saved |
| J. G. Boxhall | Fouth Officer | Saved |
| J. Boyd | Saloon Steward | Lost |
| H. Boyes | Saloon Steward | Lost |
| F. Bradley | Assistant Boatswain | Lost |
| P. Bradley | Fireman | Lost |
| J. Bradshaw | Plate Washer | Lost |
| H. Brewer | Trimmer | Lost |
| G. H. Brewster | Bedroom Steward | Lost |
| W. Brice | Assistant Boatswain | Saved |
| Harold S. Bride | Second Marconi | Saved |
| W. Brigge | Fireman | Lost |
| A. Bright | Quartermaster | Saved |
| R. Bristow | Steward | Lost |

# *Titanic* Crew

| Name | Occupation | Lost/Saved |
|---|---|---|
| H. Bristowe | Saloon Steward | Lost |
| J. Brookman | Steward | Lost |
| J. Brooks | Trimmer | Lost |
| H. Broom | Bath Steward | Lost |
| Athol Broome | Assistant, Veranda Café | Lost |
| E. Brown | Saloon Steward | Saved |
| J. Brown | Fireman | Lost |
| J. Brown | Fireman | Lost |
| W. Brown | Saloon Steward | Lost |
| H. Buckley | Assistant Vegetable Cook | Lost |
| E. Buley | Assistant Boatswain | Lost |
| W. Bull | Scullion | Lost |
| H. Bully | Boots | Lost |
| F. Bummell | Plate Washer | Lost |
| C. Burgess | Extra Third Baker | Saved |
| R. Burke | Lounge Attendant | Lost |
| W. Burke | Saloon Steward | Saved |
| E. Burr | Saloon Steward | Lost |
| A. Burrage | Plates | Saved |
| A. Burroughs | Fireman | Lost |
| E. Burton | Fireman | Lost |
| R. Butt | Saloon Steward | Lost |
| W. Butt | Fireman | Lost |
| J. Butterworth | Saloon Steward | Lost |
| J. Byrne | Bedroom Steward | Lost |
| H. Calderwood | Trimmer | Lost |
| J. Camner | Fireman | Lost |
| D. S. Campbell | Clerk | Lost |
| W. Carney | Lift Attendant | Lost |
| R. Carr | Trimmer | Lost |
| F. Carter | Trimmer | Lost |
| J. Cartwright | Saloon Steward | Lost |
| T. Casey | Trimmer | Lost |
| C. Casswill | Saloon Steward | Lost |
| E. Castleman | Greaser | Lost |
| Miss Caton | T. B. Attendant | Saved |
| W. Caunt | Grill Cook | Lost |
| H. Cave | Saloon Steward | Lost |
| G. Cavell | Trimmer | Saved |
| C. Cecil | Steward | Lost |
| J. Chapman | Boots | Saved |
| A. Charbolson | Roast Cook | Lost |
| J. Charman | Saloon Steward | Lost |
| W. Cherrett | Fireman | Lost |
| W. Cheverton | Saloon Steward | Lost |
| G. Chisnall | Boilermaker | Lost |
| G. Chitty | Steward | Lost |
| G. Chitty | Assistant Baker | Lost |
| J. Chorley | Fireman | Lost |
| H. Christmas | Assistant Steward | Lost |
| T. Clark | Bedroom Steward | Lost |
| W. Clark | Fireman | Saved |
| G. Clench | Assistant Boatswain | Lost |
| F. Clinch | Assistant Boatswain | Saved |
| H. Coe | Trimmer | Lost |

# *Titanic* Crew

| Name | Occupation | Lost/Saved |
|---|---|---|
| A. Coleman | Saloon Steward | Lost |
| J. Coleman | Mess Steward | Lost |
| J. Colgan | Scullion | Saved |
| John Collins | Scullion | Saved |
| S. Collins | Fireman | Saved |
| P. Conway | Saloon Steward | Lost |
| George Cook | Saloon Steward | Lost |
| G. Coombes | Fireman | Saved |
| C. Coombs | Assistant Cook | Lost |
| H. Cooper | Fireman | Lost |
| J. Cooper | Trimmer | Lost |
| B. Copperthwaite | Fireman | Lost |
| E. Corben | Assistant Printer | Lost |
| D. Corcoran | Fireman | Lost |
| M. Cornaire | Assistant Roast | Lost |
| A. Cotton | Fireman | Lost |
| F. Couch | Assistant Boatswain | Lost |
| J. Couch | Greaser | Lost |
| R. Couper | Fireman | Saved |
| A. Coutin | Entrée Cook | Lost |
| W. Cox | Steward | Lost |
| F. E. G. Coy | Junior Third Assistant Engineer | Lost |
| H. Crabb | Trimmer | Lost |
| F. Crafter | Saloon Steward | Saved |
| A. Crawford | Bedroom Steward | Saved |
| H. Creese | Deck Engineer | Lost |
| J. Crimmins | Fireman | Saved |
| H. Crisp | Saloon Steward | Lost |
| W. Crispin | G. H. Steward | Lost |
| J. B. Crosbie | T. B. Attendant | Lost |
| W. Cross | Fireman | Lost |
| L. Crovella | Assistant Waiter | Lost |
| G. F. Crow | Saloon Steward | Saved |
| C. Crumplin | Bedroom Steward | Lost |
| C. Cullen | Bedroom Steward | Saved |
| A. Cunningham | Bedroom Steward | Saved |
| B. Cunningham | Fireman | Lost |
| A. Curtis | Fireman | Lost |
| S. Daniels | Steward | Saved |
| W. Dashwood | Saloon Steward | Lost |
| Gordon Davies | Bedroom Steward | Lost |
| J. Davies | Extra Second Baker | Lost |
| T. Davies | Leading Fireman | Lost |
| Angus Davis | Steward | Lost |
| S. J. Davis | Assistant Boatswain | Lost |
| J. Dawson | Trimmer | Lost |
| G. Dean | Assistant Steward | Lost |
| M. De Breueq | Assistant Waiter | Lost |
| A. Deebie | Saloon Steward | Lost |
| Dennarsisco | Assistant Waiter | Lost |
| A. Derrett | Saloon Steward | Lost |
| P. Deslands | Saloon Steward | Lost |
| L. Desvernini | Assistant Pastry | Lost |
| J. Diaper | Fireman | Saved |
| W. Dickson | Trimmer | Lost |

# *Titanic* Crew

| Name | Occupation | Lost/Saved |
|---|---|---|
| J. Dilley | Fireman | Saved |
| T. P. Dillon | Trimmer | Saved |
| J. Dinenage | Saloon Steward | Lost |
| E. C. Dodd | Junior Third Engineer | Lost |
| Geo. Dodd | Second Steward | Lost |
| F. Doel | Fireman | Saved |
| J. Dolby | Reception Room Attendant | Lost |
| Italio Donati | Assistant Waiter | Lost |
| F. Donoghue | Bedroom Steward | Lost |
| A. Dore | Trimmer | Saved |
| S. Dornier | Assistant Fish | Lost |
| W. Doughty | Saloon Steward | Lost |
| F. Doyle | Fireman | Lost |
| William Duffy | Writer | Lost |
| W. Dunford | Hospital Steward | Lost |
| H. R. Dyer | Senior Fourth Assistant Engineer | Lost |
| W. Dyer | Saloon Steward | Lost |
| F. Dymond | Fireman | Saved |
| A. J. Eagle | Trimmer | Lost |
| C. Eastman | Greaser | Lost |
| F. Edbrooke | Steward | Lost |
| G. B. Ede | Steward | Lost |
| F. Edge | Deck Steward | Lost |
| C. Edwards | Assistant Pantryman | Lost |
| W. H. Egg | Steward | Lost |
| E. Elliott | Trimmer | Lost |
| J. Ellis | Assistant Vegetable Cook | Saved |
| W. Ennis | T. B. Attendant | Lost |
| A. Ervine | Assistant Electrician | Lost |
| H. S. Etches | Bedroom Steward | Saved |
| F. Evans | Lookout | Saved |
| F. O. Evans | Assistant Boatswain | Saved |
| Geo. Evans | Saloon Steward | Lost |
| Geo. Evans | Steward | Lost |
| W. Evans | Trimmer | Lost |
| H. Fairall | Saloon Steward | Lost |
| M. Fanette | Assistant Waiter | Lost |
| W. Farquharson | Senior Second Engineer | Lost |
| E. Farrendon | Confectioner | Lost |
| R. Faulkner | Bedroom Steward | Saved |
| F. Fay | Greaser | Lost |
| Carlo Fel | Sculleryman | Lost |
| A. Fellows | Assistant Boots | Lost |
| G. Feltham | | Lost |
| F. Fenton | Saloon Steward | Lost |
| Auto Ferrary | Trimmer | Lost |
| W. Ferris | Lodge Fireman | Lost |
| H. Finch | Steward | Lost |
| C. W. Fitzpatrick | Mess Steward | Saved |
| H. Fitzpatrick | Junior Boilermaker | Lost |
| E. Flarty | Fireman | Saved |
| Frederick Fleet | Lookout | Saved |
| P. Fletcher | Bugler | Lost |
| J. Foley | Storekeeper | Saved |
| W. C. Foley | Steward | Saved |

# *Titanic* Crew

| Name | Occupation | Lost/Saved |
|---|---|---|
| E. Ford | Steward | Lost |
| F. Ford | Bedroom Steward | Lost |
| H. Ford | Trimmer | Lost |
| T. Ford | Lodge Fireman | Lost |
| F. Forward | Assistant Boatswain | Saved |
| A. Foster | Storekeeper | Lost |
| W. T. Fox | Steward | Lost |
| A. Franklin | Saloon Steward | Lost |
| J. Fraser | Fireman | Lost |
| J. Fraser | Junior Third Assistant Engineer | Lost |
| W. Fredericks | Trimmer | Saved |
| E. Freeman | Deck Steward | Lost |
| R. Fropper | Saloon Steward | Saved |
| A. Fryer | Trimmer | Saved |
| F. Gardner | Greaser | Lost |
| L. Gatti | Manager | Lost |
| A. Gear | Fireman | Lost |
| R. Geddes | Bedroom Steward | Lost |
| Jacob W. Gibbons | Saloon Steward | Saved |
| V. Gilardino | Waiter | Lost |
| J. Giles | Second Baker | Lost |
| P. Gill | Ship's Cook | Lost |
| S. Gill | Bedroom Steward | Lost |
| G. Godley | Fireman | Saved |
| Mrs. Gold | Stewardess | Saved |
| M. W. Golder | Fireman | Lost |
| C. Gollop | Assistant Cook | Lost |
| J. Gordon | Trimmer | Lost |
| F. Goree | Greaser | Lost |
| A. Goshawk | Saloon Steward | Lost |
| B. Gosling | Trimmer | Lost |
| S. Gosling | Trimmer | Lost |
| T. Graham | Fireman | Saved |
| S. Graves | Fireman | Lost |
| G. Green | Trimmer | Lost |
| D. Gregory | Greaser | Lost |
| Miss Gregson | Stewardess | Saved |
| E. Grodidge | Fireman | Lost |
| Claude G. Gros | Assistant Coffee Man | Lost |
| Casail Guillio | Waiter | Lost |
| J. Gunn | Assistant Steward | Lost |
| G. Gunnery | Mess Steward | Lost |
| J. Guy | Assistant Boots | Saved |
| J. Haggan | Fireman | Saved |
| A. Haines | Boatswain's Mate | Saved |
| R. Halford | Steward | Saved |
| F. Hall | Scullion | Lost |
| J. Hall | Fireman | Lost |
| G. Hallett | Fireman | Lost |
| S. Halloway | Assistant Clothes Presser | Lost |
| E. Hamblyn | Bedroom Steward | Lost |
| E. Hamilton | Assistant Stateroom Steward | Lost |
| B. Hands | Fireman | Lost |
| G. Hannam | Fireman | Lost |
| W. Harder | Window Cleaner | Saved |

# *Titanic* Crew

| Name | Occupation | Lost/Saved |
| --- | --- | --- |
| A. Harding | Assistant Bedroom Steward | Lost |
| J. Hardwick | Kitchen Porter | Saved |
| John Hardy | Chief Second-Class Steward | Saved |
| C. H. Harris | Bell Boy | Lost |
| C. W. Harris | Saloon Steward | Lost |
| E. Harris | Assistant Pantryman | Lost |
| E. Harris | Fireman | Lost |
| F. Harris | Fireman | Saved |
| F. Harris | Trimmer | Lost |
| A. Harrison | Saloon Steward | Saved |
| N. Harrison | Junior Second Engineer | Lost |
| J. Hart | Steward | Saved |
| T. Hart | Fireman | Lost |
| Wallace Hartley | Band Leader | Lost |
| F. Hartnell | Saloon Steward | Saved |
| H. G. Harvey | Junior Second Assistant Engineer | Lost |
| R. Hasgood | Fireman | Lost |
| J. Haslin | Trimmer | Lost |
| H. Hatch | Scullion | Lost |
| John Hawkesworth | Saloon Steward | Lost |
| W. Hawksworth | Assistant Deck Steward | Lost |
| A. Hayter | Bedroom Steward | Lost |
| A. Hebb | Fireman | Lost |
| J. Helnen | Saloon Steward | Lost |
| S. Hemmings | Lamp Trimmer | Saved |
| C. Hendrickson | Lodge Fireman | Saved |
| E. Hendy | Saloon Steward | Lost |
| W. Henry | Assistant Boots | Lost |
| J. Hensford | Assistant Butcher | Lost |
| J. H. Hesketh | Second Engineer | Lost |
| T. Hewett | Bedroom Steward | Lost |
| H. Hill | Steward | Lost |
| J. Hill | Trimmer | Lost |
| J. Hill | Bedroom Steward | Lost |
| G. Hinckley | Baths | Lost |
| G. Hines | Third Baker | Lost |
| W. Hinton | Trimmer | Lost |
| S. Hiscock | Plate Washer | Lost |
| R. Hitchens | Quartermaster | Saved |
| Leo Hoare | Saloon Steward | Lost |
| C. Hodge | Senior Third Assistant Engineer | Lost |
| W. Hodges | Fireman | Lost |
| L. Hodgkinson | Senior Fourth Engineer | Lost |
| C. Hogg | Bedroom Steward | Lost |
| G. A. Hogg | Lookout | Saved |
| E. Hogue | Plate Washer | Lost |
| T. Holland | Assistant Reception Room Attendant | Lost |
| H. Holman | Assistant Boatswain | Lost |
| R. Hopgood | Fireman | Lost |
| F. Hopkins | Plate Washer | Lost |
| R. Hopkins | Assistant Boatswain | Saved |
| A. E. Horswill | Assistant Boatswain | Saved |
| G. F. Hosking | Senior Third Engineer | Lost |
| W. House | Saloon Steward | Lost |
| A. Howell | Saloon Steward | Lost |

# *Titanic* Crew

| Name | Occupation | Lost/Saved |
|---|---|---|
| H. Hughes | Assistant Second Steward | Lost |
| F. Humby | Plates | Lost |
| H. Humphreys | Assistant Steward | Lost |
| S. Humphreys | Quartermaster | Saved |
| S. Hunt | Trimmer | Saved |
| T. Hunt | Fireman | Lost |
| C. J. Hurst | Fireman | Lost |
| W. Hurst | Fireman | Saved |
| J. Hutchinson | Vegetable Cook | Lost |
| J. H. Hutchinson | Joiner | Lost |
| L. Hylands | Steward | Saved |
| H. Ide | Bedroom Steward | Lost |
| C. Ingram | Trimmer | Lost |
| H. Ingrouville | Steward | Lost |
| W. Ings | Scullion | Lost |
| T. Instance | Fireman | Lost |
| H. Jackson | Assistant Boots | Lost |
| John Jacobson | Fireman | Lost |
| J. Jago | Greaser | Lost |
| H. Jaillet | Pastry Cook | Lost |
| Thos. James | Fireman | Lost |
| W. Janaway | Bedroom Steward | Lost |
| C. Janin | Soup Cook | Lost |
| W. Jarvis | Fireman | Lost |
| W. Jeffrey | Controller | Lost |
| H. Jenner | Saloon Steward | Lost |
| Violet Jessop | Stewardess | Saved |
| A. Jewell | Lookout | Saved |
| N. Joas | Fireman | Lost |
| A. Johnson | | Lost |
| W. Johnson | | Lost |
| H. Johnston | Assistant Ship's Cook | Lost |
| J. Johnston | Saloon Steward | Saved |
| A. Jones | Plates | Lost |
| H. Jones | Roast Cook | Lost |
| R. V. Jones | Saloon Steward | Lost |
| T. Jones | Assistant Boatswain | Saved |
| G. Jouanmault | Assistant Sauce | Lost |
| Charles Joughin | Chief Baker | Saved |
| C. Judd | Fireman | Saved |
| J. Jukes | Greaser | Lost |
| H. Jupe | Assistant Electrician | Lost |
| F. Kasper | Fireman | Saved |
| C. Kearl | Greaser | Lost |
| G. Kearl | Trimmer | Saved |
| Jas. Keegan | Leading Fireman | Lost |
| P. Keene | Saloon Steward | Lost |
| T. Kelland | Library | Lost |
| Jas Kelly | Greaser | Lost |
| William Kelly | Assistant Electrician | Lost |
| G. Kemish | Fireman | Saved |
| Thos. Kemp | Executive Fourth Assistant Engineer | Lost |
| Fredk. Kenchenten | Greaser | Lost |
| C. Kennell | Kosher Cook | Lost |
| A. Kenzier | Storekeeper | Lost |

# *Titanic* Crew

| Name | Occupation | Lost/Saved |
|---|---|---|
| W. T. Kerley | Assistant Steward | Lost |
| T. Kerr | Fireman | Lost |
| H. Ketchley | Saloon Steward | Lost |
| J. Kieran | Chief Third-Class Steward | Lost |
| M. Kieran | Assistant Storekeeper | Lost |
| A. King | Lift Attendant | Lost |
| E. W. King | Clerk | Lost |
| G. King | Scullion | Lost |
| T. King | Master-at-Arms | Lost |
| W. F. Kingscote | Saloon Steward | Lost |
| L. Kinsella | Fireman | Lost |
| J. Kirkham | Greaser | Lost |
| A. Kitching | Saloon Steward | Lost |
| H. Klein | Barber | Lost |
| Geo. Knight | Saloon Steward | Saved |
| L. Knight | Steward | Lost |
| T. Knowles | Firemen's Messman | Saved |
| Bert W. Lacey | Assistant Steward | Lost |
| T. Lahy | Fireman | Lost |
| W. Lake | Saloon Steward | Lost |
| A. E. Lane | Saloon Steward | Lost |
| A. Latimer | Chief Steward | Lost |
| Miss Lavington | Stewardess | Saved |
| A. Lawrence | Saloon Steward | Lost |
| A. Leader | Assistant Confectioner | Lost |
| M. Leaonard | Steward | Lost |
| Mrs. Leather | Stewardess | Saved |
| H. Lee | Trimmer | Lost |
| R. R. Lee | Lookout | Saved |
| G. Lefever | Saloon Steward | Lost |
| L. Leonard | | Lost |
| G. Levett | Assistant Pantryman | Lost |
| A. Lewis | Steward | Saved |
| C. Light | Plate Washer | Lost |
| C. Light | Fireman | Lost |
| W. Light | Fireman | Lost |
| Charles H. Lightoller | Second Officer | Saved |
| W. Lindsay | Fireman | Saved |
| A. Littlejohn | Saloon Steward | Saved |
| H. Lloyd | Saloon Steward | Lost |
| W. Lloyd | Fireman | Lost |
| A. Lock | Assistant Cook | Lost |
| F. Long | Trimmer | Lost |
| W. Long | Trimmer | Lost |
| J. Longmuir | Assistant Bedroom Steward | Lost |
| J. Lovell | Grill Cook | Lost |
| Harold G. Lowe | Fifth Officer | Saved |
| W. Lucas | Saloon Steward | Lost |
| W. Lucas | Assistant Boatswain | Saved |
| C. Lydiatt | Saloon Steward | Lost |
| W. H. Lyons | Assistant Boatswain | Lost |
| J. Mabey | Steward | Lost |
| J. MacGrady | Saloon Steward | Lost |
| C. MacKay | Saloon Steward | Saved |
| G. MacKie | Bedroom Steward | Lost |

# *Titanic* Crew

| Name | Occupation | Lost/Saved |
|---|---|---|
| W. D. Mackie | Junior Fifth Assistant Engineer | Lost |
| W. Magee | Senior Sixth Assistant Engineer | Lost |
| E. Major | Bath Steward | Lost |
| W. Major | Fireman | Saved |
| Paul Manga | Kitchen Clerk | Saved |
| R. Mantle | Steward | Lost |
| J. Marks | Assistant Pantryman | Lost |
| G. Marrett | Fireman | Lost |
| J. W. Marriott | Assistant Pantryman | Lost |
| Miss Marsden | Stewardess | Saved |
| F. Marsh | Fireman | Lost |
| A. Martin | Scullion | Saved |
| Miss Martin | Second Cashier | Saved |
| Mrs. Martin | Stewardess | Saved |
| L. Maskell | Trimmer | Lost |
| F. Mason | Fireman | Saved |
| J. Mason | Leading Fireman | Lost |
| D. Matherson | Assistant Boatswain | Lost |
| M. Mathias | Mess-Room Steward | Lost |
| A. Mattman | Ice Man | Lost |
| J. Maxwell | Carpenter | Lost |
| A. May | Fireman | Lost |
| A. W. May | Firemen's Messman | Lost |
| J. Maynard | Entrée Cook | Saved |
| W. Mayo | Leading Fireman | Lost |
| A. Maytum | Chief Butcher | Lost |
| T. Mayzes | Fireman | Saved |
| Thos. McAndrew | Fireman | Lost |
| W. McAndrews | Fireman | Lost |
| W. McCarthy | Assistant Boatswain | Saved |
| F. McCarty | Bedroom Steward | Lost |
| W. McCastlen | Fireman | Lost |
| T. W. McCawley | Gymnasium | Lost |
| H. W. McElroy | Purser | Lost |
| J. McGann | Trimmer | Saved |
| E. McGarvey | Fireman | Lost |
| E. McGaw | Fireman | Lost |
| J. McGough | Assistant Boatswain | Saved |
| J. McGregor | Fireman | Lost |
| T. McInerney | Greaser | Lost |
| W. McIntyre | Trimmer | Saved |
| Mrs. McLaren | Stewardess | Saved |
| A. McMicken | Saloon Steward | Saved |
| J. McMullen | Saloon Steward | Lost |
| W. McMurray | Bedroom Steward | Lost |
| W. McQuillan | Fireman | Lost |
| Wm. McRae | Fireman | Lost |
| W. McReynolds | Junior Sixth Assistant Engineer | Lost |
| A. Mellor | Saloon Steward | Lost |
| A. Middleton | Assistant Electrician | Lost |
| M. V. Middleton | Saloon Steward | Lost |
| Geo. Milford | Fireman | Lost |
| R. Millar | Extra Fifth Assistant Engineer | Lost |
| T. Millar | Assistant Deck Engineer | Lost |
| C. Mills | Assistant Butcher | Saved |

# *Titanic* Crew

| Name | Occupation | Lost/Saved |
|---|---|---|
| W. Mintram | Fireman | Lost |
| A. Mishellany | Printer | Lost |
| B. Mitchell | Trimmer | Lost |
| J. Monoros | Assistant Waiter | Lost |
| J. Monteverdi | Assistant Entrée | Lost |
| J. P. Moody | Sixth Officer | Lost |
| A. Moore | Saloon Steward | Lost |
| G. Moore | Assistant Boatswain | Saved |
| J. Moore | Fireman | Saved |
| R. Moore | Trimmer | Lost |
| R. Moores | Greaser | Lost |
| A. Morgan | Trimmer | Lost |
| T. Morgan | Fireman | Lost |
| W. Morgan | Assistant Storekeeper | Lost |
| R. Morrell | Trimmer | Lost |
| A. Morris | Greaser | Lost |
| F. Morris | Bath Steward | Saved |
| W. Morris | Trimmer | Lost |
| H. Moss | Saloon Steward | Lost |
| T. Mullen | Steward | Lost |
| L. Muller | Interpreter | Lost |
| W. Murdoch | Fireman | Saved |
| W. M. Murdoch | First Officer | Lost |
| F. Nannini | Head Waiter | Lost |
| H. Neale | Assistant Baker | Saved |
| G. Nettleton | Fireman | Lost |
| C. Newman | Storekeeper | Lost |
| A. Nichol | Boatswain | Lost |
| T. Nicholls | Saloon Steward | Lost |
| A. Nichols | Steward | Lost |
| W. K. Nichols | Assistant Steward | Saved |
| John Noon | Fireman | Lost |
| J. Norris | Fireman | Lost |
| B. Noss | Fireman | Lost |
| H. Noss | Fireman | Saved |
| W. Nutbean | Fireman | Saved |
| J. O'Connor | Trimmer | Saved |
| T. O'Connor | Bedroom Steward | Lost |
| W. F. H. O'Loughlin | Surgeon | Lost |
| C. Olive | Greaser | Lost |
| E. R. Olive | Clothes Presser | Lost |
| H. Oliver | Fireman | Saved |
| A. Olliver | Quartermaster | Saved |
| W. Orpet | Saloon Steward | Lost |
| J. Orr | Assistant Vegetable Cook | Lost |
| W. Osborne | Saloon Steward | Lost |
| F. Osman | Assistant Boatswain | Saved |
| C. Othen | Fireman | Saved |
| L. Owens | Assistant Steward | Lost |
| R. Pacey | Lift Attendant | Lost |
| J. Pacherat | Assistant Larder | Lost |
| R. Paice | Fireman | Lost |
| C. Painter | Fireman | Lost |
| F. Painter | Fireman | Lost |
| A. Paintin | Captain's Steward | Lost |

# *Titanic* Crew

| Name | Occupation | Lost/Saved |
|---|---|---|
| T. Palles | Greaser | Lost |
| G. Pand | Fireman | Lost |
| E. Parsons | Chief Storekeeper | Lost |
| F. A. Parsons | Senior Fifth Assistant Engineer | Lost |
| R. Parsons | Saloon Steward | Lost |
| C. H. Pascoe | Assistant Boatswain | Saved |
| A. Pearce | Steward | Lost |
| J. Pearce | Fireman | Saved |
| A. Pearcey | Pantry | Saved |
| S. Pedrini | Assistant Waiter | Lost |
| G. Pelham | Trimmer | Saved |
| F. Pennell | Bath Steward | Lost |
| W. Penny | Assistant Steward | Lost |
| J. Penrose | Bedroom Steward | Lost |
| L. Perkins | Telephone Operator | Lost |
| W. Perkis | Quartermaster | Saved |
| A. Perotti | Assistant Waiter | Lost |
| W. Perrin | Boots | Lost |
| H. Perriton | Saloon Steward | Lost |
| E. Perry | Trimmer | Saved |
| H. Perry | Trimmer | Lost |
| W. C. Peters | Assistant Boatswain | Saved |
| A. Petrachio | Assistant Waiter | Lost |
| S. Petrachio | Assistant Waiter | Lost |
| E. Petty | Bedroom Steward | Lost |
| H. Phillamore | Saloon Steward | Saved |
| G. Phillips | Greaser | Lost |
| J. Phillips | Storeman | Lost |
| Jack T. Phillips | First Marconi | Lost |
| P. Pigott | Assistant Boatswain | Saved |
| W. Pitfield | Greaser | Lost |
| H. J. Pittman | Third Officer | Saved |
| W. Platt | Scullion | Lost |
| L. Platti | Assistant Waiter | Lost |
| P. Plazza | Waiter | Lost |
| J. Podesta | Fireman | Saved |
| E. Poggi | Waiter | Lost |
| J. Ponjdestai | Assistant Boatswain | Saved |
| R. Pook | Assistant Bedroom Steward | Lost |
| F. Port | Steward | Saved |
| G. Pregnall | Greaser | Saved |
| F. Prentice | Assistant Storekeeper | Saved |
| T. Preston | Trimmer | Lost |
| E. Price | Barman | Lost |
| J. A. Prideaux | Steward | Lost |
| J. Priest | Fireman | Saved |
| H. J. Prior | Steward | Saved |
| Mrs. Pritchard | Stewardess | Saved |
| C. Proctor | Chef | Lost |
| R. Proudfoot | Trimmer | Lost |
| W. Pryce | Saloon Steward | Lost |
| A. Pugh | Steward | Saved |
| P. Pugh | Leading Fireman | Lost |
| R. Pusey | Fireman | Saved |
| Jno. Puzey | Saloon Steward | Lost |
| R. Randall | Saloon Steward | Lost |

# *Titanic* Crew

| Name | Occupation | Lost/Saved |
|---|---|---|
| T. Ranger | Greaser | Saved |
| Jas. Ranson | Saloon Steward | Lost |
| E. Ratti | Waiter | Lost |
| F. Ray | Saloon Steward | Saved |
| J. Read | Trimmer | Lost |
| C. Reed | Bedroom Steward | Lost |
| R. Reed | Trimmer | Lost |
| F. Reeves | Fireman | Lost |
| W. Revell | Saloon Steward | Lost |
| R. Ricardona | Assistant Waiter | Lost |
| C. Rice | Fireman | Saved |
| J. H. Rice | Clerk | Lost |
| P. Rice | Steward | Lost |
| H. Richards | Fireman | Lost |
| G. Rickman | Fireman | Lost |
| C. Ricks | Assistant Storekeeper | Lost |
| W. Ridout | Saloon Steward | Lost |
| A. Rigozzi | Waiter | Lost |
| F. Roberts | Third Butcher | Lost |
| G. Roberts | Fireman | Lost |
| H. Roberts | Bedroom Steward | Lost |
| Mrs. Roberts | Stewardess | Saved |
| G. Robertson | Assistant Steward | Lost |
| J. Robinson | Saloon Steward | Lost |
| Mrs. Robinson | Stewardess | Saved |
| E. J. Rogers | Assistant Storekeeper | Lost |
| M. Rogers | Saloon Steward | Lost |
| R. Ross | Scullion | Saved |
| A. Rotta | Waiter | Lost |
| A. Rous | Plumber | Lost |
| P. Rousseau | Chef | Lost |
| G. Rowe | Quartermaster | Saved |
| M. Rowe | Saloon Steward | Lost |
| H. Rudd | Storekeeper | Lost |
| S. Rule | Bath Steward | Saved |
| G. Rummer | Saloon Steward | Lost |
| R. Russell | Saloon Steward | Lost |
| T. Ryan | Steward | Lost |
| W. E. Ryerson | Saloon Steward | Saved |
| G. Saccaggi | Assistant Waiter | Lost |
| G. Salussolia | Glass Man | Lost |
| W. Samuels | Saloon Steward | Lost |
| C. Sangster | Fireman | Lost |
| A. Saunders | Trimmer | Lost |
| T. Saunders | Fireman | Lost |
| W. Saunders | Fireman | Lost |
| W. E. Saunders | Saloon Steward | Lost |
| C. Savage | Steward | Saved |
| R. F. Sawyer | Window Cleaner | Lost |
| Joseph Scarrott | Assistant Boatswain | Saved |
| C. Scavino | Carver | Lost |
| Scott | Assistant Boots | Lost |
| Archd. Scott | Fireman | Lost |
| Frederick Scott | Greaser | Saved |
| R. Scovell | Saloon Steward | Lost |
| S. Sedunary | Steward | Lost |

# *Titanic* Crew

| Name | Occupation | Lost/Saved |
|---|---|---|
| A. Self | Greaser | Lost |
| E. Self | Fireman | Saved |
| H. Senior | Fireman | Saved |
| Gino Sesea | Waiter | Lost |
| W. Sevier | Steward | Lost |
| H. Seward | Pantryman | Saved |
| H. Shaw | Scullion | Lost |
| J. Shea | Saloon Steward | Lost |
| Thos. Shea | Fireman | Lost |
| F. Sheath | Trimmer | Saved |
| J. Shepherd | Junior Second Assistant Engineer | Lost |
| A. Shiers | Fireman | Saved |
| C. Shillaber | Trimmer | Lost |
| J. Siebert | Bedroom Steward | Lost |
| A. Simmonds | Scullion | Saved |
| F. C. Simmons | Saloon Steward | Lost |
| W. Simmons | Pass Cook | Lost |
| J. E. Simpson | Assistant Surgeon | Lost |
| W. Skeats | Trimmer | Lost |
| E. Skinner | Saloon Steward | Lost |
| H. J. Slight | Steward | Lost |
| W. Slight | Larder Cook | Lost |
| Miss Sloan | Stewardess | Saved |
| P. Sloan | Chief Electrician | Lost |
| Mrs. Slocombe | T. B. Attendant | Saved |
| W. Small | Leading Fireman | Lost |
| J. Smillie | Saloon Steward | Lost |
| C. Smith | Bedroom Steward | Lost |
| C. Smith | Scullion | Lost |
| E. Smith | Trimmer | Lost |
| Capt. Edward J. Smith | Commander | Lost |
| F. Smith | Assistant Pantryman | Lost |
| J. Smith | Assistant Baker | Lost |
| J. M. Smith | Junior Fourth Engineer | Lost |
| Miss Smith | Stewardess | Saved |
| R. G. Smith | Saloon Steward | Lost |
| W. Smith | Assistant Boatswain | Lost |
| H. Smither | Fireman | Lost |
| Mrs. Snape | Stewardess | Lost |
| G. Snellgrove | Fireman | Lost |
| W. Snooks | Trimmer | Lost |
| E. Snow | Trimmer | Saved |
| H. Sparkman | Fireman | Saved |
| M. Stafford | Greaser | Lost |
| J. H. Stagg | Saloon Steward | Lost |
| A. Stanbrook | Fireman | Lost |
| Miss Stap | Stewardess | Saved |
| S. Stebbing | Chief Boots | Lost |
| R. Steel | Trimmer | Lost |
| J. Stewart | Veranda Café | Saved |
| H. Stocker | Trimmer | Lost |
| E. Stone | Bedroom Steward | Lost |
| E. Stone | Bedroom Steward | Lost |
| A. Street | Fireman | Saved |
| E. A. Stroud | Saloon Steward | Lost |
| H. Stroud | Saloon Steward | Lost |

# *Titanic* Crew

| Name | Occupation | Lost/Saved |
|---|---|---|
| Jno Strugnell | Saloon Steward | Lost |
| H. Stubbings | Cook and Mess | Lost |
| H. Stubbs | Fireman | Lost |
| S. Sullivan | Fireman | Lost |
| W. Swan | Bedroom Steward | Lost |
| J. Symonds | Saloon Steward | Lost |
| S. Symons | Lookout | Saved |
| G. F. C. Talbot | Steward | Lost |
| F. Tamlyn | Mess-Room Steward | Lost |
| C. Taylor | Steward | Lost |
| C. Taylor | Assistant Boatswain | Lost |
| J. Taylor | Fireman | Lost |
| J. Taylor | Fireman | Saved |
| L. Taylor | T. B. Attendant | Lost |
| T. Taylor | Fireman | Lost |
| W. Taylor | Saloon Steward | Lost |
| W. H. Taylor | Fireman | Saved |
| D. Terrell | Assistant Boatswain | Lost |
| F. Terrill | Assistant Steward | Saved |
| E. Testoni | Assistant Glass Man | Lost |
| M. Thayler | Steward | Lost |
| A. Thessinger | Bedroom Steward | Saved |
| A. C. Thomas | Saloon Steward | Saved |
| B. Thomas | Saloon Steward | Saved |
| J. Thomas | Greaser | Lost |
| H. Thompson | Second Storekeeper | Lost |
| J. Thompson | Fireman | Saved |
| W. Thorley | Assistant Cook | Lost |
| T. Threlfall | Lodge Fireman | Saved |
| G. Thresher | Fireman | Saved |
| C. Tietz | Kitchen Porter | Lost |
| A. Tizard | Fireman | Lost |
| F. Toms | Saloon Steward | Saved |
| T. Topp | Second Butcher | Lost |
| F. Toung | Fireman | Lost |
| J. Tozer | Greaser | Lost |
| R. Triggs | Fireman | Saved |
| B. Tucker | Second Pantryman | Lost |
| R. Turley | Fireman | Lost |
| G. F. Turner | Stenographer | Lost |
| L. Turner | Saloon Steward | Lost |
| W. Turnquist | | Saved |
| C. Turvey | Page Boy | Lost |
| R. Urbini | Waiter | Lost |
| P. Vaivarlarge | Assistant Soup | Lost |
| E. Valvarsori | Waiter | Lost |
| A. Veal | Greaser | Lost |
| R. Veal | Saloon Steward | Lost |
| H. Vear | Fireman | Lost |
| W. Vear | Fireman | Lost |
| J. Vicat | Fish Cook | Lost |
| H. Vine | Assistant Controller | Lost |
| R. Vioni | Waiter | Lost |
| H. Voegelin | Coffeeman | Lost |
| S. Wake | Assistant Baker | Lost |
| Mrs. Wallis | Matron | Lost |

# *Titanic* Crew

| Name | Occupation | Lost/Saved |
|---|---|---|
| J. Walpole | Chief Pantryman | Lost |
| Miss Walsh | Stewardess | Lost |
| A. Ward | Junior Fourth Assistant Engineer | Lost |
| E. Ward | Bedroom Steward | Lost |
| J. Ward | Leading Fireman | Lost |
| P. Ward | Bedroom Steward | Lost |
| W. Ward | Saloon Steward | Saved |
| F. Wardner | Fireman | Lost |
| R. Wareham | Bedroom Steward | Lost |
| F. Warwick | Saloon Steward | Lost |
| E. Wateridge | Fireman | Lost |
| W. Watson | Bell Boy | Lost |
| W. Watson | Fireman | Lost |
| T. Weatherstone | Saloon Steward | Saved |
| B. Webb | Smoke-Room Steward | Lost |
| S. Webb | Trimmer | Lost |
| F. Webber | Leading Fireman | Lost |
| W. H. Welch | Assistant Cook | Lost |
| R. Weller | Assistant Boatswain | Saved |
| J. Wheat | Assistant Second Steward | Saved |
| E. Wheelton | Saloon Steward | Saved |
| A. White | Assistant Barber | Lost |
| A. White | Greaser | Saved |
| F. White | Trimmer | Lost |
| J. White | G. H. Steward | Lost |
| L. White | Saloon Steward | Lost |
| W. White | Trimmer | Saved |
| T. Whiteley | Saloon Steward | Saved |
| A. H. Whiteman | Barber | Saved |
| A. Whitford | Saloon Steward | Lost |
| J. Widgery | Baths | Saved |
| Henry T. Wilde | Chief Officer | Lost |
| A. Williams | Assistant Storekeeper | Lost |
| E. Williams | Fireman | Lost |
| W. Williams | Assistant Steward | Saved |
| W. Willis | Steward | Lost |
| B. Wilson | Senior Second Assistant Engineer | Lost |
| Wm. Wilton | Trimmer | Lost |
| W. Wiltshire | Assistant Butcher | Lost |
| J. Windebank | Sauce Cook | Saved |
| W. Winn | Quartermaster | Saved |
| A. Witcher | Fireman | Lost |
| F. Witt | Trimmer | Lost |
| H. Witt | Fireman | Lost |
| J. Witter | Smoke-Room Steward | Saved |
| H. Wittman | Bedroom Steward | Lost |
| J. T. Wood | Assistant Steward | Lost |
| H. Woodford | Greaser | Lost |
| H. Woods | Trimmer | Lost |
| Oscar S. Woody | Postal Clerk | Lost |
| T. Wormaid | Saloon Steward | Lost |
| F. Wright | Racquet-Court Attendant | Lost |
| W. Wright | G. H. Steward | Lost |
| J. Wyeth | Fireman | Lost |
| H. Yearsley | Saloon Steward | Saved |
| J. Yoshack | Saloon Steward | Lost |
| F. Young | Fireman | Lost |
| L. Zarracchi | Wine Butler | Lost |

# INDEX



*Page numbers of illustrations are in *italic* type.

# About the Contributors

Beverly McMillan is a writer, editor, and Vice-President of Marketing and Publications at The Mariners' Museum. Her recent credits include *Oceans*, a popular book on marine life and ecology that she co-authored with her husband, John A. Musick, and which was published by Monark Press in 1997.

Stanley Lehrer is a renowned collector of *Titanic* artifacts and memorabilia that have been exhibited in galleries and museums in the United States and England. Over a quarter-century, his quest evolved into the largest, most prestigious, privately held *Titanic* collection in North America. Lehrer is the founder, publisher, and editorial director of *USA Today,* and he has published eight books on a wide range of topics. His collection was featured in the recent bestseller *Titanic: Legacy of the World's Greatest Ocean Liner*, published by Time-Life Books in 1997.

The Mariners' Museum 1998 exhibition *Titanic: Fortune & Fate*, an evocative chronicle of the social history of the *Titanic*'s passengers and crew, was the vision of Museum Director Claudia L. Pennington. This commemorative volume would have been impossible to produce if it were not for the creative talents of Matt Hahn of ThinkDesign and the dedicated staff of the Museum's departments of Exhibit Production and Photographic Services and Licensing.

To commemorate the legacy of the world's greatest maritime tragedy, The Mariners' Museum in Newport News, Virginia, has produced the exhibition *Titanic: Fortune & Fate*, on view there exclusively throughout 1998. Founded by Archer M. and Anna Hyatt Huntington in 1930, the Museum preserves and interprets maritime history through an international collection of ship models, figure heads, paintings, and other maritime artifacts. The Mariners' Museum is a nonprofit, educational institution accredited by the American Association of Museums in 1972.

*The Mariners' Museum and the South Street Seaport Museum of New York City are partners in the National Maritime Museum Initiative, an alliance to share collections, exhibitions, and other endeavors.*